My Maggie

My Maggie

Richard King

HPH Publishing
Chicago, IL

First printing 2007 (Publication date: Ocotber 13, 2007)

Library of Congress Cataloging-in-Publication Data
King, Richard, 1947-
  My Magie / Richard King.
     p. cm
  ISBN-13: 978-0-9776281-6-2 (alk. paper)
1. King, Margaret, 1948–2002–Health. 2. King, Margaret, d. 2002–Health 3. Cancer–Patients Illinois–Chicago–Biography.
4. Blind–Illinois–Chicago–Biography. I. Title.
  RC265.6.K55K5 2007
  362.196'994009—dc22

                        2007026992

To
Margaret King

Contents

ACKNOWLEDGEMENTS

Peter Mowbray has one of those James Bond type English accents that you could listen to endlessly. He also possesses the good looks and sophistication that might have landed him a Bond role in his younger days. We met quite by chance in a small restaurant across the street from my condo in downtown Chicago.

Peter has a marketing firm with international connections, but he is based in the United States with offices in Chicago and Orange County, California.

Peter was the first one to make the move towards conversation by saying he recognized me as the sportscaster from WGN-TV Channel 9, and we began to have casual talks that evolved quickly into discussions about U.S. and International politics, business, religion, sports, philosophy and , of course, women.

"I used to see you here many mornings hunched over that newspaper and eating by yourself," he told me one day. "Is there no woman in your life?"

A sad grin swept across my face. "There used to be," I said, "but she's gone. Her name was Maggie."

I explained to Peter that Maggie and I had been childhood sweethearts and then husband and wife for thirty-two years. I told him she had died of ovarian cancer in 2002. "Do you care to talk more about her?" Peter asked. Three cups of coffee and two hours later we were still sitting at the table, and I was still talking about Maggie. It was pretty obvious she had been my whole life. I could tell Peter was at times stunned by her story and, at times, bordered on tears. He would react with expressions of disbelief about all that had happened to Maggie. "It is an incredible story," he said "and you talk about her with such deep passion. Have you ever considered writing a book?"

That is how all this began. Peter quickly placed his marketing hat on and pointed out that the book might not only be inspirational to some people but also make some money for Maggie's favorite causes. "And even if it never gets published, the whole experience might be cathartic for you," he added. The more I thought about it the more it made sense. At least, it was worth a try. So I owe Peter Mowbray my first thank you because he and his fiancée Amanda Prescher gave me the kick start to try to emerge from the mostly gloomy life I had lived since Maggie's death. They have become good friends, and I am grateful. Maggie would have loved them both. She would have shared their zest for life, their busy schedule, and their willingness to embrace people. That is the very way she had lived.

Maggie was an inspiration to me and to almost all the people she had touched in her fifty-three years on this earth. The great Radio and Television commentator, Eric Sevareid, once summed up the life of his hero, legendary news broadcast pioneer Edward R. Murrow, this way: "There are no 100 percent heroes. About 50 percent is the best you can be and Ed was all of that." So was Maggie. But she was not without contradictions.

The title of this book is *My Maggie* but that is not the name she had for most of her life. She was born Margaret Smith and when we were growing up in the old neighborhood in Chicago all the kids, including me, called her "Margie." When we got married it was still "Margie" sometimes shortened to "Mar." But then suddenly in her 45th year of life, she abruptly told me she was adopting the name "Maggie."

"I have a new career now, and all my new friends and colleagues call me Maggie. My business cards will say Maggie so you can call me Maggie from now on," she said.

"Maggie?" I shot back. "Forget it, you'll always be Margie to me."

That response triggered one of our classic and often hilarious verbal scuffles.

The disagreement lasted for months until I finally gave in but not completely.

I began calling her "Mags" and then eventually "Bags" to symbolize her favorite hobby, shopping. To my surprise, she liked that name and it lasted for the rest of our lives together. But I have to admit that when I think of her now or talk about her to some old friends, the name "Margie" always finds its way into the conversation. But in the end she won. She almost always did win. The title of this book is what she would have wanted, *My Maggie.*

While Peter Mowbray and Amanda Prescher gave me the inspiration to write this book the person to whom I owe the most is Arlana Fako. To say she was Maggie's best friend seems an understatement. Her love and commitment to Maggie passed all human levels. Her capacity for giving seems boundless. Without Arlana's help, I would not be writing these words right now, because I may not have made it through all the ordeals we faced.

I also have to thank Arlana's husband, George. He grew up with us in the old neighborhood on Chicago's Near West Side. He lived just a half a block away from Maggie's family. He has filled in information about dates, people, places and events that I had almost forgotten. Maggie epitomized the old neighborhood and, quite frankly, before I began to write I did not realize how great an impact it had on both of us.

Karen McCulloh became one of Maggie's best friends later in life. They shared the common bond of fighting blindness, deafness and other diseases. They also both had been registered nurses before their eyesight failed. Karen and Maggie seemed to share a positive energy field. Karen was an inspiration to Maggie and Maggie to Karen.

There are also many people to thank at the Chicago Lighthouse for the Blind, which is in its 100th year of service for not only Chicago clients but people all across the entire United States. Rob Cummings is the chief fund raiser for the Lighthouse, and he has become a good friend. He is a truly remarkable man who is driven about his cause. Rob worked with Maggie at the Lighthouse on a couple of fund raising ventures, and when I talked to him about this book he confided to me a feeling that also tells part of Maggie's story.

"Now that we have become close friends I can tell you this without offending you," he said. "When I was with Maggie I never thought of her as being blind. I always just felt like I was with a 'babe'." I burst out laughing. Maggie would have enjoyed the story also because she always prided herself in her personal appearance. She dressed elegantly and enjoyed doing it. But to everyone in her life, it was Maggie's inner beauty that was most compelling.

I owe a debt of gratitude to the staff of CRIS (Chicagoland Radio Information Service) at the Chicago Lighthouse who generously volunteered their time to record the audio version of the book.

I would also like to thank two close friends at the American Cancer Society, Anita Guerrero and Dee McKinsey.

The staff at WGN is like family, and I would like to thank Tom Ehlmann, vice president and general manager, for supporting the promotion of this book. I would also like to thank Nancy Helzing of WGN, who gave me huge assistance in getting this book done.

My closest friends also offered their constructive criticism of the first draft of this book. Jim Benes and his wife Andrea Wiley are both excellent journalists, and its hard to go wrong getting advice from professionals. Andi is like a sister to me and Jim is like a brother. So is Ron Gorski who also happens to be the chief editor for broadcast icon Paul Harvey at ABC Radio. I would also like to thank Gail Gorski for her many years of support.

Another good friend who helped inspire me to write this book is Jerry Reinsdorf. As I write this, he is celebrating his victory in the World Series as owner of the Chicago White Sox. I have dined many times with Jerry over the last 25 years, and when I was going though tough times he would offer the kind of encouragement that only good friends can provide. Maggie always notice dthe difference. "You seem to have a little more spunk when you come back from dinner with Jerry," she said on quite a few occasions. It was true.

I know exactly what Maggie would have said about this project. We were connected so strongly that even though she has been gone for awhile I still can hear her words in my head. Initially she would have ripped me.

"Oh, c'mon, Richie!" she would say, "let it go already and get on with your life. Who wants to read a book about all of this. People have their own problems." But when I explained the benefits for the Chicago Lighthouse for the Blind and for the American Cancer Society, she would have had second thoughts.

But she would not have wanted a somber book mainly about all the challenges she faced. She was a woman who battled poverty, severe hearing loss at an early age, progressive blindness, melanoma, breast cancer, and finally ovarian cancer. Yet she was the happiest person I have ever known. Through it all she maintained a childlike zest for living, and she always described herself as "a bit goofy." So don't expect one series of depressing stories after the other. This is not that kind of book. Hopefully, you will be laughing through a good portion of it. That's the way Maggie would have wanted it.

My Maggie

I Love You So

The eyes I loved so much were open. But just as they had for the past several days, they stared straight-ahead, devoid of awareness. As Maggie lay in a coma, it was as if she was looking into her next life.

Still, I could not be sure. Even if she showed no hint of emotion, could she feel my hand grasping hers? Could she feel the touch of my kisses on her cheeks and lips? Could she hear my voice—even as a distant echo—saying for the last time, "I love you"?

Since she lapsed into a coma, I spent hours and hours watching her. Lying in our proper positions on the usual sides of our bed, I pretended it was just another day. I kept hoping for one last miracle. I wanted one last moment of consciousness that she could share with me. She had overcome so much. Surely, she could muster one last ounce of energy to say, "I love you so, Richie."

I was living through a nightmare, numbed by the fear that my entire reason for living would soon disappear. I was losing a part of myself, losing it for eternity. My soul felt sick and empty.

Deep down, I knew the end was closing in. Perhaps it would

come in a day and a half. Perhaps it would come in less than twenty-four hours—or perhaps it would come in less than four. I knew there would be no miracle awakening. So I was resigned to the simple pleasure of holding her. As long as I held her in my arms, we were still together. She was still mine.

Gazing into her bright, blue eyes, a flood of memories crossed my mind. We truly enjoyed a lifetime of love and happiness. "Mags, it was a helluva party. Wasn't it?" I know she would not respond. Still, as I looked lovingly at Maggie and at the photo of her late mother on the bed stand beside us, it took me to a place that seemed like a different planet and to a time that seemed not so long ago.

1

Distant Memories

The focus of distant memory can be very soft. So, when I say the first time I laid eyes on Maggie was in the second grade, keep in mind, it's only my best estimate. While I am not exactly sure of the time, I am sure of the place. It was in the play lot of St. Procopius Elementary School on Chicago's Near West Side. Maggie was playing a game we called "dodge-ball," which involved trying to avoid being hit by a volleyball thrown by the other team. Because there was not a patch of grass on the entire play lot, the game usually resulted in a scraped knee or two, the result of diving on the asphalt to avoid taking a hit. I do recall it was a sunny and warm morning in September when classes had just begun. During this so-called recess period, one of my classmates, Eddie Smith, pointed out Maggie. She was his sister and about seven years old at the time. Maggie was born on October 14, 1948, one year and seven months after I had entered the world.

We were the first wave of baby boomers born into a country made rich and powerful after World War II. "The dawn of the American century" they called it, but while some look back on the 1950s with longing nostalgia, it was far from a carefree era. Even as a child, you could sense the fear around you. There were ads on Chicago buses showing Soviet Prime Minister Nikita Khrushchev with his fist in the air saying he would bury the United States. Talk of the atom bomb was everywhere. Each Tuesday, the air raid sirens went off in Chicago at 10:30 a. m., and we had to run out of our classrooms and into the hallways. We got down on our knees and hunched over in a fetal position, our hands covering our heads—as if this "duck and cover" drill would do any good against the inferno an A-bomb would unleash.

Maggie and I were both raised Roman Catholic, which in the 1950s was a strict and seemingly unforgiving religion, even if it did feature the Sacrament of Confession. The church was paranoid about the Soviet system dominating the world. They feared it would end Catholicism and, consequently, heaped a whole bunch of fear our way. One of the nuns told us the Communists might someday burst into our classroom with machine guns and ask us if we were Catholics. At the risk of being cut down in a hail of gunfire, we were told to stand up for our faith and become martyrs. Pretty heavy stuff for a ten year-old mind, as was the holding up of such heroes as St. Francis of Assisi who pounded himself bloody with rocks as penance for his sins. The child's mind accepts the idea that such acts are heroic rather than macabre. There was also the ever-present crucifix. It was in the classroom, in the church, in the home, and even in the car. Most often it was in graphic color; the tortured crucified body of Christ, a daily reminder we were all worthless sinners. How a ten year-old could be responsible for such a horrible event two thousand years ago was never considered.

Despite the underpinning of fear that guided our childhood, the innocence of youth could not be denied. The seemingly innate optimism of the child's mind lays waste to the concept of original sin. As I looked at Maggie on that warm September morning so long ago, I saw a skin-and-bones tomboy who looked almost exactly like her brother. And I recall the one feature that stood out and would always stand out for the rest of her life: strikingly beautiful golden blonde hair that radiated in the brilliant morning sunlight. One of her close friends, Sylvia Presecky, said they used to play "Beauty Shop" with Maggie's hair because it was so thick and gorgeous. Maggie was always the client in "Beauty Shop," as the other girls would style her hair. And Maggie wore it gloriously long, in part to hide hearing aids in each ear. Back before small batteries, she was forced to carry two long wires connected to each of the devices. They draped down to a silver battery case, the size of an old cigarette lighter, which attached at her waist. The wires could be seen clearly over the front of her dress and so could the battery case. She was diagnosed with general hearing loss at the age of four. Doctors told her mother it was caused by nerve damage from a fever she suffered during pregnancy. They also assured her Maggie's condition would not get any worse.

I watched Maggie run around the play lot—wires and all—just trying to be like the rest of us. But, in the sometimes-merciless world of children, that was impossible. Maggie was painfully ostracized many times. It created a childhood shyness that lingered to adulthood. Throughout this book, you will read her own accounts of how it felt to be Maggie Smith and then, later, Maggie King. She wrote them late in her life while attending classes at Loyola University in downtown Chicago. Some of the stories I knew. Others I was fascinated to learn. She was a great writer, and I know how much work she put into her class papers. I will cherish them forever. This excerpt from a college essay in 1999 touched on her hearing aids:

"As a child I was keenly aware that I appeared to be different from the people in my surrounding environment.

The large silver box with a cord that plugged into my ears was hard to miss. I learned early in life about human nature and curiosity. People often pointed their fingers and/or asked questions about my hearing aids. I was often the target of many questions and stares. Moreover, I had a speech impediment that attracted additional attention. When I was six or seven, I remember playing a game with the girls in the neighborhood. I could not hear anything that was gong on; thus, some of the girls thought I was too stupid to play the game. I ran home and sat on the back of the porch stoop and sobbed. My mother heard me crying and came out to see what was going on. She put her arms around me until I was able to control my tears. When I told her what happened she continued to hug me and explained that there would always be people who would not take the time to understand my situation. However, she said it was their loss because they did not get the chance to know me. My mother said she would always love me and asked that I do the best I could in any given situation. She then leaned over the banister and yelled for my brother. He was told what happened and took me to play with the boys. I was a tomboy from that day forward."

Maggie and I came from similar families. Her hard-drinking father worked at a nearby printing company. My hard-drinking father drove a truck that carried live poultry from Illinois farms to Chicago for slaughter. Both mothers for the most part stayed at home, ran the household, and worried about money, which nobody had a lot of in a neighborhood of second generation Eastern Europeans—mostly Polish and Czech. There seemed to be a tavern on almost every block. Maggie's father would pick up his check on Friday and head for a place called Locko's on Carpenter Street. There he got properly hammered and spent a good part of the weekend singing old vaudeville songs with his equally smashed buddies. My dad took me to the liquor store every Sunday at noon sharp: the precise minute it was legal to buy booze on Sundays in Chicago. He could not even wait until 12:30 to make it look less conspicuous. But both men were sober during the week and worked hard to support their families. And for those who might judge the drinking with a harsh eye, consider that both were in World War II.

Maggie's dad was in the Navy repairing ships. My father had the worst of all jobs. He was in the infantry and fought in the Battle of the Bulge in 1944–5, during the push to Germany. God alone knows what carnage he saw. He and Maggie's dad were part of what Tom Brokaw called "The Greatest Generation." They were great, but they smothered their fears with stoicism and booze.

While I knew Maggie, I can't say I paid much attention to her in the years at St. Procopius. She was an angel at my First Holy Communion in second grade. All first grade girls had to assist in what is perhaps the most important of all the sacraments— receiving a piece of bread and drinking wine to symbolize Christ's body and blood. During those years, Maggie and I exchanged what amounted to childhood small talk. I did not realize she confided to friends in third grade that I would be her husband some day!

I was actually closer to Maggie's mother, Ann, a wiry chain-smoking bundle of energy. Unlike Maggie, she had jet-black hair and a booming voice. Her maiden name was Sevcik—Slovakian. Maggie's dad was Irish. Ann Smith had to be tough. She raised three kids, essentially by herself, on a low income. She was not adverse to vulgarity when she got incensed, and I saw her many times unload on her husband after he had waddled home from a trip to Locko's. Some people feared her.

But she was always very nice to me. For some reason, we hit it off from the moment we met. When I went to Maggie's house to play with Eddie, their mom would always greet me with a smile and kind words. It was as if I possessed some intangible quality that brought out the softness in her. The truth was, beneath all her bluster, she was a warm and sensitive woman.

Ann was also light years ahead of the times. She was a humanitarian in a time and a place that was awash with distrust. Many of the ethnic people in our neighborhood carried with them the prejudices of the old world. The neighborhood itself was called Pilsen, after a city in the country then known as Czechoslovakia. If you were outside the Eastern European culture in our neighborhood, you did not get the benefit of the doubt. But Ann was the exception. She seemed to accept change and welcome diversity long before most everyone else.

During the fifties, an influx of immigrants from Mexico changed life in Pilsen. Many people moved out, fleeing to different neighborhoods but mostly to the suburbs. The so-called "greatest generation" feared African-Americans and Latinos, as much as the Roman Catholic Church feared the "Commies." Jews were also on the bottom of the list. I often wondered why some of the very men who had risked their lives in war, fighting Hitler's master race theory, came home and hated just about every minority that existed.

I wondered why they weren't more like Maggie's mother. She welcomed the Mexican culture, talking freely with the new residents and exchanging recipes with Mexican women. Because of her mother, Maggie was ingrained with a wonderful diverse outlook on life. She wrote about the experience in a college essay.

"The majority of my Mexican-American classmates were bilingual. How I envied them! I have always regretted the fact that my mother did not teach me how to speak Slovak, her native tongue. I can appreciate my ancestors' assimilation into the mainstream American culture. However, I really believe that we would have benefited from the knowledge of more than one language. I envy other cultures, which have the ability to speak more than one language.

Furthermore, I admire Latinos for holding on to their beliefs and values. The older generation in Pilsen could not accept the fact that Mexican- Americans were successful in advocating for Spanish to be incorporated into the American culture. It is very interesting to me that people who have so much in common could not live in harmony.

Since communication has always been an issue for me, I think I was more sensitive to the issue on both sides. What difference does it make what language we speak, as long as we can communicate? It is very difficult for me to learn a foreign language, but my husband speaks fluent Spanish. It is so much fun to travel and speak to people all over the world, not to mention how educating it can be. Therefore, I celebrate with cultures that respect and value their traditions and are empowered to advocate for themselves."

When Maggie said the cultures had a lot in common, she was right on the money.

Both Maggie and I had older brothers. I would wear all of my brother's used-up clothes, and I recall Maggie had it worse. She had to wear some of Eddie's old coats. Boy's clothes! Add that to the hearing aids, and it's a wonder Maggie had any friends at all.

But every penny counted in Pilsen whether you were Slovak, Irish, Polish, or Mexican. Once a week, my parents would drag a steel tub into the kitchen to give my brother and me a bath. Our house had no tub or shower. On a salary of twenty-four dollars a week, even a Coke was a luxury. My mom made us Kool-Aid to drink with our meals. Old coats, patched up pants, and penny candy were the realities of life during an era that dims in memory with each passing year. We had the basics of life, but that was about it.

Even though money was tight, our childhood offered a few indulgences. The biggest one was bowling, which was huge in the 1950s. It seemed as if all the neighborhood kids gathered at the Pilsen Bowl each Saturday morning. A line, which is a single game, was something like fifteen cents. Nobody seemed to have his own bowling ball or shoes. The shoes had to be rented. The balls were selected off the racks. It was at the bowling alley that I began to flirt with Maggie.

The hormones of puberty were beginning to kick in. While I paid some attention to Maggie, my first real infatuation was with her best friend, Pat. She was the exact opposite of Maggie; Pat was a pretty brunette with an outgoing personality. But she had absolutely no interest in me. And who could blame her. Like Maggie, I was as thin as a rail and had the look of a nerd. My deep religious beliefs also made me afraid of girls. Any impure thoughts would have sent me straight to hell if I could not have found a confessional box before I died. It is laughable to realize now that at that age you really don't have any idea what an impure thought would entail.

While I focused on Pat, I also noticed Maggie was losing

her tomboy look. She wore her pretty blonde hair in a ponytail now. Thanks to rapidly improving technology, the hearing aids had become much smaller, and the dangling wires were gone. Although Maggie had a speech impediment, it was not that bad. Her mother sent her to a speech therapist regularly, and Maggie applied herself thoroughly to the task, as she always would. She later told me she practiced incessantly. It served her well because for the rest of her life experts in the field were amazed she spoke so well with such a great loss of hearing. To me, the speech impediment was barely noticeable.

After I finally realized I had no chance at all with Pat, I started kidding around more and more with Maggie. Her sister Patty would tease me about Maggie—sometimes in Maggie's presence. It would embarrass her to no end. I knew she liked me, but she didn't want to tip her hand. It was typical of the awkward teen years back then—breaking through into a relationship was almost like mission impossible. But while Maggie was extremely shy, I had just a tad more confidence and kept up the dialogue when we crossed paths.

I recall one occasion when Maggie and Pat baked a birthday cake for the sixth grade teacher, an ailing nun named Sister Thomas who could not control her gas attacks. You wonder how the poor lady dealt with the muffled giggles and laughs at her frequent explosions during class. Sadly, she was always sick; but the week after she received the cake, Sister Thomas was hospitalized with a gastrointestinal disorder. Eddie and I never let Maggie forget that she and Pat had sent Sister Thomas over the edge with their "poison" cake.

We were a close-knit group of kids, and as we got older, Maggie felt more comfortable. After the silver box and wires were gone, the hearing aids became a non-issue: she concealed them with her long blond hair. Eddie, however, always made fun of her feet. Maggie had a habit of falling over things around the house. He laughed at her for being a "klutz." Everyone, including Maggie, also laughed. It was just the usual childhood play. Only later in life did all the falling down make sense. Unknown to all—her mother, her brother, her entire family, her friends, and even Maggie herself—an insidious eye disease lay in her cells. It would take a while, but the disease ultimately shaped both her life and mine.

2
That's Old Fashioned

As Maggie and I hit our high school years, the country was awash in change: political and cultural. It was pretty much a complete upheaval in American society. The first three years of the sixties were a copy of the 1950s. But all you had to do was listen to the music of that era to note the change after 1963. I thought November 22, 1963 would be the one historical milepost of our generation; then 9-11 took place. Now tragically, we have two. Still in 1960, John F. Kennedy brought to the presidency a youthfulness that inspired most Americans. He sure inspired me. The line that changed my life most came from Kennedy's inauguration speech where he talked about the heavy burdens of the time—"the long twilight struggle" that would be needed to overcome the threats of war, tyranny, and the other evils of mankind. On that clear and cold day in January with his hand pointed in the air, he said "... some people might fear the burden ... I do not shrink from this responsibility, I welcome it." That became a way of life for me. It seemed like such a noble undertaking to dig in and try to make the world a better place. It also spoke to the chief value we had learned as Catholics, sacrifice. It seems even if you lose your faith, at some point during your life, the basic beliefs still stay with you.

Religion was central to Maggie's life as she was growing up, but she really got most of her values from her mother. In one of her college papers on cultural diversity, she shared these thoughts:

> *"I had a mother who was able to nurture my mind, body, and soul. I soon learned that despite my hearing aids, I was human like everyone else, and all she ever would ask of me was to do my best in any given situation. My mother also explained that everyone has challenges in life, and the goal is to meet those challenges to the best of our abilities. It is from her values that I draw strength in my personal and professional life."*

When Maggie was getting this tender nurturing back in the 1960s, she paid no attention to what John Kennedy, Lyndon Johnson, Nikita Khrushchev, or any other leader had to say. Her interests were school, sports, and—what all girls at that age talk about—boys. And I was now beginning to take an interest in Maggie. It's funny to look back on it, but my interest in her was in the purest form. American culture had not yet become inundated with sex, and since I was deeply religious at the time, I simply wanted to go on a date with Maggie and hold her hand.

The Everly Brothers had a song called *That's Old Fashioned*, detailing a series of simple, sincere values about courtship. One line stood out: "That's old fashioned, and that's the way love should be." I thought this was ideal and talked to Maggie more and more with the idea of taking her out to hold hands. Unfortunately, the memory of our first date is completely out of focus. I believe her mother took a group of us somewhere, and I kind of made Maggie my target. I don't think I even held her hand, but she knew I was interested.

I do, however, recall the first time I really got close to her, and it scared me out of my wits. It scared Maggie, too. Every St. Patrick's Day, St. Procopius held a dance in the small school theatre. It was a dingy place with booze-soaked floors that reeked of the same smell you find in an old neighborhood tavern. The St. Pat's party was an excuse for the men in the neighborhood to get "hooched-up." Then again, they didn't need that much of an excuse. A change of wind direction was enough to order another round in celebration, and the wind changes a lot in Chicago. Still for us teenage kids, the dance was an opportunity to share some intimacy in the form of dancing.

I saw the slow dance as a great chance to show Maggie my affection. But when the moment came, we were both so nervous. I don't think we said a word. I could hear Maggie breathing heavily as Richie Valens sang *Oh Donna,* and I was weak in the knees because Maggie and I were dancing so close. But oh, how good she felt! I recall she had on a powder blue dress. And, I remember that neither of us was smiling. Maggie, in fact, was looking down. It was almost as if we were afraid to enjoy it. The moment was both awkward and beautiful.

We truly lived in a vacuum of innocence, and looking back on it, I am glad we had the opportunity. Nowadays, the mass media with its endless peddling of sex has taken away from most children something that had been basic—innocence. It seems now that kids aren't allowed to grow up. I am very grateful Maggie and I both had the chance to be children who learned through guidance how to grow into being adults.

After those initial encounters, Maggie and I dated only sporadically in the early years of high school. She attended St. Procopius High School, and I went to De La Salle, another Catholic school a few miles away. While we did not date that often, we saw each other almost every day.

I had gotten close to Eddie, George Fako, and a few of the boys on May Street where Maggie lived. We became quite a happy group. Baseball was supreme back then; we were all White Sox fans and played the game of baseball endlessly. I recall being in two hardball leagues and two softball leagues at the same time for a few summers. Maggie and the rest of the girls came to watch us quite often. Even when there was not a game, we hung around on Maggie's porch and got involved in all forms of teenage nonsense. This was the life that defined the "old neighborhood." None of us watched TV in the evening—it was a wonderfully communal experience almost every night. In the winters, we played basketball at the local park district field house. But summers were the best. We stayed out until 9 or 10 o'clock, and I remember walking home every night with no fear of getting mugged. Can you imagine? No fear whatsoever. It is a feeling I will never have again no matter where I am walking.

As for Maggie, well, she fit in flawlessly. While her brother still laughed at her heavy feet, she appeared to be quite normal. However, what nobody knew, including Maggie, was that she had night blindness. She ran around and seemed to function like the rest of us, but because of a genetic malfunction, her night vision was non-existent, as was her peripheral vision. What carried her through was strong central vision that no doubt compensated for a great deal of her vision loss in other areas. The street lamps also must have provided some help. When she was finally diagnosed later in life, she realized she was lucky something tragic had not happened as a teenager.

"How in the hell were you able to play with us and get around so well?" I once asked her. She would laugh and say:

"I really don't have a clue." Later, she found out and wrote about it:

"The loss of peripheral vision is soon manifested in the inability to maneuver in familiar surroundings. While I could still function for many years in a familiar environment, it was very difficult to function in unknown territory. Needless to say, this is a very confusing and frightening occurrence."

Maggie was familiar with the streets and sidewalks of Pilsen because she saw them during the daylight hours. She was safe in the old neighborhood, and since she possessed strong central vision, she was just one of us. And that's all she ever wanted to be.

During my last year of high school, our family moved out of Pilsen to a neighborhood five or six miles farther south. For me, it was a painful experience. All my friends were in the old neighborhood, and I really had a decision to make: would I make new friends near my new home or try to maintain my friendships in the old neighborhood? I opted to make the daily bus trips to my old stomping ground. Almost every night, I took the bus back to Pilsen—always carrying a transistor radio to listen to the White Sox game on the way home. It was not easy, but I didn't mind. I was happy with my old friends, and what a fateful decision that turned out to be. Had I made a new life for myself in my new neighborhood of Brighton Park, I would have lost Maggie.

Money was more abundant for our family by now because my mother began working. With that change in lifestyle, the two incomes gave us the ability to move to a bigger house and enjoy some of the freedom that money brings. People always drop clichés on you. Money, they say, does not buy happiness. Well, I can tell you first hand: it really does. I saw it in Maggie's life and in my own. Because we had more money, my dad gave me the old family car when he bought a new one. I was able to drive back to see my old friends more often. It also gave me a chance to drive Maggie to the movies. That series of circumstances led to the beginning of our serious courtship. Money, used wisely, can make good things happen.

When we first started to date on a regular basis, Maggie was still extremely shy. We would talk a little bit, then she would clam up. As we sat on the front stairs of her house for hours, I did most of the talking. It was almost as if Maggie feared me. She was reluctant to reveal anything. I really didn't know what to make of it. But her mother once told me that even she had trouble understanding Maggie.

There were times, however, when she was more quiet than usual. One situation stands out in my mind because it epitomizes the fears she faced almost daily.

"What's wrong?" I asked, after a brief exchange of small talk.

"Nothing."

I held her hand in silence then repeated my question. It was obvious to me that Maggie had shut down. But, I kept trying for almost an hour until finally I cracked.

"Look," I demanded. "You have something on your mind, and it's all bottled up. Let it out."

Nervously, she shared with me that she had a big chemistry test the next day and was worried she had not heard enough of the teacher's lecture to pass it. She was as close to tears as Maggie ever got in those early years. I looked into her eyes, and for the very first time, I tried to turn her fear around. By dumb luck, I responded in the best way possible.

"Hell," I said. "Just give it your best shot. That's all you can do. If you fail, screw it, and go on."

It seemed to work because Maggie opened up about how

difficult it was for her to hear even with hearing aids. She seemed to feel better having talked to me and walked home happier that night. Of course, she passed the exam the next day. We all carry fears and doubts about ourselves. But in Maggie's case, they were exacerbated by her physical challenges.

3
With God On Our Side

Those last years in high school and our early courtship turned out to be the last years of the old me. Back then I was an obedient, narrow-minded religious nerd. The soul that the church was trying to save was lifeless. I had an almost Calvinistic view of life. I was resigned to my fate devoid of real dreams. Like many kids in the old neighborhood, I figured I would eventually marry, get a job in a factory, have some kids and learn to drink and smoke cigarettes like my father. That was it. Fortunately for me and for a whole bunch of others, then-Mayor Richard J. Daley built a campus on the Near West Side called the University of Illinois at Chicago Circle. Interestingly, part of the Pilsen neighborhood was demolished so that the university could be built, but what was lost in homes was gained in creating better lives. I was one of many beneficiaries.

Maggie was in her last year of high school when I began my college studies at UICC, as it was then known. The "Circle" name, which represented the tangle of merging expressways near the campus, has been taken out. It's now called UIC. Whatever the name, this was the salvation of my life, which transformed me into a whole different person. I put into motion the John Kennedy bravado about accepting responsibility to change the world for the better.

We all now recognize the 1960s as being among the most radical times in US history, and colleges as being the hotbed of that change. Well, I got so caught up in it that most of the values I hold dear today can be traced to my college days. These were values Maggie also grew to eventually share.

I had no trouble getting into UIC. I was in the top 25 percent of my class at De La Salle High School, and that's all you needed. It may seem hard to believe, but tuition was seventy-five dollars for a ten-week period. So back then, you could go to school for $300 a year plus about $100 for books. The four years cost my parents less than $2,000! That's for an entire college education! I cannot believe what it costs today and really don't know how most parents are able to finance it. For our families, even a $2,000 education was not easy. I worked part-time as a stock boy and a doorman to help my parents pay for school. Still, each step along the way was a struggle.

When you are from a poor neighborhood, you always feel it tugging you back. I get angry when more prosperous people, afraid to set foot in the city, say people should pull themselves up by their bootstraps. Yes, that's a noble idea, but oh how hard it is to accomplish! The odds are stacked against you. While we have made some progress in this country since the 1960s, it's still a hard road for most poor people. It's almost as if your neighborhood keeps sucking you back in and making your dreams seem impossible to attain.

My goal of getting out of the old neighborhood was not made easy by one member of the Christian Brothers, the religious order that ran De La Salle. This guy was in charge of counseling kids on their college careers. When I came into the room for my mandatory meeting, he put my grades up on a screen from the college ACT test.

"Look," he said. "Here is where you finished, and here is the average of Illinois students."

Needless to say, I was well below the curve.

"You'll never make it at UIC," were his exact words. "My advice to you is to talk to your parents about attending Lewis College in Lockport." His advice did not shock me because the Christian Brothers also ran Lewis College. This guy's job was not to give advice, but to recruit. So what if he tried to destroy what little confidence a young man had—money was at stake.

As usual, I was polite and controlled my anger. I did not tell my parents about the conversation and applied to UIC. But this wonderful religious teacher of young men had one parting shot: he held up my transcripts. My mother had to call him to release the papers to UIC. I wonder how he explained all this when he met St. Peter.

The incident created an intense resentment that I carried into my first year at UIC. That first semester was a bit overwhelming. With my evening work as a stock boy at Marshall Field's department store, I did not have enough time to study and quickly fell on the probation list. Walking across campus one day, I began to think the counselor might have been right. Perhaps, I was overmatched. But then as my anger and frustration boiled up, I pumped my right fist in the air and muttered under my breath.

"No, you son of a bitch, you're wrong. I am going to make it!"

As it turned out, the incident was the best thing that could have happened. A negative became a positive. This man's misguided values became a catalyst for my success at UIC. I have never come close to facing the horrific obstacles Maggie faced and would face, but that moment in my freshman year gave me the courage to look at life differently. No one should ever tell you that you don't have a chance under any circumstances. Maggie always believed she had a chance, and this "can do" spirit motivated us throughout our lives.

Though I struggled along that first year in college, my relationship with Maggie blossomed. We saw each other on a regular basis, which allowed our mutual appreciation for each other to deepen. Sometimes, though, I felt Maggie thought I would leave her because of her hearing aids or because she was not good-looking.

The truth was, Maggie became very attractive. She stood five feet seven inches tall, with a lean athletic body. Her body had filled out to womanhood, and her face had taken on a mature beauty that was classic Irish. It was long and elegant, with a small turned up nose that gave her the look of a Barbie doll. She draped her long blonde hair over her shoulders again, as she had the day I first saw her in the playground. Ironically, however, the most striking thing was the beauty of her physically troubled eyes. They were a pretty blue; yet, it was not the color that stood out. It was something intangible: the sparkle that would now and then pierce through. Maggie had summer eyes. They were warm and sincere. If you look at her high school picture contained in this book, I think you will see her eyes also had an intangible goodness that reflected her soul. As our bond grew, I was a witness to the flashes of happiness and excitement that existed within her. I could see it especially when she looked at me. If I could have seen a reflection of my own eyes, I would have seen the same happiness and excitement when I looked at her. The feeling is impossible to put into words.

I recall the exact day we fell totally in love. Maggie and I felt it was like a scene out of a movie—but it really happened. We were at a picnic in Wauconda, a beach in Illinois. We were part of a big group of kids that had gone up there on a warm and sunny

Saturday in summer. I don't think Maggie and I ever went into the water. We spent the day talking and laughing and eating and having a wonderful time. I sensed she realized I wanted to make her my life.

As things quieted down in the afternoon, Maggie and I went to sit on a blanket. As I laid down, she grabbed my hand and leaned over me. While lying on my back and looking up at her, our eyes met. Not in laughter anymore but a more serious gaze. Maggie stared at me with a deep longing look of love in her eyes, and thank goodness, her eyes were still good enough to see the same look in mine. As I glanced up at her, happiness surrounded me. There was a feeling of eternity about it. I think we both knew we were crossing over some kind of line that was hard to define. We both knew something big had happened. We held our loving gaze for quite some time and not a single word was exchanged. We were both euphoric and held each other a lot tighter on the way home. A flame had been lit.

After our moment together on the beach, I called Maggie everyday. She would go into her closet at home, lock the door, and talk to me in private. Slowly, she revealed more and more about her inner thoughts. Maggie was trying to overcome a whole bunch of fears. It seems we all had self-esteem problems in the old neighborhood, but hers were exacerbated by a hearing problem. Soon, she would be heading off to college, and she revealed her dread about leaving home. She was scheduled to go to Eastern Illinois University in Charleston, Illinois, where her brother had enrolled. I kept telling her it was a piece of cake, and I wondered why she doubted herself. Though she never let on completely, she had a fear of being in a strange environment that I did not understand at the time.

When Maggie graduated from high school and the date

of departure to college approached, I could tell she was getting really uptight. She wanted to cancel the whole thing, but on my urging—and her mother's—she took off in August of 1966. As it turned out, that September would be the beginning of a two decade mystery about what was really wrong with her eyes.

On her first day of school, Maggie called her mother, almost in tears, wanting to come home. Ann asked me to talk to her, and I urged Maggie to stay in school. I thought that maybe in a few days, she would get adjusted. We all thought it was just home sickness. But her misery continued for a week.

Every day she would tell me she wanted to come home. Her mother instructed Edward to stay close to her, so one night near the end of the week he took Maggie to a concert. He had the best of intentions, but away from the familiar streets of Pilsen, with very few street lamps in a country setting, Maggie was literally in the dark. When she told me she felt totally lost and barely found her way back to her dorm room, it was the first time she and I realized perhaps there was something seriously wrong with her eyes.

I no longer believed it was a matter of homesickness. Because I loved her so deeply and selfishly I wanted her back for myself, I told her to trust her instincts. If Eastern Illinois was not where she wanted to be, she should come home and join me at UIC. Her mother also changed her mind. Maggie came home; but she felt like a failure. It took a lot of talking and hand wringing before she regained her confidence. That, plus being back in familiar territory in the old neighborhood, soon pushed the Charleston experience into the background. She truly did not understand it. Maggie acted as if her night blindness was a fluke and life would go on as it had. Over time, it pretty much did.

No, actually, life got better because we were falling madly

in love. Still, in the cultural and religious climate of the time, there was no thought of sex. The big thing for us was to park at a lover's lane on the South Side in Marquette Park. There, all the kids would "make out." Kissing was it for us and, even then, I still feared winding up in the blazing inferno of hell at the wrong end of a pitchfork. And think of it—for eternity! Other kids were not as fearful, however, and I do remember driving up to our spot one night and seeing discarded panties from the night before on the grass. Maggie never allowed such shenanigans; kissing was it.

I proposed to Maggie at Marquette Park, though it was hardly romantic. We were talking about our plans. She wanted to go to nursing school. I was going to major in speech and theatre with the idea of becoming a sportscaster. I then blurted out, rather casually, that after college we would get married. Maggie said that sounded good to her and that was it. I told her later, however, I thought our mutual proposal came in that longing glance of love on that warm Saturday at the beach in Wauconda.

Maggie enrolled at UIC halfway through my second year, as I was working through a process of enormous personal change. By the time I graduated, I had become a completely different person. It's amazing that Maggie and I were able to stay together through this difficult period. Yet, reflecting back, I realize that it laid the groundwork for us to grow individually and as a couple for the rest of our lives together.

Whoever devised the liberal arts tradition of education is a genius in my eyes. It allows you to sample a variety of classes in your first two years. Importantly though, it makes you think about the world. The shackles of Pilsen and the resignation of never reaching my dreams were suddenly replaced by bold visions. Our parents told us that they sent us to school for a chance to have better lives than theirs. In my case, and later in Maggie's, our parents were absolutely correct.

At UIC, I read things I never heard about in high school, and I met a cross section of kids from all cultures. Our generation has a lot of flaws, but I think our strength was that we challenged everything. We asked questions and did not believe a lot of the answers. Why did high school history books gloss over the tragic injustices in the South when black men were lynched just for looking at white women? Why is it they seldom stressed the race riots that had boiled over in the United States? Why was there no discussion of the segregated military where black men risked their lives for their country only to be treated like second-class citizens when they came home? We were told blacks were lazy, and we were a better race of people. It was the mind-set of the Third Reich and the Inquisition. The more I learned, the more I grew to despise what I was.

Then there was my total change regarding religion. That was the toughest one. I was still deeply religious when I went to UIC. It was the foundation of my life. But in the 1960s, even religion came under serious attack, and I joined the fray. I realized that the religion of my time controlled people by guilt. If you were a sinner, you needed a priest to absolve you. That kept them in business since they told us we were all sinners. How did they figure out that Christ died for our sins? How can a ten or eleven year-old boy commit so great an evil that a man has to suffer and die for it? Could it be that Christ was just a great preacher whose teachings offended the powers of the time? Could it be that he was crucified for his own alleged sins against those powers as the philosopher Friederich Nietzsche claimed? And why did a Holy Ghost conceive Christ? Things I had believed without question sounded like ancient mythology written under dim candlelight in a remote dungeon.

There was a folk song at the time written by Joan Baez called *With God on Our Side*. It was a litany about the great wars: the Spanish-American War, the Civil War, and the First and Second World Wars. In each war, the claim is made that God was on their side. The last line of the song brought home the point, "If God is on our side, he'll stop the next war." Earlier in my life, I would have viewed the song as sacrilegious. Now, it made sense. My mind had been opened up. It was scary, and it was painful. But it was also exhilarating.

How Maggie felt about these changes is another story. She was not pleased with the changes she saw in me at all. Thanks to the views of her mother, Maggie embraced my changes regarding racial issues. However, she was not happy with my loss of religion. It boiled over one evening when one of her friends, Amy, was sharing a Saturday with us on Maggie's porch. Somehow, the discussion drifted towards the Church, and I rattled off my new belief that it was all nonsense to me. Amy had just come from confession and challenged me. Suddenly, she lost her cool and lashed out.

"I am in the state of grace, and you are offending everything I believe in," she shouted. I responded equally loud and dripping in sarcasm.

"I don't know where the state of grace is. All I know is that I am in the state of Illinois."

With that she bolted in tears and left. Then I received a worse broadside from Maggie. For the first time, her temper boiled over. She called me every name in the book, saying I had no right to defame anybody's religion. Whenever she was serious with me, happy or angry, she called me "Richie."

"You are warped, Richie. Totally warped," she yelled.

Of course, she was right. I felt I had to be warped to cleanse myself from a lifetime of mindless obedience. The change was painful. Part of me longed to believe in a God and in an order to life where the just are rewarded and the evil are punished. I simply could not rationalize it anymore. Ironically, many people that are skeptical about almost everything in their lives—politicians, journalists, even doctors—accept religious teachings without question. The Roman Catholic Church still tells us women can't become priests because that was the mandate of Christ. How do we know what Christ meant two millennia ago when we can't even figure out what happened to John F. Kennedy in 1963? Maggie did not care to hear such arguments from me, and while there were a lot of unhappy moments during that time in our courtship, I never stopped loving her. Even so, she did break up with me three times—flat out dumped me!

The separations did not last long. Maybe each was a month or six weeks. Maggie accused me of taking her for granted the first time. The second time, she wanted to play the field. The third time, well, I can't recall what it was. During the last separation, I dated one of Maggie's friends, Sally. We hit it off pretty well, but she dumped me for a tennis player. That's a total of four "dumpings." I guess I was warped!

Maggie and I got back together in my junior year in college, and we never parted again, until her death. I recall when we made our peace she held me extremely tight, kissing me like she had never kissed me before. Years later, when we lived on Chicago's Magnificent Mile, in a high rise overlooking the sparkling lights of Michigan Avenue, I could not resist poking fun at her.

"And to think you might have missed all this because you wanted to play the field," I joked.

"Oh hell," she laughed. "That wasn't the reason. Every time I broke up with you it was because I despised the fact my mother liked you so much." Then she put a finger in her mouth as if to throw up adding, "What girl at that age likes a mama's boy?"

It was when we got back together for the last time that Maggie left UIC to pursue classes at a South Side hospital. She was on her way to a career in nursing, her childhood dream. As it turned out, she would also meet the dream friend of a lifetime.

Maggie had to take two buses to get to class. One morning, she stuck up a conversation with a girl who had gotten on the bus at 26th Street. Maggie found out that the girl was attending the same nursing school but that was all she said, except to add that her name was Arlana. To say she was shy would be an understatement. Still somewhat shy herself, Maggie persisted and after three or four tries, Arlana began to talk to her. Slowly, but surely, they became good friends. Maggie told me about the painstaking way she made friends with Arlana. It was an interesting experience for Maggie because she was in the reverse role of being the talkative one.

Arlana loosened up, and quickly let Maggie into her life, becoming part of the family. She would come over for dinners where Maggie's mother had huge pots of chicken paprikash on the stove. Paprikash is a mixture of meats, vegetables, herbs, and spices too numerous to mention. It was all part of a huge feast in a raucous setting—like a scene from a movie. Verbal barbs and food seemed to fly around the kitchen at the same time. Arlana was always the quiet one.

But when she was alone with Maggie, she was not. Maggie had drawn Arlana from a shell of mistrust that surrounded her. It seemed to me that Arlana and I had similar backgrounds: anything different was no good; most people were not to be trusted. College changed me; Maggie changed Arlana. Both women wound up benefiting from their strong relationship. By the time they graduated from licensed practical nursing school, they were like sisters. Maggie would bark at Arlana just the way she barked at me. This was a sure sign of love.

Maggie was grateful for their friendship. Through Arlana, Maggie discovered a part of herself—the ability to bring out the best in other people. In addition, she received a form of independence. Arlana was able to drive a car while Maggie could not. These were not simple token gestures of friendship, and Maggie deeply appreciated Arlana for them, especially having mobility.

It was not that Maggie didn't try to learn to drive. Through some political chicanery, Ann got her a state-learning permit to drive a car. One afternoon, she took Maggie to an empty parking lot to practice. Well, the lessons were short-lived. Ann herself did not know how poor Maggie's eyesight was and quickly figured out that she had no peripheral vision at all. Maggie often joked about her three or four days behind the wheel.

"Thank God I was in a parking lot," she said, "or someone would have lost their toes."

With Arlana at her side, and our approaching marriage, Maggie headed for the best years of her first life. She got emotionally stronger and more confident each year. And we were sailing off on a stretch of intense happiness that we thought would never end.

4

We've Only Just Begun

When I graduated from UIC in the summer of 1969, I started my career in broadcasting at WGN-TV and Radio as a news writer. Maggie and I were at a White Sox game at the old Comiskey Park on the South Side when I asked her when she wanted to get married. Again, hardly a romantic setting. Later, she never once passed up an opportunity to rip me for it when we were with friends. "Rich proposed to me at a ballpark," she would say sarcastically.

We agreed to a ceremony in May. Maggie was adamant that it not be a big wedding. She said her family could not afford to rent a hall, pay for food, or anything else that went along with the standard wedding. I really didn't care what kind of wedding it was, but as the time approached Maggie surprised me by saying she would like to elope: take off in the middle of the night. While that had romantic appeal, I managed to talk her out of it. I pointed out that it would be too hard on our parents. After busting their butts raising us for twenty-one and twenty-three years, respectively, they didn't deserve to pick up a note in the morning to find out we were gone. I was not about to begin a new life that way, and Maggie agreed.

Soon afterwards, the fun began! In early May, we walked into the rectory of St. Procopius to set things up. A young priest named Father Terrance heard us out. When we picked out May 23rd as the date, he quickly said that was impossible. He said you had to have "bans." This involved a priest making a public announcement at a Sunday Mass for three weeks that Richard King planned to marry Margaret Smith on May 23rd. We didn't have enough time. Since I no longer feared burning in hell, I challenged Father Terrance.

"What kind of tradition is that? Who cares about bans?" I asked.

"Well," he replied, "it is a practical necessity because six months ago we made an announcement in church and found that the guy who was getting married was already married to another lady sitting in a pew and attending the Mass!"

But he did agree to call the archdiocese to see if a two-week series of bans could be arranged.

The next order of business for Father Terrance was the type of ceremony. He made a simple enough suggestion that we should have Mass before exchanging our vows. I quickly cut him off, having seen enough masses in my short life.

"No, Father," I said. "We don't need a Mass. Just give us the vows at the altar."

"But surely," he responded. "This is a big moment in your lives. It has to be marked with a fitting ceremony. Everybody has a Mass."

Full of myself, I went into a long discourse about why ceremony had never been important to Maggie and me. Having just graduated from college, my vocabulary was quite extensive. I told the beleaguered priest we viewed each moment of our lives as a special ceremony. Waking up every morning to a world of opportunities, enjoying the gift of happiness and health with family and friends, seeing the love in Maggie's eyes were all part of the same joy. I quoted the Henry David Thoreau theory about "seizing the moment" and ended with a discourse about how people are overly fixated on the trappings of life—one of the trappings being ceremony.

"People are too intense today about everything, Father," I added. "People deify everything and deification of ceremony or success or whatever is commensurate with human meanness." It was another stolen thought from Nietzsche, and it was a reach at best in trying to nail home my point.

When I was done, however, Father Terrance looked stunned.

"Did you just graduate from college?" he quipped. When I replied yes, he threw his hands in the air and laughed.

"Well, then you can get whatever you want." We were lucky to have had such a liberal priest.

Before we left, there was one more order of business. Separately, we each went into a room with Father Terrance where we were submitted to a series of questions. I guess it was designed to "weed out" lies, and it sure worked.

Maggie went in first. After she was done, I went in. Father Terrance asked me to put my right hand on two Bibles stacked on his desk and vow to tell the truth. Though I did this, the truth was, Bibles no longer scared me. The only religious value I cherished was Christ's human command to "do unto others as you would have them do unto you." I felt the rest of it was pretty much mythology. So when the Father asked me a rather simple question: "Do both sets of parents know about the wedding?" I paused. No, we hadn't told them. Believing the truth would open up a rat's nest and delay things, I lied. I told him both sets of parents knew, gambling that Maggie had also lied. What was I thinking! Of course, she hadn't. When the three of us came back together, Father Terrance pointed out the discrepancy. It was an awkward moment. His job was to test our truthfulness to others and to ourselves. Maggie and I, just as all couples do, needed to be able to rely on one another. Without honesty in our relationship that would be hard to achieve. Father Terrance understood this. Importantly, he understood I wanted nothing to stand in the way of Maggie and me becoming husband and wife as soon as possible. Without hesitation, I told him the reason I was not truthful. Being an understanding person, he simply laughed it off.

In spite of my irreverence for the church and its ceremonies, Father Terrance gladly set our wedding date for May 23, 1970.

Maggie, however, did not let me off so easily. As we left the rectory, she stared daggers at me. I knew that I was in serious trouble.

"How could you lie with your hand on a stack of Bibles?" she growled at me deservedly. I could not argue with her. What I did was wrong, and we both knew it.

One cool spring night, not long before our wedding, Maggie stunned me. We were sitting on her front stairs, and I saw the look of misgiving in her eyes. I wondered what I had done wrong because the sense of longing we shared was still there. Yet, for the first time ever I saw real doubt there, too. Enduring the silence nearly killed me as I waited for her to tell me what was on her mind.

"Richie, I know I have bad ears, and I can live with that, but I don't know what the future will hold for my eyes. They seem okay, but I know they are not right, even though I pass the eye exams."

She told me she loved me deeply but wouldn't hold it against me if I bailed out. It was as if she knew something bad was going to happen down the road.

Stunned, I found the suggestion absurd! First, she could see pretty well as far as I was concerned, and second, there was no indication at all her eyes would get worse. I understood she had trouble seeing peripherally and at night, but that was it. Quickly, I told her she was crazy. I told her I loved her, and whatever happened the rest of our lives would be dealt with together. I grabbed her, kissed her, and held her tight. The sense of relief in her body was obvious. This had been a really tough thing for her to do. She was sincerely willing to risk giving it all up. At that moment, I realized I loved a woman who was truly pure of heart. Maggie was an extremely proud woman and did not want to be a burden of any sort. She placed my happiness above her own. This was the first of many acts of courage that punctuated her life.

My mother was not surprised when I told her about the marriage. She was surprised, however, that it was just three weeks away. Maggie's mother, on the other hand, was ecstatic. Sometimes, I think she prayed for this from the first day she met me. She once told a close friend (George Fako's mother) that she never worried about Eddie or her youngest child, Patty. But she did worry about Maggie. I think she felt I was the kind of guy who would be true to her and take care of her the rest of our lives.

Only two pictures still exist of our wedding day. That's two too many. We both looked terrible, and it really was uneventful. Maggie looked tired and nervous. She cut her hair short for the wedding, and it did nothing for her. I looked fat, tipping the scales at close to 200 pounds. Many years later, my mother was looking at our remaining wedding pictures. She paused and said, "Who is this guy?" Well, it was me. Her fat son!

The short twenty-minute exchange of vows took place on a warm late-spring morning. Simon and Garfunkel were on the top of the record charts with *Bridge Over Troubled Waters*, and The Carpenters were singing *We've Only Just Begun*, a fitting title for what was taking place. *Patton* was the movie of the year, and George C. Scott was the best actor. The average price of a three-bedroom home was $23,000. The world and our lives were very different then.

Can you believe our entire wedding cost just fifty bucks? Perhaps just a bit of ceremony wouldn't have been such a bad idea! Nevertheless, the gathering after the ceremony symbolized the way Maggie and I would lead our married lives, with a small group of family and friends gathered around us. About twenty of us went to Maggie's house where her mother cooked up a great feast. Later that night, the group drove from Pilsen to my parents' house in Brighton Park for more food—polish sausage and sauerkraut, of course. In so many ways, Maggie and I were extremely lucky. Close family and friends always surrounded us.

Maggie and I left around ten o'clock to start married life in our newly rented apartment on the North Side of Chicago. It cost $100 a month, and it lived up to its price. It was a dump, one of those depressing brick apartment complexes where "the view" was the equally shabby brick apartment complex across the courtyard. Our apartment was on the top floor of a three-story building. The place had a flat roof, which meant you baked in the summertime unless you had a good air conditioner. We did not. The walls were also filthy, so before we were married Maggie went there to clean them. In another sign her eyes were not quite right, somehow, she fell off the ladder and got a huge, ugly bruise on her thigh. When I asked her how it happened, she snapped back it was just an accident. But it was the first of a series of such mishaps that Maggie would suffer. To add insult to her injury, the effort spent cleaning the walls was fruitless because the dirt streaks had become ingrained in the paint. We had to throw a new coat of paint on the walls just to make them look decent.

When we got to our apartment the night of our wedding, it was a rather sobering experience. We were far too exhausted, both physically and mentally, to even think about sex. Because of the rush-rush nature of the wedding, our apartment was almost empty. Our furniture consisted of a kitchen table and two chairs, given to us by Maggie's mother; an aluminum folding rocking chair, given to us by my parents; a box spring and mattress (no support); an electric coffee percolator; a bedroom lamp; and a ladder. It was quite the ensemble. Ralph and Alice Kramden had better furniture. Footsteps even made eerie noises as you walked on the wooden floor. Everything about the apartment was cheap and did not match up with the life I wanted to create for my new bride.

Seated at the kitchen table, I began to feel a real sense of responsibility. The reality of being married and starting a family sunk in almost immediately. I was scared. I loved Maggie so much, and I wanted our lives to be beautiful. More importantly, I didn't want to waste any time. Even at twenty-three, I knew time was precious. With tears in my eyes, I looked at Maggie and said, "Let's not waste anything. I want to enjoy every moment. Let's live hard and squeeze every ounce of happiness out of this thing." Maggie, somewhat frightened, asked me why I was weeping.

"Because this is a milestone, and I get emotional with milestones. This is the beginning of our adult lives. We have responsibilities now."

She got out of her chair, walked around the table, and sat on my lap. Stroking my hair, she tried to console me.

"We will have a good life, Richie. I know it."

Maggie and I went to sleep on our luxurious box spring and mattress. They were so low it felt like sleeping in a hole. With no end tables, Maggie left her hearing aids on the floor beside the bed. Naturally, I almost stepped on one of them and crushed it. She slept like a rock, but I couldn't. The emotion of the day and sleeping with Maggie for the first time made me toss and turn. Eventually, I fell asleep; however, a rather loud echo awakened me. It was morning already, and Maggie was making coffee. The percolator resonated through the empty flat like a gurgling stream through a lonely mountain pass. But as we woke up, husband and wife for the first time, the fatigue and gloom of the night were replaced by the glow and optimism of a sunny spring day. We were headed for the airport and then the foothills of Denver, Colorado for our honeymoon.

Just like our apartment, I had gone cheap. We stayed at a deluxe Ramada Inn west of Denver. The rooms faced the foothills but that was the only redeeming quality unless you consider a pool, color television, and clean towels among the extras. Like our arrangement of the wedding, our first night of sex turned into a comedy of errors. We had planned to wait a few years to have a family, so Maggie bought a diaphragm as a birth control device. She did not want to take birth control pills and did not want me to use a condom. The problems arose when Maggie put the thing in the wrong way. I was all set for my first big night of lovemaking, and it went nowhere. I felt like I was making love to the Great Wall of China. And there was another problem: Maggie, for some reason, clung to the bed sheets for fear of being totally naked. This was a remnant of her youthful shyness. I remember asking her to take the damn sheets away. She apparently was worried about showing her entire body nude.

"You haven't got an ounce of fat on you. You're as hot as can be, and you want to hide?" I joked. She got the message and tossed the sheets aside. It was an awkward session at best, and the second night was not much better.

On the third day of the trip, we both had extremely sore throats, which turned out to be the advent of a bad virus that led to bronchitis for both of us. A lot of time the rest of the week was spent in Walgreen's getting drugs. That was the honeymoon!

When we got back home, we went about the task of furnishing the house. I got my first real taste of Maggie's spending habits. They would become legendary later in her life, but I learned early that Maggie had a philosophy totally alien to my mother. Maggie believed in buying the best. So when I took her to my mother's favorite furniture store, Joe Shwenk's Discount Furniture on 26th and Kedzie, she took one look and said: "We're not buying any of this cheap crap!" The word "discount" was not in her vocabulary. I fought her on this philosophical difference, as well as on other matters, during the first few months of our marriage. It's hard to adjust to the lifestyle of another person, even if you love them deeply. But a few months into our marriage, I made a decision. Since I had vowed to make her happy, I decided to pretty much give in to her, whatever she wanted, within reason. I recommend that for any husband. Most men have no feel for household things or the desire to mess with them. After I gave Maggie control of all that stuff things really clicked in, and we became a team in every sense of the word. Instead of thinking about my own habits of living, I focused entirely on making Maggie happy. I gave myself to her, and for me, that was rather easy.

5

No Stinking Insurance

The "Joe Shwenk" episode was my first and last attempt at buying anything important for any of the places we lived. Maggie did it all and loved it. I often told her shopping was the second big love of her life and the margin between one and two was not all that great. I did go with her to buy the furniture, but it was always her call. Who cared anyway? I really only needed a decent chair, a TV, and a corner of the living room. She could have the rest. Sadly, even furniture did not help the appearance of our place. It was now a furnished dump.

There are few good memories of that apartment, but one was priceless and really sums up Maggie's philosophy of life and her amazing fortitude. Since we planned on having a family, I decided we needed life insurance. Through a friend at work, I set up a meeting at our apartment with a young insurance salesman named Ron Rugo. Making the mistake that most rookie husbands make, I forgot to tell Maggie about the meeting, figuring she would have no objection. For all you young husbands out there— never assume your wife will go along with anything.

Maggie was extremely upset.

"Who wants to talk about life insurance? We don't even plan on having kids for a few years," she barked.

My weak explanation that it was good to get life insurance

early, to protect her, made little sense to Maggie. In a style that exemplified her mother, Maggie said, "We don't even have mortgage payments, and if you croak, I will be fine. I don't need anymore money." She was fiercely independent. When I told her it was too late to cancel the meeting (Rugo was already on his way), she became more upset.

As it turned out, poor Rugo wound up suffering for my mistake. When he walked in the door, Maggie was as cold to him as an ice cube. Being the salesman he was, he gave it his all but the small talk and the attempts at humorous banter just made Maggie's eyes even more piercingly cold. Maggie quickly shot down Rugo's first proposal. His sales pitch went nowhere. For me, it quickly evolved from an awkward scenario into a humorous one. I learned how dogged and determined my new wife could be. Rugo began back peddling and lowered his offer then lowered it again over a half hour period. Maggie simply said, "No, we don't want it." Rugo had the look of a beaten man. He tried to rework plans to please her but Maggie was having none of it. We all know that insurance salesmen almost never give up and watching Rugo and Maggie battle it out was like a heavyweight test of wills. After about an hour, Maggie had Rugo on the ropes; he was totally exasperated.

"Okay, Mrs. King," he said, "so you don't want anything big now but how about this—a $5,000 policy to cover burial costs for you and Rich?"

"We're not getting buried," Maggie coldly replied.

"What?" Rugo replied with a startled look on his face.

"No," Maggie replied. "We're donating our bodies to science."

"You're going to end up in a bottle?" Rugo sputtered.

"You got it!" Maggie responded.

With that, the fight was over. Maggie won by a unanimous

decision. Rugo left the apartment in a daze, lugging his heavy volumes of insurance books under his arm. I have never seen a man look more defeated. When he left, Maggie was still fuming, but I had a good laugh.

"You realize," I said, "that you may have put the poor guy on suicide watch. He'll probably get home tonight, close the garage door, keep the motor running, and take the gas pipe." That seemed to lift the anger, and Maggie began to laugh while still pointing a finger at me.

"We don't need any stinking insurance," she laughed.

A few months later Maggie also suggested strongly that we get out of the dump we were living in. I could hardly argue. We found a much fresher and lighter brand new apartment on the South Side near my parent's home. What a difference! Even though we had a lot of truck traffic noise, the new place lifted our spirits. We were getting happier everyday, and both our careers were off and running.

I was a news writer and producer for WBBM Radio, the all-news station in Chicago. It was an important time to be in news. There was plenty of it in the early 1970s. Viet Nam, Watergate, the Tate-LaBianca murders, the Middle East, then-Mayor Richard J. Dalcy ... all were huge stories. I felt like I was part of history by informing the public.

Maggie and Arlana received their licensed practical nursing degrees from the Chicago Board of Education School of Nursing in 1969 then joined Rush Presbyterian-St Luke's Hospital, which at the time was one of the biggest and best in Chicago. While working as practical nurses, they went to school for two years at St. Mary of Nazareth Hospital to obtain their diplomas as Registered Nurses. Arlana drove them to work and school everyday. They loved their careers and thrived on the hard work demanded of them.

Then about a year and a half into the start of our new lives, Maggie's mother suffered a perforated ulcer. Luckily, she was rushed to the hospital in time to stop the internal bleeding, which controlled the ulcer. But while there, the doctors discovered she had lung cancer. Smoking for so many years had taken its toll. She was just fifty-five years old. Maggie and her sister Patty took her to most of her monthly chemotherapy sessions. I took up the slack whenever they needed. It was pretty obvious to me from these interactions with Ann that she was not going to make it. So what was truly an eye opening learning experience for me was how the entire Smith family handled it: with dogged determination and no show of emotion. Maggie took care of her mother religiously but we never talked about the obvious: death. I loved Ann, and when I tried to express it, I got no response from Maggie. Now, the Rugo experience made sense.

"Hey, she's not dead yet," she would say. "Maybe the chemo will work."

It didn't.

I remember Ann's response after we got back from one grueling chemo session. She told me she was done with the stuff. It wasn't worth feeling so horribly bad. Her exact words were "to hell with it." It was a sad time but not without its humor.

As usual, a bizarre "only in Pilsen" type story developed during Ann's illness. I had saved $10,000 by then and made the mistake of telling my father-in-law that I was thinking of putting a down payment on a summer home. Suddenly, his usually laid back nature changed.

"King," he said jumping up (Maggie's mother and father called me King because they both knew my father when they were growing up), "there's a nice place for sale up in Prairie du Chien."

When you are young, you sometimes do things that you can't later explain, but I actually thought this would be a good idea, even though I hated fishing, which was the big thing up there. Prairie du Chien is a small town up in Wisconsin on the backwaters of the Mississippi. So I drove to Wisconsin with Maggie to check it out, and boy was I impressed. It was right on the water and had a wonderfully rustic smell to it. There were two bedrooms and a big living room, which featured a moose head on the wall. I wanted to buy the place, but Maggie had reservations.

"You have no idea what you're doing," she said. "Let's just drive back and later you can come back with your father and have HIM check it out."

She was wise beyond her years.

When my father saw the place he laughed.

"Where's the washroom?" he asked.

"Oh, it's in the back, it's an outhouse," I said.

"You want to buy a place with an outhouse?" he asked, shaking his head. He also looked at the beams supporting the structure and found one rotting. Some of the cabinets inside were not finished. He went to look at the outside and laughed again.

"Look at these mosquitoes, they look like dive-bombers!" he said. That pretty much sealed the deal. I felt deservedly stupid and ended "negotiations" to buy the place. He and Maggie had saved my butt.

When I got back, I visited Ann in her bedroom. She was almost totally emaciated from cancer. Her eyes, circled by huge black rings, made her look like one of the victims of the Holocaust. It was frightening to see. As I told her negotiations for the summerhouse were off, she looked relieved. In her dying voice, made raspy from cancer, she said, "Thank goodness. All Ed (her husband) wanted was to use your cottage for free and booze it up with his drunken bums. It would have been a huge mistake."

That was the last time I saw her.

Ann died on a Friday morning in July of 1972. I was working at WBBM, but Maggie was at her mother's side along with Ann's sister, Irene, known as Auntie "I." Maggie called the funeral parlor. In the immediate hours after Ann's death, Auntie "I" and Maggie were sitting at the table when a man knocked on the door and, looking rather somber, asked to see Ann. He was dressed in a sports jacket and dress shirt so they naturally thought he was the funeral director. They sent him to the bedroom and heard him sobbing. He was on his knees leaning over the body, "Oh Ann, oh Ann," he cried. Auntie "I" got suspicious and walked into the room. "Oh. She's gone!" the man moaned with teary eyes.

"Who are you?" she asked.

"I'm Whitey, one of Ed's friends from Locko's."

Showing the toughness of her recently departed sister, Auntie "I" immediately kicked the guy out. If Ann had known what had happened, she would have been furious that one of the "drunken bums" from the tavern had gotten in to see her.

Taking her mother's death stoically, Maggie never once cried. In fact, the wake and funeral amounted to endless stories and jokes about Ann's life. At the time, I did not understand, but that was the typical Irish wake. They buried their pain deep inside and covered it up with black humor. I was in tears most of the time. Ann was really the first person I loved that had passed away. I felt a kinship with Ann's soul in our mutual love for her daughter and shared with her the promise that I would take care of Maggie. I felt I had lost my only ally, not knowing at the time how deep the relationship between Maggie and her best friend Arlana had become. I don't know if Ann realized it either before she left this earth. She would have been very happy.

Arlana and Maggie were similar in a lot of ways. They both cared deeply about helping people inside and outside their jobs. They were both religious in those years. They enjoyed the same hobbies, cooking and working out. Still what made the relationship really work is that they were also very different. Maggie was more bold and daring and willing to try anything. Arlana was less adventurous and provided an anchor for Maggie. Throughout her life, Arlana was there by Maggie's side. Upon completing their coursework to become registered nurses, Arlana and Maggie would work side-by-side over the next twenty years.

Sadly, Ann was not there to see Maggie realize her dream of becoming a Registered Nurse in 1973. If ever there was a person suited to be a nurse, it was Maggie. She even looked the part in her white uniform with the long blonde hair cascading from underneath the white cap. Besides looking good, she was extremely efficient at her profession. You have to preface anything you say about Maggie by pointing out she had no peripheral vision or night vision and had two hearing aids. What often overcame these setbacks in her life was an adamant determination to show people she could do the job. Also, her intellect and memory were amazing. Fellow workers were always amazed at Maggie's extreme intelligence and incredible photographic memory. She had it in her brain what she had to do and from all accounts almost never forgot to do it. When lives are at stake, quite literally, you really can't afford any slip-ups. Maggie never had a major one in her career.

As registered nurses, Arlana and Maggie settled in at Rush Presbyterian Hospital. They were selected to work on floor 10K in the old building of the hospital: the largest ward in the place with forty-seven beds in four modules. Each module had twelve patients with all kinds of ailments: cancer, kidney problems, even

AIDS before they knew what it was. Can you imagine the risk? Yet Maggie always told me her AIDS patients were the kindest people she had in the hospital, treating the nurses with dignity and respect and seldom causing a problem. There were two or three nurses that handled a 12-bed module. Maggie was especially adept at kidney dialysis since it involved a lot of mathematics. Her central vision was quite good during that time. She did not even need glasses. There were also an endless variety of pills to handout and medications to inject. It was serious and complex work.

Maggie and Arlana were put on the overnight shift, 11 p.m. to 7 a.m., and while it's a graveyard in most professions, in nursing the best people are placed on the overnight shift. They sometimes have to make quick decisions since there are not a lot of doctors around during those hours. So they have to be good. Maggie and Arlana always got in early to check their charts and set things up.

"The amazing thing about Maggie," Arlana said, "is that when she talked to the nurse going off duty, Maggie never took a lot of notes. She memorized a good portion of the information about each patient. She seemed to remember every detail. The rest of us had to make our lists."

At times, Maggie and Arlana would have to "float," which meant the nurses on another floor might need extra help. So they would have to fill-in in a totally different area with totally different patients. Nobody really liked to "float," but they all did it because it was part of the job. Maggie never seemed to have a problem when she "floated," handling a strange floor with the same sharpness as 10K.

Maggie was also a floor supervisor at times. She would oversee the whole ward handling admissions, emergencies, and handing out assignments. Maggie and Arlana had gripes about nursing but they were never about having too much work or not enough wages. They would always talk about patient care. They were dedicated to it even at the risk of their own health. When I heard some of the extreme measures nurses in New Orleans had taken during the aftermath of Hurricane Katrina I thought of Maggie and Arlana. Nurses will do almost anything to help people get better, and in some cases, even save their lives. As for me, I get queasy just walking past a hospital. I never understood how Maggie could do her job with such relish.

Any slight pain for me is the beginning of the end. I don't know how many times I bothered her about things that a simple aspirin could correct. One day, Maggie came home with an article from a trade journal that suggested taking huge amounts of Vitamin A would improve one's eyesight. Naturally, Maggie bought a case of the stuff for herself, and since I didn't want to be left behind, I popped the pills without telling her. When I returned from work one afternoon, I went to the toilet and to my utter shock my urine was dark, as if there was blood mixed in. I got so weak I had to lie down in bed. When Maggie came home a few minutes later, and saw me in the sack, she looked concerned.

"Are you sick?" she asked.

"Worse than that," I replied. "I'm finished. I have blood in my urine. I guess we better call the doctor. I may have the "big C."

I was dead serious, no pun intended.

"Wait a minute!" Maggie said. "What were you doing? Did you strain yourself lifting something? Did you fall down or have any kind of trauma?" She rattled off a list of possibilities and then asked me if I had eaten something different. At first I said no then thought about the Vitamin A. The second I mentioned it, Maggie burst into a hysterical laughter. She was laughing so hard she had to leave the room.

"What?" I asked.

"When you take too much Vitamin A your body excretes it. The urine comes out dark," she explained.

It wasn't blood at all. I was perfectly fine. I wasn't going to die, not yet anyway.

It was very comforting being married to a nurse, and in the course of our marriage, I lost track of the times Maggie would set me straight. At various points in my life I thought I had a heart condition, brain tumor, polio, cancer of the tooth and a myriad of other ailments. We would always have a good laugh about it. For me, a trip to the dentist was being "under the knife." Every annual physical might reveal some terminal illness.

"So," Maggie would joke after I would come home from a physical, "did the doctor give you six months to live?"

She knew her stuff and cared greatly about her patients. This was evident in her anger with hospital administrators when they made financial decisions overriding the welfare of her patients. She also got angry about the sloppiness and sometimes incompetence of doctors. Most of us exalt doctors because of their education and power over life and death matters. But Maggie saw doctors as no better or worse than the rest of us.

"There are good ones and bad ones," she would say. "Just like plumbers."

I think about this every time I meet an arrogant doctor, and sadly, I have met quite a few. It scares you to think that your life might be in the hands of an incompetent doctor, but there are more around than the average person might think.

Regardless of the challenges in providing quality patient care, Maggie loved her profession. She had a direct impact on people's lives, and throughout the years, she and Arlana befriended scores of patients, even seeing a good many outside the hospital.

"Things were so good in the old days," Arlana said. "You had time, and you had enough people to give the patients top-notch care."

Maggie was content being a part of that noble endeavor even if she was poorly paid. I made five times the money she made because I was in the entertainment business. You wonder why people value a sportscaster, or any entertainer, more than a nurse or any health care professional whose responsibilities are so much greater. The values are totally out of whack. But what else is new!

Importantly, Maggie and Arlana's friendship was sealed by their years together in the trenches of nursing. When you deal with illness, death, and sadness on a daily basis, it's got to feel like being in a war. War buddies are close for life. When Maggie's mother died, I lost a huge force in helping me make Maggie happy. As it turned out, Arlana took up a lot of the slack.

6
The Rat Pack

Maggie and I were also fortunate to enjoy the friendship of a lifetime with two other young couples. It was amazing to experience the process of casual friendship becoming a family-type bond. Ron Gorski and Jim Benes became my best friends at UIC when we all were in the Broadcasting Club. We had a lot in common. Jim is Czech, and he grew up in the western suburb of Cicero, and later in North Riverside. He and I shared the same religion and the same family background. His father was also a World War II veteran and was quite a character. He once came down in the living room during one of our parties dressed in long underwear and a coon-skin cap using a broom as a shot gun. It was his inebriated imitation of Davy Crockett. It was something my or Maggie's father would have done. Jim is extremely intelligent and was the president of the Broadcasting Club at UIC. He also is the most generous man I have ever met. We became friends almost instantly.

The same thing happened with Ron. His family originally was from Brighton Park. Yes, it's the same area that my family had settled in when I was in high school. What's amazing is that he, too, had a hard-drinking father. It makes you wonder whether anyone from that era didn't have a father who sucked up the booze to excess. Ron is the funniest man I have ever met. He has a Gene

Wilder sense of timing, with the facial expressions to match. He was the anchorman during our Broadcasting Club days at UIC, and we all had a blast.

What made the friendship work so well is that we always supported each other. We quickly became brothers sharing pretty much the same political views, meaning we were against everything in the 1960s. We also shared the same views on women—none of us ever got close to all of the so-called "free love" of the 1960s. Ron dated one woman who burst into tears after he took her to see a movie called *Rosemary's Baby*, in which Mia Farrow gets impregnated by the devil.

"She got in the car and started crying, calling me a pervert for taking her to the movie," he told us. She never went out with him again. That summed up our luck. Jim dated sporadically and I, of course, was involved with Maggie, getting dumped three times.

Jim and Ron accompanied me to buy a car one day, and both had a bright idea about how to get a better deal.

"Look," they said, "the guy is going to low-ball you when he gives you the price for your car on the trade-in. So no matter what he says tell him you have somebody waiting, maybe your brother, to buy it for a $1,000 more. He'll have to come up." It seemed like good advice, so we were all sitting there when the dealer came back after analyzing my car.

"Okay, Mr. King, I'll give you $3,500 for your Chevy." Seizing the moment, I employed the Gorski-Benes strategy.

"Well," I said, "that's a bit too low. My brother wants to give me $4,500."

"Fine," the dealer shot back, "sell it to him, come back and we'll make a deal."

He didn't go up a penny! Benes and Gorski looked stunned. When we left we joked about the Polish-Czech car buying technique that accomplished nothing except to give the salesmen a good chuckle. Sales guys have heard it all.

Jim became a news writer and producer at WBBM–AM Radio after college and later Ron also joined the station as a writer. He later left to try his luck as a TV news producer in St. Louis and Green Bay. At that point, I left WGN-TV then later joined WBBM–AM as a news writer. A few months before Ron left WBBM AM, he got married. He had met Gail while at UIC. She was part of our gang that gathered for coffee at the student union on a regular basis. Gail had a pretty heart-shaped face with dainty features, beautiful hazel eyes, and long, flowing 1960s style hair. She was on the quiet side and extremely intelligent. Her love was plants and gardening, which led her to an associate's degree in horticulture. Ron and Gail were married in 1969 a year before Maggie and I exchanged vows.

As for Jim, he married three years later. Andrea Wiley was born on the South Side in the Chatham neighborhood. She also had long black hair, a classically beautiful face, and the slender body of a model. She is warm, outgoing, and extremely well-read, having been a broadcast major at Southern Illinois University in Carbondale. She began her career at WBBM–AM Radio as a desk assistant and worked with Jim and me in the newsroom. One day Andi, as we call her, asked me about Jim, who was interested in another woman at the time. I happened to mention to her that whatever woman Jim marries would be lucky because he would make a great husband. About six months later when I went to visit Jim at his apartment in Hinsdale, it was Andi who opened the door dressed in a bathrobe. About a year later, they were married in a beautiful ceremony at Bond Chapel on the campus of the University of Chicago. Ron and I were the best men for Jim, but the wedding was not without a degree of sadness. Andi is African-American, and Jim's parents boycotted the wedding out of a misguided prejudice ingrained in their lives at the time. Eventually, they embraced Andi, forming a typical family relationship where the color of her skin didn't matter. It was a happy ending after all.

As it turned out, Andi, Gail, and Maggie also became close friends. They were all similar in that they were well-educated and part of a generation that changed things for women. Gail's mother, like Maggie's, had been a homemaker. Andi's mother had been a Registered Nurse. Maggie, Gail, and Andi were feminists in the truest sense. They made sure they were equals in the marriage. While they were strong-willed, they were not hard-boiled. They were able to mix it up pretty well when it came to fun. I often told Maggie that I did not understand men who wanted to subjugate their partners. I don't know whether the present generation appreciates what these women of the 1960s did. By their own will power, they made life better for everybody, including men. Intelligence is extremely sexy.

If you were designing a blue print for compatible couples, you could not design a better one than the one we all enjoyed. What was amazing about it was that it was not just all the women sharing their lives with each other, or just the men. It was a total mixture. I could talk to Andi, Ron could talk to Maggie, and Gail could talk to Jim as friends. It was a total sharing of ideas, and boy, did we have some times. We became the "Hinsdale Rat Pack" because we all lived in that affluent suburb southwest of Chicago. We had long wine-soaked talks about every issue you could imagine: race, religion, politics, and sex. We exposed our inner thoughts because we got support from the group, even if there was a difference in philosophy. It's amazing how much your life can be enhanced when you let people in. Maggie and I learned a lot about ourselves from these discussions. We always felt good afterwards, reaching the kind of security, perhaps, that we never received from our families.

Everyone in our group had something valuable to offer, but Andi and Maggie probably had the most. Andi offered us the realities of being black. Most white people never really get to know a black person. By that, I don't mean a casual or friendly relationship; I mean really get to know them on a deep and personal level. That's the way we felt about everyone in the group. Andi told us things we never knew. She spoke of light-skinned blacks, who had ill feelings towards darker-skinned blacks. In 1984, a movie came out called *A Soldier's Story* that addressed the divisions within the black community itself. This story hit home for Andi, and she shared with us how her father had served in the Army Air Core during World War II only to be called a "nigger" while wearing his Army uniform. She also explained the extra pressure on blacks to make sure they did not fail in the business world because it would show poorly on their race. Andi said she dealt with the situation by smoking. It allowed her to exhale the anger and anxieties of dealing with whites who did not know or want to deal with educated blacks. Back then a business meeting usually meant a big group of white males. She would be the only woman and the only black in her meetings. In short, she told the truth on a variety of racial issues, but not in a vindictive manner. It made us all think. The Civil Rights movement of the 1960s seemed to die with Dr. Martin Luther King, and while blacks may have made major legal and business strides over the years, it doesn't appear the country, in general, has any better moral outlook than it did back then. During our discussions among the couples, I used myself as an example of how things can change, and it involves education. The facts are there, from lynching to "whites only" toilets. When you read this stuff, you realize all the nonsense that had been drummed into you as a child was based on total ignorance. How it still exists in many forms today is tragic.

Because of her mother, Maggie did not need the transformation I needed. She related to Andi especially well because in a different way, Maggie was also a victim of discrimination. When you are laughed at as a kid because of hearing aids, or when people think you are dumb because you can't hear, it stays with you. Maggie shared these experiences and more with the group. On a daily basis, she dealt with sickness and dying. I will never understand how she did it. Because of her warm heart, she really cared for her patients. She would have to hold someone's hand as he or she lay near death. She would see the pain in the faces of family members who arrived at the hospital right after a loved one had died. She spoke of young men dying from some disease that caused an immune system disorder, never realizing at the time that one slip of a needle might cost her own life. The name AIDS had not yet been applied to the disease. A nurse gives more than physical care, and if you have ever been in a hospital, you know the difference between a nurse going through the motions and one that cares about you. Maggie cared deeply.

We all had different beliefs in religion. We were all raised Roman Catholics but saw the traditional church as pretty much a farce. Yet none of us was quite willing to write-off God. When issues were raised such as why God allowed the Holocaust, there were explanations. Andi thought that God is like a scientist. Just like a scientist who does experiments, even if He thinks He knows the outcome, God doesn't interfere. He lets the experiment play itself out. Jim believed God was a life force too complex for us to understand. Maggie and Gail felt pretty much the same way, but they believed in a spiritual realm beyond the physical. Ron and I were the closest to being non-believers, but even we held out hope that our existence was due to something greater than evolution. We were agnostics.

The amazing thing is that we could talk about religion and politics and still remain close friends. I think it was because we had a sense of humor. Ron and I always used to throw in a zinger to lighten up the conversation. When Jim would be talking about socialism, Ron would call him a "pinko Commie," and everyone would laugh. Or when someone defended a right wing cause, someone would shoot a left hand in the air and say "Heil, Hitler." I remember one conversation about how much brainpower you need to play the game of golf. "That's right," Ron would say. "That's why those of us who are Polish are so deficient."

In discussing music, I pointed out to Maggie that 8 of every 10 Irish songs make some reference to whiskey or getting drunk. It was all politically incorrect, but when you share love and respect with friends, it's taken for what it is—fun.

We had plenty of it. All of us loved to drink wine, and Jim befriended a Bulgarian wine salesman named Dimitri Dimitroff. His claim to fame was that he escaped communism by making it out of his country in a rowboat—or, so he said. He had such a thick accent you could barely understand him. When his presentation was done and all the crackers and free wine were consumed, we had such a "buzz" we would each buy four or five cases. I learned to imitate Dimitroff so well that I would call Jim on the phone the following day posing as Dimitroff. I would address Jim as "Meester Benesh" and then explain that his bill amounted to an additional $200 because of new Bulgarian tax laws enacted in the past twenty-four hours. We were all totally fried.

There was also the time Jim ordered parts to build a living

room chair. Every time we came to visit, he would show us the progress of his brown-varnished creation. When completed, it did look pretty good. One evening, Jim was sitting in the chair when we all became engrossed in a heated discussion. He pointed a finger at me and said, "Your bullshit argument just doesn't stand up." As if on cue, at that exact moment, his new chair collapsed, and he went down in a heap—glass of wine and all! The place went up for grabs, and thirty years later, we are still laughing.

On another occasion, Maggie and I went out to dinner with Andi and Jim and arrived at the restaurant early. There was a word we always used in Pilsen when we thought a guy was a jerk. We called him a "haufnaut." I have no idea where it comes from. One explanation is that it means horse manure. Of course, it could be that someone made up the word. Well, Jim thought it was hilarious, and we always called each other "haufnauts." At the restaurant, the young lady who was the maitre d' invited Maggie and I to sit at the bar to have a drink while we waited for Jim and Andi. "May I ask your name, sir?" "Haufnauts, Charles Haufnauts," I explained, with a straight face. I even spelled it out for her as she tried hard not to laugh. Maggie just shook her head. When Jim and Andi arrived, we greeted them at the desk and you could see the young lady holding back again. "Okay, Mr. Haufnauts, this way please." Jim was dying all the way to the table. When we finally sat down, and the young lady was gone, Andi said, "Rich, why do you do things like that?" I replied, "I guess because *I'm* a haufnaut."

Those were wonderful days. There is a song by John Denver that came out at just about that time called *Poems, Prayers, and Promises*. Some of the lines fit our group perfectly.

"We talk of poems and prayers and promises and things

59

that we believe in: How good it is to love someone, how right it is to care, how long it's been since yesterday, what about tomorrow, what about the dreams and all the memories we shared."

We were sharing a good life, and we were in our prime. Maggie's central vision was fine. She could walk anywhere. Read paperback novels. Do most of the things the rest of us could do. While she occasionally would have trouble hearing, it was not a major problem especially since everyone in the group made sure they spoke up. Once when Jim was mumbling, Andi blasted him. "Speak up so Maggie can hear," she demanded. It was that kind of group. Everybody was very caring. While we had loads of fun at home, it got even better and more titillating when we began to take our mid-winter vacations.

I do not use the word "titillating" lightly. Our first one was with Ron and Gail, and it was something special. We had planned to get in tip-top shape for the trip. Ron and I, at that time, were hooked on racquetball, playing almost everyday. Our talent level was about the same so the games were long, drawn out grueling affairs. We sometimes played three matches over an hour and a half, leaving both of us drenched with sweat. We also lifted weights so our bodies were well-cut. Maggie and Gail also worked out. They both wanted to be in top form in their bikinis.

We left Chicago in the middle of January on our very first winter vacation with the temperature at 10 degrees. Four hours later, we arrived in Jamaica and the thermometer at the airport read 85 degrees. The bus ride to our resort in Ocho Rios featured an onboard ice cooler with drinks courtesy of the hotel. The pressures of home and work evaporated quickly as I spent most of the bus trip looking at Maggie. She was in her prime now.

Her beautiful face, with those long elegant features, barely had a wrinkle. Her fair complexion radiated with a healthy glow. Her blonde hair was still breathtaking and very long, blowing over her shoulders by the warm tropical breeze pouring through the open windows, as the bus sped along a narrow highway. As always, it was Maggie's eyes that got to me. They were so full of life, reflecting the happiness within her. There was not a cynical bone in her body. I loved her to the bottom of my soul.

On the first day of our vacation, I realized Maggie's shy days were over. When she took off her robe on the beach, she revealed a skimpy purple string bikini that did not leave much to the imagination. Gail matched her with a white-knit bikini that was as close to being see-through as you could get. They were both stunning and set the tone for the trip, which turned into the hedonistic adventure of our lives.

We were on a package deal, which included drinks. On the first morning of the trip, we sat in the lounge, watching people storm the bar when it opened at eleven in the morning.

"Look at that," Ron said. "It's like a pack of lions heading for raw meat." Once we sampled the drinks, we were among the lions the rest of the week. Those Jamaican rum drinks were incredible. A Jamaican Delight featured rum, whipped cream, and crushed ice. A Dirty Banana was a concoction that featured crushed bananas, rum, and cream. Each drink had to be about 500 calories. We consumed four or five in a sitting. It was a booze-soaked week of fun. Ron and I were tipsy about 70 percent of the time. The only thing that saved us was our physical activity, which included swimming, volleyball, and sex.

Whoever said women reach their sexual peak in their thirties was right on the money! For the first three days, we just drank, ate, and frolicked in the bedroom. Maggie was into it everyday.

Ron had the same thing going with Gail. On the fourth day of the trip when we were in the washroom at pool side, Ron told me he had had it.

"We have to get a break," he moaned. "I am actually sore." We got the wives to give us one day off. We had met our matches.

The week turned into a trip to Paradise. There were pool side games for all the couples and fashion shows with women's and men's bathing suits. The men, of course, were modeling the latest Speedos, getting great reviews from Maggie and Gail. One night when Maggie and Gail really got tipsy, Ron and I talked them into visiting the nearby nude beach the next day. It was actually a small island. Boldly, both ladies said they would do it. The next day, in the sober light of the morning, they both conceded they were drunk the night before.

"Are you crazy? Go to a nude beach?" Gail responded. "Forget it."

When the seven days were up I had gained about eight pounds and actually had a small gut. Considering we piled on about 5,000 calories a day, it was quite understandable. The two-hour bus ride from the resort to the airport was perhaps the most peaceful time I have ever had in my life. Maggie said she felt the same. We were completely relaxed and satisfied, entertained by the driver who sang Jamaican folk songs as he took us to the airport. I told Maggie I had never been as happy in my life and hoped it would never end. She said she felt the same way. It didn't end, at least for about six or seven years. The Jamaican trip was just the beginning of a series of adventures that we shared as couples, and as friends.

Andi and Jim joined us for other vacations during the next few years. Four of them were spent in Acapulco. Though we never got close to a nude beach, Maggie and Andi went topless, accidentally that is. Andi was standing in the shallow water at Paradise Beach in Acapulco when an unexpected wave clocked her pretty good in the face. She was stunned and trying to clear the water from her eyes not realizing the wave had ripped off her bikini top, which was now strung around her neck. Jim and I were not about to tell her to fix it. It was about a minute or so before she realized what had happened. The men on the beach were praying for another wave. The same thing happened to Maggie on a different trip. She also did not realize what had happened and, actually, an old man standing next to her told her. Ron and I almost attacked the old guy.

The strip in Acapulco is full of people asking for handouts of money. One day as we were walking along, good-hearted Jim was handing out coins to just about everybody who asked. When we got back to the room, he suddenly could not find the key to the condo.

"Jesus," he said, looking startled, "I think I may have given our room key to a beggar." We all cracked up telling Jim that if anybody showed up, they would be taking his room.

The wonderful trips, the days, the weeks, and the years all seemed to fly by. Maggie took a pass on some activities because of her vision problem. Ron, Gail, and I made the tricky walk up the Dunn's River Falls in Jamaica, while Maggie watched. She also took a pass on parasailing in Acapulco. Still, she pretty much did the rest, even horseback riding in Colorado and snorkeling in Aruba, where the water was a bright blue providing Maggie's eyes with enough light. She was also able to take part in bicycle riding at Washington Island in Door County, Wisconsin. But perhaps her favorite place of all was Las Vegas.

We went to Vegas at least once a year for about ten years. It's a perfect place for people who have trouble seeing. It's always bright, day and night, in the casinos. Maggie loved the slot machines because she could see them perfectly with her narrow central vision, and she loved the jingle of the coins when they pelted happily in the tray after she had won. As for me, I played blackjack exclusively, and I always controlled the amount of money we could lose. Ninety percent of the time you do lose in Vegas, no matter what people tell you. Arlana and Maggie would disappear into the casino, but in about a half hour they would reappear at my blackjack table with long faces. Maggie especially looked forlorn and would look at me with sad eyes saying she was wiped out. Naturally, I would take another $50 from my wallet and give it to her. This would happen quite often in the course of our trips, and only later did I find out from Arlana that on many occasions Maggie was actually *winning* at the slots. She was pocketing the extra money I gave her for later shopping excursions! She had developed a foolproof system.

Her spending habits became legendary. She truly lived for the moment. I did my best to control things, but my heart was simply too soft. In our first house in Hinsdale, Maggie insisted on remodeling every room, picking out bathroom tile or a sink or a stove was happiness to her. I once joked that if it came down to a new couch or an intimate evening with me, she would have chosen the couch. We could afford a lot because we both worked and my income, especially, was increasing rapidly, and we had no children.

Being a registered nurse, Maggie knew exactly what her cut-off age for having children would be.

"All these studies saying women can now have babies in their forties are nonsense. Maybe some can, but it's still a greater risk for the mother and the child. If we don't have kids by the age of thirty, forget it."

I pointed out at the time that because of better nutrition and better care women's bodies had become stronger over generations, and it was okay to have children even as late a forty years old. Maggie did not buy it. So, when she was twenty-nine we sat down one night to have a long talk. Did we really want to have kids? Maggie was still concerned about her eye problem, and she knew for sure she carried the genes for hearing loss. There were other reservations as well. We were so much in love and so happy with our lives that we didn't want to change anything. We were both willing to have children if the other really wanted. We both decided to forgo a family. Maggie was happy with the decision, and the honest truth is, neither of us ever second-guessed it. In fact, Maggie always told me kids were not in the cards for us.

Our careers meantime were going really well. I had advanced from a news writer to a news producer at WBBM–AM Radio. In 1977, I got my break on the air as a sportscaster. Maggie and Arlana had settled into the overnight shift at Rush Presbyterian, and they seemed to thrive on it. Maggie would work from 11:30 p.m. to 7:30 a.m., so she would go to bed around four in the afternoon. My shift was three until eleven p.m. Our bed was in use sixteen hours a day, five days a week. We slept together only on weekends and vacations. What made life so easy for us is, we never pressured each other. She never demanded more of my time, and I was content to let her do her thing. If she wanted to go out with Arlana on my day off it was of no consequence. The emphasis was always on the quality of time, not the quantity.

I had the time I needed for my friends and my activities. Maggie never demanded to know where I was every day. If I was on a road trip for work she would tell me it was not necessary to call unless it was an emergency. It was the same for her. I recall one time she and Arlana were at a nursing conference out of town. On the third day, I was talking with my mother. She asked me how Maggie was doing. When I said I hadn't heard from her, she was shocked.

"She'll surface soon enough," I said. She did. We were always overwhelmed with the excitement of our reunion. "Richie!" She would squeal with delight when she walked in the door. Running to meet me, she would rope her arms around my neck. I would pick her up and squeeze her with all I had. It was a touch of heaven. We would then go out to some expensive restaurant where she would tell me about her trip, and we would get caught up.

She also never once bugged me about the hours I had to work, which in broadcasting are erratic and sometimes extensive. She had her own life and had plenty to do. The only pressure I ever received was from my in-laws, particularly from my brother-in-law, who was brutally honest.

"How come King gets to miss all these boring parties?" he would say sarcastically. Over the years, I missed almost all of them because I was always working weekends. Maggie never cared a bit.

Our transition from the city to the suburbs had worked out extremely well. We bought our house in Hinsdale using the money I almost wasted on that run-down fishing cabin in Wisconsin. Living in Hinsdale was like living in a doll house. We had a cute three bedroom, red brick ranch house on a tree-shaded street. The downtown area is something out of a Rockwell painting. The old, brown brick city hall building sits atop a grassy hill overlooking quaint stores, an old movie house, an ice cream shop, and the best feature of the town, a train station. Maggie and I loved it. We would spend endless hours walking around town shopping. There was a fresh pastry store, a big well-stocked fruit and vegetable store, a newsstand, and an exotic pen store. We would hit them all then sit by the train station to rest with a cup of Starbucks's coffee. The freight and passenger trains would roll in and out in the late afternoon sunshine of summer. I would hold her hand just as we had on the brick stairs in the old neighborhood in Pilsen, and we would talk and laugh the evening away.

In Pilsen, we grew up in a totally different environment where, at times, there was raw garbage on the concrete in the alleys and where, from dirty horse drawn carts, peddlers sold fruits and vegetables in the street. Once, I spotted one of the peddlers urinating behind a garbage can. It seemed like a million years ago.

Hinsdale became our life. Our friends were all in the area, and there were more wine tasting parties, more dinners, and more great vacations to look forward to. And Maggie's eyesight was pretty good.

Her pre-marriage warning about her eyes began to look like a useless concern. Granted, she could not see at night and, granted, her peripheral vision was bad. But she worked at a major hospital, read paperback novels all the time, and was able to work around the house with ease. It seemed we would live the rest of our lives in a comfortable rhythm of happiness. We really had very few fights. Perhaps we got all our disagreements out before the marriage, because we rarely had a knockdown, drag-out battle. If we did, we always made up quickly then laughed about it. Maggie many times blamed it on her Irish temper. I used to always point out how short life is, so why fight over what time you take out the garbage or other such trivialities. When you get older, it's funny. You can't even recall what you had argued about.

In the mid 1980s, we again took off for Acapulco with Andi and Jim. We rented a gorgeous two-bedroom villa with its own pool. The trip, as usual, was outstanding. Jim, as usual, provided the levity. He had a habit of bringing heavy reading material with him. On this trip, it was Aleksandr Solzhenitsyn's *Gulag Archipelago* about the horrendous conditions in the hospitals and prisons of the Soviet Union. Both Andi and I ripped into him, "How can you read that depressing stuff amid the sunshine and bikinis of Mexico?" we asked. Jim just shrugged his shoulders. He also got nailed with food poisoning when he ate some bad chorizo in a restaurant on the strip. His remedy to combat the ailment was Tylenol and beer. That's all he had for a couple of days.

We were having the usual great time when near the end of the trip I woke up late one morning and saw Maggie sitting on a lounge chair beside the pool. Her hair was wet, and she was shivering. The temperature was 90 degrees. As I got close to her, I noticed she had tears in her eyes. My step increased, and I knelt down at her feet.

"What happened?" I asked.

"Richie," she cried. "I fell in the pool. I didn't see it."

She was frightened beyond belief over what I saw as a harmless accident. But nothing like this had ever happened before, and a swimming pool is hard to miss, even with bad peripheral vision. I tried to calm her down, saying perhaps the morning clouds had darkened the area. I knew this was a stretch, because there were no clouds. To stop her trembling, I held her in my arms, and she soon felt a little better. I also managed to convince her it must have been a fluke. Though she agreed, I sensed a concern that her central vision was not as strong as it had been. Still, she was able to shake off her incident in the pool to enjoy the rest of the trip. This was a turning point that would challenge the sweet life we enjoyed and would also test to the limit her courage.

7
The Beginning and The End

When Maggie got back from vacation, she went to visit her ophthalmologist. He was a bright young doctor and put her through the usual battery of tests. They showed the usual lack of peripheral vision and night blindness, but there was very little deterioration in her central vision. It was not perfect by any means, but the change was not drastic enough to cause concern. Being the constant worrywart that I am, I cornered the doctor when Maggie was out of the room.

"Doctor," I said in a low voice, "is she losing her vision or is this just the same nerve damage she suffered at birth?" He looked straight at me and said there was nothing to be overly concerned about. If we came in for eye exams every year, he would keep monitoring the situation. That's all. I was greatly relieved. Maggie was thirty-seven years old at the time, and I thought perhaps this was just a slight wearing down of the eyes due to age. If this was as bad as it got, we could live with it.

So we jumped back into our lives, but I never felt Maggie was the same after that incident in the pool in Mexico. She was not one to sound alarms, and she was also not one to cry and moan about things. Her solution was to keep working at life. She kept her problems to herself as long as she could, and above all, she did not like to burden me. She always thought of me first. She went to great lengths to spare me any worry.

That same year, we took a trip to Aruba, and I bought Maggie another skimpy bikini. It had become a tradition by then for Andi, Gail, and Maggie. Every trip, the bikinis seemed to get smaller. On this trip, Maggie was noticeably reserved. She was obsessed with putting on the strongest sun block, and most of the trip, she wore a long white robe that draped all the way down to her feet. I joked she would have been better off staying in Chicago. The sun tan level would have been the same. Maggie just laughed it off and did her best to enjoy the trip, as she had in the past. I sensed there was something wrong. The old carefree spark was not there. When I asked her about it, she simply said there was nothing bothering her.

A month after we returned, we were in bed one night. Maggie leaned over to tell me something. A few weeks before the Aruba trip, she had gone to a dermatologist to have a mole removed from the back of her neck. The biopsy shocked her when it came back with a positive result for melanoma, which is skin cancer. She said the doctor told her there was no danger; it had not spread beyond the outer layer of skin. It took her a half hour to convince me she was not holding back any information: she used every medical term in her vocabulary to calm my fears. The word "cancer" makes my heart stop, and my stomach turn over. It is not easy to shake off, no matter how minor the condition. I was somewhat placated, but still angry with her for not telling me. I *knew* something was going on in Aruba. Maggie laughed, and told me she saved me two months of worry. I was still angry. At first I thought she had kept the whole thing to herself, but that was not the case. Arlana knew. That made me even more furious. She did apologize but said she had a good reason for not telling me.

"You don't handle medical problems well," she told me.

"Arlana is a nurse. In any event," she said "things turned out okay."

They did, but I was still concerned. A neighbor across the street from us in Hinsdale died of skin cancer. No matter how hard I tried to be positive, I kept thinking of the neighbor who was just thirty-five years old when she developed a spot on her thigh from excessive sun bathing. From that moment on, I kept a close watch on every mole Maggie had on her body.

Maggie continued to live at the same hectic pace. It seemed every week we hired workers to do something to the house. She wanted walls knocked down, rooms expanded, new furniture, and new lights. You name it. We had the money, and she was determined to spend it. She once got a tip from a friend about a painter named Lars. Maggie was told he was the best, so she hired him to put a new coat of paint in the bathroom, which was very small, about four feet by ten feet. I was there when Lars came in with his buckets. He was a distinguished looking guy whose white painting clothes looked better than my daily casual wear. He looked like a doctor, sporting a salt-and-pepper goatee. I have to admit the guy looked like a class act. Maggie was ecstatic with the job, which lasted about an hour. I then saw her hand Lars his check, and he was gone. Later that night when I looked at the bill it was $300! I got up from my desk and walked into the living room laughing.

"Who is this guy, a descendant of da Vinci?" I asked. We both laughed uncontrollably although I must admit there was a tinge of pain in my laughter. Maggie had Lars back a few times before she too finally got fed up with his prices. Whenever we passed an art gallery the rest of our lives, I would always ask sarcastically if the place had any of Lars' creations. A nasty profanity became her standard response.

She went from one adventure to the next. She convinced me to buy a $2,000 piano so she could take lessons. They were short-lived but still provided an embarrassing moment for me. When her prissy schoolmarm-type piano teacher lifted the lid of the piano bench to look for some music books, she found a dirty magazine instead.

"Oh, that's Rich's," Maggie quickly responded. Thanks a lot! We wound up selling the piano within the year for $1,400, a $600 loss.

Another time, she forced me to lug forty pounds of seashells back home from Sanibel Island, Florida, in my garment bag. The long walks in the airports in Fort Myers and at O'Hare just about killed me. Her idea was to make a lamp out of the shells, but I don't think she ever even bought the glue! The shells were placed in a bag near the fireplace. There, they sat for a few weeks before Maggie noticed an odor.

"Hey," she said, "there must be a dead bird in the chimney. Go look."

So, I got a broom and a flashlight, put on an old football helmet, white worker's gloves, and swim goggles—for protection—and poked up the chimney. I looked like Jackie Gleason's "Man from Mars" in the Honeymooners. It took me about fifteen minutes to realize the smell was not coming from inside the chimney but from the rotting meat in the seashells. She finally threw them out.

For awhile our house had little stones and rocks in every room. She had gotten into the art of painting them with a mixture that smelled like model airplane glue. You could get high just being in the room. She had me looking for rocks everywhere, and if I brought home a "bad" one she would say, "Please, no more boring rocks!"

"There's an exciting rock?" I would ask in response.

When her nieces and nephews were small, she loved to take care of them.

She and Arlana would crawl around the floors with toy guns, having a blast with the kids. She also wrote children's books. They were pretty good, but as hard as she tried, she never got one of them published.

Maggie's activity schedule seemed to get more hectic with every passing week. I noticed that she was not as relaxed as she had been in the first ten years of our marriage. It was very subtle at first, but there was a change. She was pouring herself into project after project.

She went crazy with cooking. She bought every exotic blender, pot, and utensil on the market. We were always going to food stores and coming home with backbreaking bags of food. She would be in the kitchen for hours making a huge mess. The walls of the kitchen were always stained with tomato sauce. Just like everything else, she learned to cook really well. Italian pasta was among her favorites: a huge pot of pasta with vegetables and a vegetarian tomato sauce. She also made many kinds of fish: salmon, grouper, and halibut. All bought from a fresh fish store in Hinsdale. We would have Ron and Gail and Andi and Jim in for big feasts at least twice a month. It made Maggie extremely happy to be complimented on her cooking. Yet, it seemed to border on obsession with her.

She also got into physical fitness. Not that she was ever out of shape, but she said she wanted to increase her endurance. She and Arlana would join a health club for a few months, find a better one then switch. Maggie also bought all kinds of fitness gadgets. The Thigh Master was among the first. I tried telling her it was a rip-off, but she had her mind set on it. She used it for less than a month. There were ab-crunchers, bun busters, and endless videotapes from people I have never heard of.

Around this time, Maggie became dissatisfied with the house. For some reason, it had become too small. When we bought the place in 1972, it was Maggie who insisted on moving to Hinsdale.

"We have to get a place," she said. "You are tossing money away by renting."

Though I knew she was right, I had a tendency to drag my feet. Maggie was the one who pushed things. We had purchased our house for what then was a hefty $35 thousand. I took out a $25 thousand dollar mortgage and felt I was signing myself into bankruptcy. The pen was shaking in my hand as I signed the mortgage papers. Maggie had no such fears. She never worried about making ends meet.

Over the years, Maggie remodelled every room in the house. We put in new lighting to brighten things in every room. Our home became a showcase house. I could have lived there forever, but Maggie could not. She started a pressure campaign to move. Even though we had three bedrooms, it was not enough. They were too small, she said. As usual, I stalled for a while hoping she would back off. Of course, she didn't. This mild displeasure quickly became an aggravation for her. The contentment of the first decade of our marriage began to unravel, slowly at first.

What was happening at home was also happening at work. Maggie and Arlana were also having more disagreements. One evening, Arlana and Maggie both overslept. When Arlana got to our house to pick her up, Maggie's temper got the best of her, and she ripped into Arlana. Maggie apparently forgot that she, too, had overslept. But it was all Arlana's fault. "How could you be so stupid?" she yelled. Arlana yelled back and the battle was on. I had seen Maggie angry like this before, but always at me—never at Arlana. I knew she loved her like a sister. It was scary to see how angry she could become over a minor issue. People oversleep. People make mistakes, but in Maggie's eyes it was as if Arlana had committed a capital crime. Over the next few years, her temper would flare up often.

I also noticed that Maggie was walking into more things, getting more bumps and bruises. Because of her peripheral vision problem, she had always walked into chairs, tables, and other protruding objects. Now, she was walking into walls she had seen in the past. She would always joke about it. "I have bones of steel," she would say, after a collision. I would get concerned whenever she had a mishap, but within a few days, she was getting around perfectly again and the concern would evaporate. I repeatedly told myself that, if she was working at the hospital, her eyes must be okay. The loss of any sense is something you try to put out of your mind. And at such a young age, you think you are still invincible. There is always an excuse—fatigue, bad lighting, or whatever. Maggie and I used them all. Essentially, you try to hope your fears away.

In 1988, we went with Andi and Jim to Hawaii. Jim booked a beautiful condo on Maui overlooking the ocean. This trip was another turning point because it marked the last vacation during which Maggie could function normally. Whatever discontentment she felt at home evaporated in that gorgeous and rich land across the Pacific. We had a fantastic trip. Maggie was the only non-golfer in the group, so she stayed in the condo while the three of us took on beautiful Kapalua Country Club. She missed viewing the round of a lifetime. None of us is a good golfer. When we broke a hundred, it was rare and cause for great celebration. Why we took on a championship caliber course can be attributed to the ignorance of the unskilled. The three of us were teamed up with a nice older gentleman who shot in the low 80s. We warned him beforehand that we were bad, but he was the nicest guy you could meet.

"Oh, don't worry," he said. "Let's just have fun."

On the first hole, I was lucky enough to have four good shots and wound up with a par. The older gentleman immediately befriended me.

"Hey, you're sandbagging me, you shoot pretty well."

He thought he had a golf partner. As I teed-off on the second hole, the truth became stunningly apparent. When I hit the ball, I lost my balance. My left shoe flew completely off and landed in a water-filled ditch about fifteen feet away while the ball went just over twenty feet. Though Jim and Andi laughed hysterically, the older gentlemen looked on apprehensively. I wound up with a 9-stroke hole, and the rest of the day was a disaster. Jim, Andi, and I sprayed the ball all over the place. The older gentleman scratched his head in bewilderment. At one point, I forgot to put the brake down on my golf cart. As I was shooting in the fairway 100 yards away, Jim yelled out, "Runaway cart!" It landed in a lagoon, which meant they had to bring me a new one, holding up our play. It was embarrassing beyond belief. I had also brought along one of those goofy golf balls and tried to trick Jim into putting with it. It didn't work. Jim quickly noticed it was a different ball and told me, "Get that thing out of here!" I decided to take a whack at the ball anyway, and it bounced in fifteen different directions before landing on the fly right in the cup from thirty feet away. A one in a million shot! The older gentlemen must have thought we were "golf trash." After sixteen holes of laborious play, he finally begged off, claiming his wife wanted him back for an early dinner. Once again, we apologized for our poor play. The guy graciously replied, "no problem." You could tell he was glad to rid himself of the torture.

We were not done yet, however. As he drove away down the cart path on the left side of the fairway, Jim decided to take his tee shot. It was a low line drive way off the mark, as usual, and was going straight towards the guy's cart. It missed his head by a foot or so as Jim bellowed – "FORE!" We not only tortured the guy, we almost killed him! At dinner that night with Maggie, we told her our story about the "round from hell." We are still telling it.

We took a lot of pictures on that trip. I had brought along a camcorder, and we played around endlessly. One day, we were overlooking the Pacific from a lovely hill next to our condo. There was a grassy area about 100 yards to a cliff that overlooked the beach. When I asked Maggie to take a walk on the grass so I could get a picture, she refused.

"The cliff is a football field away," I joked. "Don't worry." In previous times, she would not have given it a second thought. But on that day, she was fearful of going even a few feet onto the area. I handed the camera to Andi then joined Maggie so we could get a picture. Though she seemed distracted, we continued to enjoy the trip. We went to a black sand beach, took the treacherous road to Hana, and indulged ourselves in the seafood-dominated cuisine of the island.

On the final day, we took a carefree walk along the beach. I played the role of pirate and "kidnapped" Maggie, carrying her away. Andi wrote "I love you" in the sand, and Maggie and I watched the waves wash it away. Andi also manned the video camera, as Maggie and I posed and waved good-bye to Hawaii. But I sensed Maggie had no idea where Andi was standing. Gently, I put my hand on the back of her head and pointed her towards the camera. Despite the warm sunshine, a chill of fear raced through my body.

8

Welcoming Responsibility

When we got back from our vacation, things changed at a rapid pace. Maggie was bumping into more walls. I noticed that she was becoming more tentative everyday. She was also finding work a lot tougher. Maggie could still read all the medication bottles and still do dialysis, but Arlana noticed she was having more trouble walking around the hospital, an environment she knew well.

"Something's going on with her," Arlana confided to me, "and it scares me to death." Maggie went in for another eye exam and got the same results. She had lost a little vision, but there was no reason given for it. Her eyes did not look diseased in any way and the loss was not that great. Once again, she walked out of the office with no answers.

Maggie's demeanor slowly changed. The bad days were more frequent now, and she was not easy to deal with. If I left a shoe out of place or a cabinet door open, she would go bananas, even if she did not bump into it. "You're stupid, Richie. I'm sick of it. You're a slob," she would shout. It became almost a daily occurrence.

Maggie had a pail she used for dirty jobs like washing out the basement or the garage and a pail for the floors inside the house. (She called it her "clean" pail) One day, with the best intentions,

I was washing the floor in the kitchen, but I had picked out the "dirty" pail to use. To me, they both looked the same. "What are you using?" she yelled, "That's the wrong pail. You're an idiot." She was not kidding. Maggie was incensed at this small breach of her rules then stomped away and refused to talk to me. It was inexplicable. There was an anger I had not seen before.

I started seeing this kind of stuff a lot in the next few years. One day when I was at my desk in my room, a shoe flew by narrowly missing my head. I had left my shoes in a place that endangered Maggie. Yet again, she lost her temper and almost nailed me. It could have been a serious injury. I told her she was nuts. I felt like a public enemy in my own house. However, she could only push me so far. It is rare that I lose my temper, but when I do, I really blow up.

One afternoon, I was painting our breezeway. Maggie had wanted me to spread newspapers on the floor to prevent any dribbles from doing damage. She was asleep when I began the job at two in the afternoon, and it was such a small job that I decided to eschew the newspapers and just paint the thing. It worked. There was not a drop on the floor. Maggie, however, woke up for some reason just as I was finishing. When she saw what was happening, she asked me where the newspapers were. I laughed and told her I had already put them away.

"You didn't," she bellowed. "You fool. You're an idiot. How stupid. After I told you to use papers."

Pointing out that there was not a drop of paint on the floor was useless. She continued to be enraged and called me every name in the book. Every time I tried to laugh it off, she got louder. It was as if she had a demon inside her. Finally, I'd had enough. I walked into the kitchen where she was sitting and yelled back, even louder, calling her an "inconsiderate bitch." I stomped all over the kitchen and, eventually, grabbed a plastic cereal container, smashing it against the floor. The top flew off and cereal went all over the place. I then swore at her again and walked away. She went back to sleep, or at least back to the bedroom, and I finished cleaning up from the paint job. She went to work that night without saying a word to me. We didn't talk for a whole day.

Maggie was not one to give in. In almost every argument we had, I was always the first at rapprochement. So the next day when I approached her, she cried and admitted she had overreacted, and I also apologized. I wondered if she was getting sick of me, although she always professed how much she loved me. She said she simply did not know why she got so angry. But deep down, she had to know it was the fear of what was happening to her eyes.

When we went out to eat, things she had taken for granted in the past now became difficult at times. It seemed she always needed more light. Granted, she could never see very well in a dimly lit restaurant; even people with normal eyesight have trouble. I recall Jim getting so upset about the lack of light in a restaurant that he lit a match to read his menu. The waiter, of course, was not amused. Still, Maggie was now having difficulty reading menus in even what I felt were well-lit restaurants. Reading the menu was becoming a real chore. Sometimes, she would ask me to go down the list of items for her. She was also beginning to knock over water glasses, wine bottles, and other things on the table. Not all the time, but enough to make me wonder why the doctors could not notice what *we* were seeing.

At work, Maggie started relying more on others. Arlana said she began asking other nurses to go with her because she was not sure about what she was seeing. Knowing Maggie, that had to be galling. Nobody wants to be dependent on anybody else, especially a nurse whose whole being is geared towards others depending on her. It was always safety first with Maggie, and Arlana covered for her time and again. She was getting by physically, but emotionally she was confused and upset.

One afternoon, when I was on the road, Maggie smelled smoke in our house but had no idea where it was coming from. She looked everywhere and became so frightened that she called Andi and Jim who lived just down the block. They came over and found that the house next door had a small fire in the backyard, and the smoke had drifted into our place. Again she was dependent on others, and it hurt.

Maggie had overcome her hearing problem, perfected her speech pattern through hard work, and studied hard to become a registered nurse at a big city hospital. She was her own woman, strong, and proud of what she had accomplished. To suddenly have to rely on others was something she did not want to face.

It seemed, I was always the chief target of her anger. Again, she peppered me about moving. The house we had completely remodeled had become a "piece of shit." She wanted to move in the worst way. Suddenly, the house was too dark and too small. So we began to look. We looked for places close to where we lived because we both loved Hinsdale and cherished our walks in the downtown area.

Still, I was reluctant to move. We bought the house in 1972 for $35,000, and it was now worth $120,000. I realized it would be a wonderful profit, but I was also very happy there. All the rooms were re-done, and our monthly 30-year mortgage payment was a mere $188 a month, including the DuPage County property tax. Can you imagine? I did not relish the idea of buying a bigger house with a bigger mortgage. When I explained all this to

Maggie, she knew it made sense, but she still wanted to move. I think she felt a change of scenery might somehow change her luck and help her eyes.

At work, fellow nurses needed to cover for Maggie more and more. As her confidence eroded so did her role as a front line nurse. She had to rely heavily on Arlana, and it was a huge blow to her self-esteem. Maggie understood that patient safety came first; therefore, she understood the changes in her workload. Still they were bitter to swallow.

Maggie tried to use her great gifts of endless optimism and dogged determination. This time, they were not working. Our life at home became more and more confusing. Most of the time, she was the wonderful woman I married sixteen years ago, while at other times, she was a shrew flying off the handle at the slightest provocation. I once sat her down and asked her why she got angry over minor things. She immediately barked at me saying they were not minor, and I was inconsiderate. Maybe I was, but I sure didn't feel that way. I thought I was doing my best to help her. I really didn't know how bad her eyes had become. She was still working, albeit in a limited capacity, and there were days when she got around pretty well. The whole thing was crazy.

I recall one day when Maggie and I went to Kramer's, a supermarket in downtown Hinsdale. I left Maggie alone with the shopping cart and went off to buy some items for myself. When I came back I saw her in the aisle for the canned goods trying to read the label on a can of tomatoes. She was almost in tears as she moved the can up and down and sideways trying to attract more light. She was simply losing the ability to see things as she had in the past. It was heartbreaking. I tried to keep her spirits up by grabbing the can and saying, "Jesus, they don't make these labels big enough nowadays. You need a magnifying glass."

"Really," she said, "I thought it was me."

"No," I said. "It's the can." Maggie looked somewhat relieved.

That incident began a new era for me because for the rest of her life, I always tried to boost her confidence, even if I had to lie a little bit. Most of the time she responded, I think, because it fed into her optimistic nature. She wanted to believe her eyes were not that bad! You can say it's a bad way to handle things but I really had no idea what was going on. How can a thirty-six year old woman suddenly begin to lose her sight?

Sadly, the disheartening episodes continued to mount as time passed. She went to Silver Lake, Wisconsin, one day to visit the condo owned by her brother-in-law, Marty Cook, and her sister, Patty. Patty was well aware of Maggie's growing problems, but like the rest of us, she was not sure of the level. Maggie had been to the place many times. But this time when she was left alone walking along the pier, she took a false step at the end and wound up in the water. Fortunately, it was deep enough to avoid injury, and they all laughed it off. But deep down Maggie was shaken. She just would never show it to her family. The only people who really knew her inner thoughts were Arlana and I. But not all the time.

When Maggie and I talked about her eyes, she was very reluctant to elaborate. She kept repeating that the doctors found no reason for her recent loss of sight. She was hoping that somehow it was a fluke thing and one day she would wake up and regain all or some of the sight she used to have. You could hardly blame her. If nobody gives you a reason for something, it may disappear as mysteriously as it appeared.

In the meantime, we tried to live our lives as a so-called "normal" couple. Thank God for our friends. Jim, Andi, Ron, and Gail treated Maggie the same as they always had even though they sensed a decline in her sight. The routine fun sustained her. One day in the Christmas season, Maggie and I went to visit Andi and Jim. Surprisingly, she opened the door with a can of Lysol spray in her hand. She had just laid into Jim for leaving a five-pound bag of rum balls on the chair in the kitchen instead of putting them in the cabinet. It seemed their dog, Tippy, had eaten the rum balls. All five pounds! The dog staggered all over the house in a drunken stupor, leaving vomit in almost every room. "Look," Andi yelled at Jim. "It's even behind the Christmas tree."

On another occasion, we were playing cards in Jim's living room and Tippy was playing in Jim's spacious backyard. Suddenly, Jim shot to his feet and dropped his cards. He pointed to his picture window and shouted "Look, it's Tippy. She got away." So, Ron, Jim, and I all chased the dog down the streets of Hinsdale and returned her to the backyard. This time Jim tied her leash tightly to the wooden railing of the stairs leading down the small wooden deck in the yard. We went back to resume the card game only to be shocked again. For flashing across the picture window, again, was Tippy this time running down the street dragging her leash and a piece of the wooden railing behind her. Tippy had ripped apart Jim's patio and escaped again. We started calling her "Super Dog."

The vacations also continued to provide comic relief. On one trip to Michigan, Jim was nursing a case of colitis only to order a dish of spicy Mongolian beef at a Chinese restaurant. "Are you sure you want to eat this?" Andi asked. "There is an asterisk next to it indicating it is one of their hottest dishes." Jim quickly brushed her off saying it would actually be good for him. On the way home we had to get off at each of the first six or seven highway exits looking for a washroom, as Jim turned green in the back seat of the car.

Besides the good times with our friends, Maggie had the total devotion of Arlana. They became even closer as Maggie's eyes began to fail. Arlana took Maggie everywhere, especially to shopping malls—filling a role I could not. Arlana knew how to shop and knew what Maggie liked. I did my best but a man's touch at shopping is not the same. Maggie leaned on Arlana more and more. Though, she really did not want to rely on anyone.

In one of her college essays years later, she wrote about the transition from relative independence to dependence.

> *"It was reassuring to have the love and support of family and friends in a time of need; however, this was accompanied by a growing sadness and unhappiness due to my waning independence. In Soul Mates, author Thomas Moore, points out that there are not enough words in the English language like 'bittersweet' that connote the contradictions in our lives. However, I found the oxymoron 'bittersweet' an excellent choice in describing the ambiguous stage of this passage. I was touched by the kindness offered by family and friends, but I was increasingly distressed by my incessant dependence on other people."*

Maggie tried her best to avoid being burdensome to all of us. She always found something to do when I was in one of my long stretches at work. Broadcasting is a demanding profession with endless hours at times. When things were going well with Maggie, I never cared all that much about my schedule. But as Maggie started having trouble seeing, I began to hate leaving town on any trip. The worst was when the Chicago Bears had their pre-season camp in Platteville, Wisconsin. It was three and a half hours from

Chicago, and usually a week or longer assignment with numerous live TV shots. I dreaded leaving Maggie at home and missed her more than I had before. While on the surface she didn't seem to care, I worried about how she would cope at home without me. Arlana, thank goodness, filled a huge role in caring for her or it would have been worse.

Having heeded John Kennedy's call to "welcome responsibility," I took on the task of trying to get Maggie through her tough times and still had an abundance of optimism that all would be well. I told Maggie that eventually she would see better or something would be invented—perhaps new glasses or implants—that would restore her sight. There is really only one course of action in life: to be optimistic. If you are pessimistic, you will waste your life and become a bore to those around you. Even a realist is hard-pressed to be happy. There are just too many bad things to swallow. You simply have to face them then regain your optimism. That is the only way to a happy life, although I fully admit it is easier said than done.

My father was a good example of a person who tried to live a happy life; he had the positive outlook. His generation had its problems, for sure, but self-pity was not one of them. My father's family faced real starvation during the Great Depression. My grandmother used to bring home table scraps from the restaurant she worked in and that was their food for a couple of years. As I mentioned earlier, my dad got drafted to fight in World War II and had his brushes with death. After the allies defeated Hitler in May of 1945, he was sent to training for the invasion of Japan. It was well known such an invasion would result in the slaughter of tens of thousands of American troops. Perhaps my father would have been among them. Harry Truman dropped two atom bombs on Hiroshima and Nagasaki, and the war was over. It was one of the few breaks my father got. He had an eighth grade education, made $44 a week driving a truck, and could only afford to give his family the basics. My dad was never one to complain. He did his job, drank more than a few beers every night, and always moved forward. He blamed nobody for his hardships; the chief trait that defined the "Greatest Generation."

Maggie and my father really liked each other. They always talked about food, carpentry, household gadgets, and other things, such as lamps made out of seashells. In spite of her voracious spending habits, she, like my father, enjoyed the small pleasures of life.

She was with my mother in 1986 when my father was taken to the hospital for surgery for colon blockage. My brother and I went to get a sandwich because they told us the operation would take several hours. We left Maggie and my mother at the hospital. The doctor came out in thirty minutes. He told them my father had cancer almost everywhere in his body.

"I can try to cut it out," the doctor said, "but he won't live long either way." My mother asked Maggie what to do, and Maggie said just close him up. The suffering and pain would not be worth it.

When we saw my father in intensive care after he awoke from the anesthesia, my mother informed him of the gravity of the situation. All he said was "doggone it." He said nothing more. He showed no emotion. The day before he died, a nun came into his room to say a few prayers. My father was not a religious man, he did not believe in any of it. He allowed the nun to perform her devotion then before she left she draped a scapular around his neck. It's a string necklace with a picture of Jesus stitched on a square piece of cloth that hangs near your heart. As soon as she left the room, my dad ripped it off and told me to get rid of the thing. Strangely, that act really impressed me. In his dying days, my father might have embraced some of the solace that religion can bring. He was no phony—he was true to his convictions. He no doubt had his regrets, but he apparently felt he had done the best he could with his time here, and if that were not good enough, then no last second prayer would help. I could see why he and Maggie got along so well. My dad did not live long enough to see Maggie begin to struggle with her sight.

By 1987, her problems had become much worse, and even with special glasses, she was having trouble reading. It really was painful because she loved to read. It was hard battling an enemy that was unknown, and each day it took a heavier toll on her dogged optimism and determination. Being a floor nurse had become tiring for her—or, so she said, complaining of sore feet and a sore back. She was also more critical of the hospital. There were cutbacks at RUSH, a by-product of the cost-cutting of the 1980s where the work force shrunk, but the workload stayed the same. The remaining staff simply had to work harder.

Ronald Reagan gave this country a much-needed dose of optimism, but when he deregulated everything, he trusted the big boys to "police" themselves. Unfortunately, many of them wound up only policing the profit margin. I would assume that most corporate CEO's are good family men and, for the most part, good people who care about their employees and their civic duty. Still in the 1980s and even now, far too many have looked the other way when it comes to the bottom line and their own careers. They let the corporate accountants hack away jobs and cause enormous suffering. All you have to do is look at the slop that passes for programming on TV to realize that ratings and money always defeat honor and duty. The best quote I ever heard about unbridled capitalism came from Herbert Hoover, the Republican president who presided over the beginning of the Great Depression.

"The only thing wrong with capitalism is the capitalists," he said. "They are too damn greedy." This is a quote from a Republican!

While Maggie complained about the changes in her job, I think deep down it was her eye problem that was at the heart of her desire to quit. She loved being a nurse. She would have done it for the rest of her life if she could, but that was becoming impossible. So she told me one night that she was giving her two-week notice the following day. My heart sank; my own optimism that, somehow, her eye problem would be taken care of took a big hit.

Then I rebounded, realizing that as long as Maggie maintained any semblance of her eyesight we could deal with it. I would take care of her, and it was a task that I truly enjoyed. It was not a life and death situation. People are restricted in lots of ways. They have wheelchairs, canes, walkers—a variety of devices that allow them to get around. Maggie was not even close to being that bad, although I noticed her relying on me more and more when we walked.

We always held hands when we walked outside. I don't know why more couples don't do it. One person told me holding hands appeared to be a phony show of public emotion. I guaranteed this person that I really loved Maggie, and she really loved me. There was nothing fake about it. Now Maggie was holding hands in a little different way. When she could see well, she held my hand loosely. Now she grabbed it harder and walked closer to me. She was using me as a guide.

It was about this time that Maggie went into the Hinsdale Hearing Center to get re-tested for new hearing aids. The technology was getting better every year, and Maggie was looking forward to the appointment. It only brought more disquieting news. The technician put Maggie in a booth with earphones and gave her a variety of sounds with different volumes and pitches. It had been five years since her last test. I could see the man looking at her charts, glancing at his readings, and he did not have a happy look on his face. When Maggie emerged from the booth, he told us she had inexplicably lost about 10 percent of her hearing during the last five years. The newer and more powerful hearing aids would make up for some of the loss, but he also recommended that Maggie see her doctor to find out why she had had such a drastic loss of hearing. He suggested maybe some illness had affected her.

Maggie told her doctor about it, and when she was examined, he found nothing wrong. Since the hearing aids worked out well, we both kind of blew it off as another fluke. We had no idea what was going on. She still heard very well with the hearing aids, so again I reasoned that even a little hearing loss would be tolerable. Perhaps it was her age? Not even the doctors could figure it out. If they were not all that worried, why should we be worried?

She also talked herself into feeling good about quitting her job as a floor nurse. After twenty years overall, including eight years on the overnight shift, she felt she was ready for a change. Her goal was to get a job she could handle in a hospital or a clinic close to home. She was happy that Arlana could get a break from picking her up every day. In a way, a new job would mean more independence. Money did not matter. I was making enough for the both of us. So Maggie quit RUSH and took some time off to rest before looking for a new job. "I'm not retiring, just taking on a new phase of my career," she explained. She was still full of steam!

But she was also full of fear. Her bravado at times was a cover. With each passing week, she became more moody. I once heard her on the phone with Arlana when the discussion became heated. They were talking about different types of jobs Maggie could handle. Arlana apparently was throwing cold water on some of Maggie's suggestions. Arlana, after all, had seen her at work and knew as well as I did she could no longer function as she had in the past. The discussion ended with Maggie literally screaming into the phone saying, "That's none of your business." She came steaming out of our bedroom. I was hoping she would not get me involved in the verbal fracas with Arlana. But she did. To make it worse, when I sided with Arlana, she barked at me. Three hours later she called Arlana back as if nothing had happened. She was totally erratic.

Maggie's time at home, after quitting her job, can best be described as purgatory. Arlana and I were both working, as were the rest of her friends and family. She hated being at home on her own without mobility. Cooking occupied some of her time, but that was about it. This was a time before computers could enlarge print, so she could not read that well anymore. She tried calling anyone she could to pick her up to go out and succeeded many times. Still, it was not enough. Accustomed to a quicker pace of life, Maggie was bored out of her mind. She wouldn't talk much and slept a lot, staying in bed until 10 a.m. I would be done with breakfast and my workout by the time she got up. At meals, she was eating less and said she was not hungry. Soon, she looked unhealthy. I urged her to get a new job as quickly as possible. I was relieved when she began to look.

Suburban Hospital, in unicorporated Hinsdale, offered her the first good opportunity. Arlana took Maggie there, and with her impressive resume, she was almost in the door right off the bat. After a day of orientation, she knew it would not work. It was an older hospital with a lot of exposed beams and unusual hallways, making it tough to navigate. Maggie said the place was just too dark.

"It's a pit," she said. "I can't work there." Arlana said Maggie never once blamed her eyesight. The hospital was no good: end of story.

She had chosen Suburban Hospital because it would have been a short, cheap cab ride from our house. Arlana and I drove Maggie everywhere. Without one of us, she was pretty much limited. She always complained about not being able to drive, and now even taking a bus was becoming a major effort. She applied for a job at a clinic that was within walking distance of our house. The rooms were smaller, and she felt they were better lit. But that was also fraught with problems. Being at a clinic, Maggie would have to answer phones. With her hearing aids, that was not an easy task. Part of the reason she never wanted to talk to me when I went on road trips is that she did not enjoy asking me to repeat things. She was not a good phone person. That, plus her diminished reading ability, made any job in the nursing field a long shot. The best hope was finding something that did not endanger people but allowed her to use her nursing skills—particularly caring for people. It seemed an almost impossible task.

Once again, my heart was bleeding for her. She was a good nurse and had so much to offer. It was painful to see her groping around for a job in what should have been the prime of her career. Then one day she came home beaming!

Maggie had gone to that small clinic in downtown Hinsdale again, which was exactly six blocks from our house. She was interviewed for the job by a fellow nurse who was sympathetic with Maggie's situation and willing to give her a shot. Maggie was hired to work in the reception office and to help with some of the medical charts. She felt she had a chance to get by in the job with a little help. Maggie happily told me she was "back in the workforce." Finally, she had found someone who understood her eye and ear problems, and I could tell she really liked the woman who had given her a chance. The job paid only $20,000 a year. It was a big cut for her, but she didn't care. It was a job. And with it, she had her dignity back. The old sparkle returned to her beautiful blue eyes, and she was bouncing around and joking about things once again. Her complexion even seemed to change.

People who have never lost a job are truly blessed. I learned that the hard way—I got fired after twenty years with CBS. I found out then how Maggie had felt when her career was yanked from her. Financial hatchet men take heed! Every time you red line a few jobs to save money, think of the consequences. It's not just a job; it's dignity. After you get the axe, people always tell you, "Oh, you can do something else, don't worry. You have the talent." I learned never to say that to people when they have just been let go. Simply say you're sorry and offer them help. You have no idea if things will ever again be okay for a person out of work. Their whole lives may change, as might the lives of their husbands or wives or children. Lack of money causes endless misery especially in the prime of your life.

The self-esteem issue is huge when you get fired. In his second inauguration speech, George W. Bush said: "We live in a new America, unlike our parents, who might have worked for the same company all their lives. Now," he said, "people will have to be more creative and have several jobs in their careers."

Maybe a lot of people can accept that kind of nonsense, but I can't. Who says you have to switch jobs? Didn't this country prosper when companies remained intact and paid fair wages?

Now jobs are being shipped overseas for "so-called" cheap labor. Does anyone wonder what's going to fuel the American economy in the next thirty years? What is going to happen when all the credit runs out? You don't need any stats to tell you that far too many Americans are mortgaged up to their eyeballs. It rivals the same sad state of affairs when most people bought stock on "margin" before the stock market crash of 1929. Now it all goes back to people losing their jobs and losing their lifestyle. The American dream is becoming available to fewer and fewer people.

The reason I feel so strongly about this issue is that I saw what happened to Maggie right after she came home with that brand new job. I will never forget it as long as I live. It is etched in my mind and still chills me to the bone every time I think of it.

Maggie was sitting on my lap. We were still in a giddy mood; so happy she had found a job close to home. Then the phone on my desk rang. I picked it up, as she continued to sit on my lap. The woman on the other end asked for Maggie. It was the nurse who had hired her just a few hours earlier. Maggie thought perhaps it was a clerical matter connected to her hiring. About thirty seconds into the conversation, I saw a wave of sadness sweep across her face. I had never seen anyone's entire appearance change so quickly. The air simply came out of her. It was as if she had just received news of someone dying. Her face sagged and wrinkled in pain as her eyes welled up in tears. She even began to hyperventilate a little bit but regained her composure and just kept saying, "Sure, I understand. Okay. Sure, that's too bad." I knew what was happening, and it made me sick to my stomach.

The conversation lasted no more than five minutes and after it was over, Maggie hung up the phone and looked at me.

"They don't want me," she gasped, bursting into tears.

The pain in her face was devastating. Seeing it was as painful as someone sticking a dagger in my own heart. Through her tears, she told me the doctor in the office felt it would not be a good idea to train someone who does not have good sight or good hearing. The nurse apparently had hired Maggie without his permission. As my profound sadness deepened, I boiled over. What kind of doctor can't give a person a two-week trial? I told Maggie it was a bullshit way to be treated. Knowing that the doctors from Hinsdale Hospital ran the clinic, I was going to call the hospital to complain then go to the clinic to give that doctor a piece of my mind. Maggie begged me not to. Quite frankly, I did not want to leave her in the state she was in. She needed me to hold her. She cried for a long time, and eventually, my anger disappeared. I just hugged her and told her how sorry I was. I regret to this day, however, not storming over to that clinic. It would not have saved Maggie's job, but it would have given that doctor pause the next time he faced a similar situation. You simply don't treat people that way.

Doctors are exalted people, and they should be. They deserve respect for their years of hard work and the awesome responsibilities they face. They also deserve the money they make. Still one should not forget that quite a few doctors are simply arrogant and talk down to others because of their knowledge. When you are younger, you are more likely to suck it up and accept such behavior. The older you get the more you realize nobody has a right to be arrogant. I wish I had possessed the attitude then that I have now. I would have given that doctor a piece of my mind and then some.

After Maggie regained her composure, we had a long talk. I told her to keep trying to find a job because if she stayed at home she would go out of her mind. She told me she didn't think she could perform a nursing job without special consideration. She also questioned how she could change professions. "How can you work anywhere when you have trouble seeing things?" she asked. "You can't sell clothes, work in any secretarial job, or be a waitress for fear of falling over somebody's feet and spilling food all over the place." She began to cry again, saying she felt suitable for nothing. It was hard to deal with.

Finally, I realized how bad her eyes had become. The doctors we were seeing had no idea what was happening, neither did we. Our only alternative was to keep going, to hope her eyesight improved, and to try to get Maggie a job somewhere. I felt her frustration of fighting an unknown enemy. The whole thing was becoming a nightmare.

The next several months did not go well. Maggie ate less and complained more. The house issue came up again. This time, she insisted we move. I finally agreed, but managed to put it off for a year. She did not, by any means, give up her search for a job—she called everybody she knew. I even asked people at work about possible openings. Nothing was happening. The happiness we had shared for so many years was unravelling. Neither of us ever considered splitting up, but Maggie was simply not the same person she had been. While her childlike optimism was far less frequent now, I had faith it would return if she somehow got a break and got a job. At that point, it appeared to be a long shot at best.

Our vacations were also becoming increasingly difficult. Maggie was now concerned about making a fool of herself by falling or knocking something over. The fun was always tempered. On a trip to Arizona, there were moments of bliss, but there were more moments of tension when I felt I had to watch Maggie closely. Years ago, I had videotaped Maggie in Florida with my mother. Maggie walked around cars, around posts, and everything. My mother was not holding her hand. On this trip to Arizona, she did not trust herself to go out alone. I always had to be with her and hold her hand. It was quite a departure from her ability to get around previously. The sticky thing about it is, when she was with me no one would guess there was a problem. She didn't even wear glasses! Those were the months and years of being in "no-man's" land. It left an unsettling feeling in the pit of my stomach.

Maggie's quest for a new job also became depressing. Sarcasm replaced the optimism that had marked the years of our married life. She sent resumes out and talked to people about job prospects, but a lot of the time she sat around doing nothing.

There were moments of joy amid this "no-man's" land. She and I would take her nieces and nephews to the Hinsdale pool during the summer. Maggie's sister had two children, Nicole and Brett. Her brother and his wife, Candy, also had two children, Zach and Annie, who was named after Maggie's mother. Maggie always loved being with the kids. We also occasionally went to restaurants with our friends. At these times, we had the old spark that made our union magic. Yet, under it all was a bad feeling about the future. Her eyesight was on our minds almost daily no matter what we were doing. Sometimes, I was able to put it out of my mind for a while but not for long.

One warm summer day, I was sitting in a lounge chair in the breezeway reading in the sunshine when she threw a piece of paper at me.

"Look," she said, "at least somebody wants me. Too bad it can't work." It was a letter from her old supervisor at Rush Medical Center. They wanted to hire her for a weekend shift, just Saturday and Sunday.

"Hey, what's wrong with that?" I beamed. "You'd be back

among friends and in a familiar surrounding."

"Oh sure," she shot back sarcastically. "Just how am I going to get there?"

"Well, just wait a minute. Let's figure this out," I responded.

It took me a few minutes, but I came up with a solution. My mother still lived in the city and driving her car. Though at seventy years old, she drove it quite slowly. I told Maggie I would take her to my mother's house on Friday. She could sleep there on the weekends, and my mother could take her to work and pick her up. My mother was retired and might welcome the assignment. Maggie loved my mother. While they did not see eye to eye on a lot of things (I think most daughters-in-law are in the same boat), Maggie considered my suggestion. After a few minutes, I could see she saw some value in it, and her spirits perked up.

"Look," I said, "even if you keep the job for a few months or just a year, it's worth it. Something better might come along in the meantime." Maggie then warmed up to the idea even more.

It became reality a month later, and Maggie was a lot happier, at first. She loved putting on the nurse's uniform again and feeling useful. I just hoped she could function well enough to keep the job for a while. Sadly, she could not. The first month or so Maggie's old friends basically allowed her an extended orientation. She did not do much. One time when she was trying to lower an empty bed, she left her foot in the wrong place and almost broke her big toe when she lowered it. She simply could not see well enough. She was never given a task that could endanger anyone. Getting ice chips and cleaning out empty rooms was hardly being a nurse, and Maggie sensed her old friends were simply carrying her out of the goodness of their hearts. It was a testament to how well she had worked in the past. These nurses respected her and wanted to get her out of her malaise.

The whole thing was simply not working. My mother also started burning out after a few months. She was not used to driving as much as her weekend assignment dictated. She was also having trouble sleeping and worried about getting Maggie to work safely. After a few months, Maggie had to quit. Arlana told me one of her friends, who worked with Maggie at that time, said she simply could not handle the work anymore. It was the end of the line for her days as a nurse. While it ended poorly, she had a great twenty years. Though it seemed little consolation at the time. Losing another job only added to her growing depression. We were back to square one. Maggie went back to moping around the house and griping about little things that had never bothered her before.

At that point, I figured a change of scenery might help by making life busy in a different way. I told her it was time to move. Immediately, Maggie's spirits took a bit of a rise.

"Okay," she said. "While we are looking, I'll begin to pack and get things in boxes to get ready."

Between packing and going with me to look for houses, Maggie's time was again well spent. Throughout our home search, she kept stressing the place had to be bright. Her sight was helped by being in light spaces. We finally settled on a three-bedroom ranch style house in an unincorporated area of Hinsdale, just a couple of miles from where we lived. Twice as big as our first home, the new house had a natural dining room, something we did not have in our old house. I did not care for the hassle of moving. I especially did not care for the wheeling and dealing that goes along with haggling for a house. When the final bidding occurred, I was in Florida, covering spring training with the White Sox. It was ridiculous. For a $340,000 house, we were haggling over peanuts. The real estate agent and I received four or five calls in a half hour period. The owner of the house was a great guy, but he thought he was Donald Trump, making a big deal and standing tough. When the difference got down to $3,000, I told my agent to make the deal. What's $3,000 in the course of a 30-year mortgage?

Maggie was extremely happy with the new place. She loved moving. One of her specialties was throwing things out. She discarded a bunch of furniture and other items so she could go shopping to replace it all. All of the old furniture ended up at my in-law's houses. It was a trend that continued the rest of our lives. She would corral Arlana or me to take her shopping and turned it into her new job. I was glad I made the move. When she was busy she was a lot happier. And, as always, spending money was part of that happiness. It pushed away, for a while at least, the gnawing psychological ache of her failing eyes. Even if it was only temporary relief; it was relief nonetheless.

When we moved into the new house there were problems. Naturally, the configuration was totally strange to her. She did more than her share of bouncing into walls. She had cuts on her hands, bruises on her legs, and even a bruise on her face. She looked like a boxer who had gone the distance in a brutal fight. Used to it, she was always able to shake it off and laugh it off. That high tolerance for pain would stay with her the rest of her life.

Two weeks after we moved in, a couple of women from the Welcome Wagon organization came to our door. Maggie was out shopping with Arlana at the time, so I greeted the ladies. At first it was the usual pleasant conversation about how nice the neighborhood was and how many activities were available to residents. Near the end of the chat, one of the ladies said, "You'll also find it very safe here. We have no blacks." (Keep in mind, this is the late 1980s) The other lady almost jumped out of her shoes.

"How do you know I am not married to a black woman?" I asked. Realizing she had made an inappropriate comment, she began an embarrassing apology. The rest of the visit lasted less than a minute. They were out the door, no doubt warning their neighbors that "riffraff" had moved into the area.

As I thought about the incident later, I wondered if we really belonged in the suburbs at all. We had moved there with the intention of having children. Now that we did not have kids, what was the point? You never quite fit in the suburbs unless you have a family. From then on, I had it in the back of my mind that we would eventually go back to where we belonged, back to the city.

Maggie was going full tilt trying to fill-up the place. But stuck at home all by herself, the nagging worry over her eyes ate at her. As the worrying escalated, so did the temper tantrums. At one point, I got tired being called stupid, her favorite word. We had a huge blowout. She kicked things throughout the house, even wrecked a transistor radio. I had never seen her so angry. It seemed the more I tried to placate her; the less it worked. Sometimes, Maggie resembled a spoiled child, and this behavior really tested me. My anxiety level was high, knowing I was living with a time bomb that could explode at any time.

Something had to give somewhere along the line, and finally, it did. A few months after we were in our new home, Maggie went for another eye exam. Again, a slight loss of central vision had occurred, but this time she was finally sent to a specialist. I was out of town and knew nothing of her visits. As she always did, Arlana took responsibility for getting Maggie to her doctor appointments.

Why Maggie did not insist on seeing a specialist earlier is unknown, as is my own neglect in not pushing her to do it.

There were likely two factors. The loss of vision was so gradual that there was no sense of real panic. During her eye exams, she always saw a lot of the letters on the wall in the doctor's office. They were lit up and straight ahead. That's why the doctor himself always scratched his head. Secondly, no one volunteers to go to a specialist for anything because that usually means trouble. Why open up a can of worms? Maggie was in no physical pain, so why not wait and hope that somehow it gets better? But now, the waiting was over. She went to see a doctor who knew everything there was to know about the eyes and eye diseases.

9

Done With Gung Ho Bullshit

In the summer of 1990, Arlana took Maggie to the office of Dr. Gerald Fishman, on the campus of the University of Illinois at Chicago where Maggie and I had both gone to college. Arlana immediately knew that Maggie was not in a great frame of mind on the day of the visit. She was complaining about everything: the walk from the car was too long, the hallways were dark, the waiting room had too many people in it, etc. It seemed the slightest thing set her off. Arlana recalls Maggie even ripped the water fountains!

Dr. Fishman is the foremost expert in the field of molecular genetics and characteristics of hereditary retinal disorders. His list of awards and accomplishments could fill half this book. He is a pleasant, short, slender, and serious looking man, and he is also not one to beat around the bush. Maggie and Arlana were seated in his office when he came in with one of his teaching assistants. He asked a lot of questions, adding to the information in the reports he had received from her doctor. She took a battery of tests, looking into every angle of her eyes. Finally, he sat back down behind his desk. He asked Maggie to get up and walk back to his door and come in again as if she was just entering the office. This time Arlana was not guiding her. Maggie walked all over the place. There was no railing, no chair, or wall to bump into. She resembled a stumbling drunk. When she finally found her chair, Dr Fishman told her flat-out she had retinitis pigmentosa. Maggie and Arlana were stunned. That news was about as bad as it could get. Being a nurse, Maggie knew it was a progressive disease, and there would be no improvement. Her eyesight would only get worse, and the only question was how much worse. Arlana said Maggie's eyes glazed over, and she was even hard pressed to ask questions. In a matter of seconds, "no man's land" had disappeared to be replaced by an even worse fate, the prospect of going blind.

Maggie did not cry. She kept everything bottled up inside. Dr. Fishman said more tests would have to be conducted to figure out the scope of Maggie's disease. The fact that she had a hearing problem pointed to a condition known as Usher Syndrome, a disease that affects both hearing and sight. Arlana and Maggie had never heard of that particular disease. When Maggie asked Dr. Fishman if she would go blind, he said he simply didn't know. More tests would be needed. He also said every case is different, which meant there would be no easy answers. One thing was clear; her eyes were diseased. The overwhelming odds were that her sight problems would only get worse and, perhaps, lead to total blindness.

Arlana noticed that Maggie got rather quiet near the end of the session with Dr Fishman. She had to be emotionally wiped out. Her mind was clearly on the future and me. When they left the office, Arlana said Maggie's first thoughts were of me. "Should I tell him now?" she asked. She really didn't want to tell me. She never wanted to give me headaches or burdens. Despite all of her nastiness and temper tantrums, she still wanted to protect me. She would have given anything to not hurt me, even if it meant going it alone in her agony. Maggie decided not to tell me until all her tests had been completed.

She went to see Dr. Fishman twice more. He examined her thoroughly. As it turned out, the doctors and ophthalmologists who had seen Maggie in the past had not really made mistakes. The disease she had is almost impossible to detect. Dr. Fishman, however, was among the best in his field in the United States and the world. It took him a few weeks, but he nailed it down. Maggie had Usher Syndrome. It had been in her body since birth. She had the bad luck to have a disease that not only affected her ears but her eyes as well. Only 10,000 people in the United States have it. Can you imagine the odds? I figured it out as a .000028 percent chance.

When Maggie was born, both parents carried the gene that causes Usher Syndrome. If one of the parents had not been a carrier, she wouldn't have gotten the disease. However, she would have also been a carrier. So the decision not to have children was a wise one. Still, even when both parents carry the gene only 1 of 4 of their children gets Usher Syndrome. Maggie's brother and sister are completely fine. So are their children. Thank goodness the odds of getting this disease are so low. Maggie was just plain unlucky. In one of her college essays, Maggie summed it up better than I ever could.

"It is a dual disability consisting of severe hearing loss at birth with an insidious onset of visual deterioration known as retinitis pigmentosa (RP). The first symptoms to occur in the visual deterioration are a decrease in peripheral vision and the inability to see in the dark (night blindness). The syndrome occurs when each parent carries a recessive gene, and it is manifested in one of every four children. I experienced a gradual loss of peripheral vision

but was undiagnosed for forty years, despite countless eye examinations from various ophthalmologists. At age forty-two, it was a shock to discover that I was legally blind with a progressive disease of the retina."

Believe it or not, it could have been worse. Maggie had USH2, which manifests itself in the later decades of your life. USH1 causes an individual to lose hearing and sight in adolescence. When you read through the brochures, it becomes mind-boggling. Deafness is due to a nerve malfunction in the cochlea of the inner ear, and the cause is unknown. Blindness involves a malfunction of the cells that convert light into electrical impulses, which transfers sight to the brain. Like cancer cells, these cells also become diseased. As Maggie always explained, the eye is so small and has so many nerve endings that it is almost impossible to figure it all out. It's easier to transplant a big organ like a heart or a liver. With the eyes the symptoms can vary more. The most depressing line in the brochure on Usher Syndrome is found in the Q&A:

> Q: *"Is there currently a treatment for Usher syndrome?"*
> A: *"Currently, there is no way to halt the degeneration of the retina or to restore normal hearing."*

The disease is hard to diagnose in its early stages because the onset is so gradual. It comes on at different rates of speed in each case. There is a mutation of the genes and the mutations give faulty messages to the sensory retinal cells and the inner ear cells. Usher Syndrome affects people from all races, cultures, and ethnic backgrounds, and the strangest thing about the disease is that the symptoms can change from day to day. Some people see better on cloudy days and some people see better on sunny days. Fatigue and emotional stress are also factors. This explains why Maggie saw better some days than others. She could always see better after she drank wine or alcoholic beverages. You could actually see her gain confidence in her step. She used to joke about it, not knowing at the time that such things really did change her eyesight.

For three weeks, Arlana took Maggie for more tests, which I knew nothing about it. Maggie digested all the information before she made the decision to tell me. Arlana explained that Maggie was in the quandary of her life. She was also in shock and really didn't want to tell me at all. After all the years of uncertainty, she now had answers, even if she did not fully understand the depth of her particular case. Some people go blind earlier in life, some later. Dr Fishman, after all, was still in the process of researching the disease himself. Not even *he* knew how long it would take for Maggie to lose her sight or whether she would retain some of it for the rest of her life. It was not an optimistic picture. The word "progressive" works well in politics, but when it comes to disease, it's the worst word you can hear. Barring some kind of a cure, the dying cells would cost Maggie most, if not all, of her vision and that was a devastating realization. Gordon Gund, the owner of the NBA's Cleveland Cavaliers at the time, also went blind from the disease in mid-life.

I remember vividly the moment Maggie told me. We were having breakfast in our TV room on a beautiful summer morning. Maggie had made bran muffins and fresh coffee brewed in a brand new pot. She had more coffee pots in her life than Wilt Chamberlain had women. Her latest was a French concoction where you placed hot water in a glass container and pressed it down over the coffee grounds. French roast. It was rich and delicious. So were the muffins, which were sweet and moist out of the oven. It was hardly a setting for bad news.

But bad news it was. This was one of the few times in her life when Maggie actually broke down in tears. I sat in stunned silence as she nervously explained what had happened. When I heard about the tests and the meetings, I asked a lot of questions. I wanted to know about possible cures; I refused to accept that nothing could be done. She said they were researching it, but at that point, there were no answers.

"Don't look for miracles, Richie," she said. "There are none." I would not give up. I also asked her if she was hiding something from me. I was worried that perhaps there was some danger to her life. Would it affect the brain? All the stupid questions you ask when your world is suddenly turned upside down. She assured me she was not in danger of dying.

I was stunned, but I also tried to regroup my thoughts. My caretaker role asserted itself, and I quickly tried to offer positive thoughts. Quite frankly, I was also trying to boost my own morale. I rationalized that she still had considerable sight and was at least getting around a little bit on her own. I rationalized that despite what she said I could find her a cure somewhere in Europe, Australia, China, anywhere. I also thought, in the worst case, even if she did go blind and deaf, she would still be alive and in my arms. I would take care of her and make her happy. I groped for a silver lining.

Maggie did not share my optimism. I held her, and we both began to cry. I consoled her and told her I would take care of her, and somehow, there would be a happy ending.

"It's not your body, it's mine," she cried. "My life will never be the same."

She was right. It's easy to talk when you are not the one with the disease. Thinking she would be happy simply by being cared for was naïve at best. Sometime it's wise not to even try to be optimistic. Maggie was grieving something she had just lost: all hope for a normal life. That is about as huge as it can get. There is nothing anyone could say, do, or promise that could make her feel better. The best thing I could have done was grieve with her. I could not. I tried to tell her things would be okay despite what had just happened. She was not buying it.

Suddenly, the summer morning was not so sweet. We now knew the enemy, but we still didn't know how many forces it had. Maggie's job prospects were bleak, and I sensed that her tough psyche was beginning to unravel. Over the next few days, she became increasingly quiet, and we lived by osmosis. Things were said that had always been said. Dinners were eaten in the same way they always had been eaten, and the work of life went on. But it was all superficial. Maggie was reluctant to talk about anything connected to her diagnosis. I went along with it, thinking she would eventually open up.

I think I also found the will to change, digging deeper into my energy pool. This was a new beginning. Now, I had even more responsibility. I would have to give Maggie all the support I could. I would have to take a larger role in taking care of the house, the finances, and the rest. We had no kids, so I was more than willing and able to handle the added responsibilities. What also set in was deep anxiety. Now I had three elements to worry about. The melanoma scare had also stayed with me. To add to it, I had major concerns about her eyes and her deepening depression. I watched her more closely on a daily basis, hoping she would hold her own. She never did. As the days and weeks went by, she struggled more and more.

She still had the ability to move around, but she often made contact with a wall or a chair or a toilet bowl. Now that I was paying more attention, her eyes seemed worse than before the diagnosis. It is funny. Once you start worrying about something, it seems to escalate. I worried about her burning herself at the stove, falling down and breaking a leg or worse, poking an eye out by failing to see a cabinet or something. This was just the beginning. From that day forward, I would never have another day without significant anxiety. As for Maggie, she was beyond worry. She was slowing slipping into a life threatening depression.

It was pretty apparent in the weeks after the diagnosis that Maggie was not going to regain her old spark anytime soon. She withdrew more everyday. I usually got home from work around 11 p. m. to find her sleeping. When I would awake in the morning at around 8 or 9 a.m., she would still be sleeping. I would get up, make coffee and warm some muffins in the microwave. At least, she was still cooking a little bit. When she got up around 10 a.m. or so, she was always in a bad mood. Try as I might, I could not bring her out of it. In the past, I could always make her laugh by doing something crazy or saying something that put a smile on her face, but not now. Whatever reactions I got were perfunctory. She simply went through the motions. Out of fear of raising a tempest, I never brought up the diagnosis.

Our walks to downtown Hinsdale were pleasant, but even then, I could tell she was not happy. The diagnosis made it plain she would be hanging onto my arm for the rest of her life. All the wonderful sights we saw and that she had appreciated so much might not be available to her in the future: not to mention going deaf and not being able to even hear me. I knew these thoughts were on her mind because they were on mine on a constant basis. Once fear takes a grip on you, it digs in and creates havoc.

We went out with Ron and Gail one night to a lovely restaurant, even they could sense something was wrong. Initially, we did not tell any of our friends and family about her diagnosis. She tried to act like her old self. But Maggie was a bad actor. Her face always told the story. If she was sick, she had such a pained expression that you knew exactly what was wrong. If something bothered her, she was quiet, as she was with Ron and Gail that night. To this day, Ron still recalls that evening when he knew something was drastically different. He just did not know what it was at the time.

Arlana also did her best to cheer Maggie up. She would take her out to her favorite shopping malls, but Arlana would come back shaking her head. Not only was it not the same, when Arlana would try to raise the issue of the diagnosis, Maggie would almost tear her head off. She was in denial.

A few months went by. She did not show any improvement. So I felt I had to bring up the issue myself. She looked physically beaten by now. That happy glow in her face, and the magic in her eyes had totally disappeared. One day after breakfast, I brought it up to force her to talk about it. I reasoned that doing nothing was not an option.

I started the discussion by saying she had gotten a tough break, and she had a right to feel awful. I also told her she deserved time to be sad. Then I tried telling her to start thinking about the rest of her life. I urged her to forge ahead somehow by getting a new career in a field that allowed for her handicaps. That's the last thing she wanted to hear. She stiffened up in her chair and moved towards me with tears of anger in her eyes. Her face was boiling red.

"Here we go again." she said, "You and Arlana are great at handing out advice, but you're not the ones going blind and deaf. You don't realize that my life is over."

I shot back that that was nonsense. I told her quitting is not an option as long as we are breathing.

"Screw you," she yelled. "I'm done with all that gung ho bullshit. I'm going to be useless. I am going to be a burden to you and everybody else—more than I am already. Think about that! So don't give me any more bullshit."

She was getting angrier by the minute. I decided this was not the time to pursue it. I was also scared stiff. After all the years of living the full life, I could not believe Maggie was recoiling. All of this was totally out of character.

The conversation not only didn't do any good, it only made matters worse. During the next week or so Maggie got sarcastic about everything. When I mentioned that perhaps we could take a trip somewhere, she would say:

"Why? So I can make a fool of myself! I don't feel like going anywhere. Forget it!" When I mentioned buying a new oven range, which she had suggested, she again blew it off:

"Why? So I can burn the house down?" After a while it got to be so ridiculous that I only talked about the most superficial things or told her about things that had happened at work. I felt I was losing her into an abyss.

Maggie's sister, Patty, even gave it a crack. Maggie was always happy in the role of big sister. She loved giving Patty advice. They were alike in a lot of ways. We had a picture of Maggie getting on a horse in Colorado, and even I had to look closely to realize it was Maggie, not Patty. The resemblance was that close. They also sounded alike. When they got a good conversation going, their rapid speech patterns and voice inflections sounded the same. They loved each other dearly. Still Patty had no better luck. I really don't know how far Patty got, but I gather it was tough being the younger sister trying to change roles and give advice.

All I know is, when Patty left that evening, Maggie was still in the pits.

The days rolled by with no change—one week, two weeks, a month. Maggie's physical appearance became worse. She was getting thinner by the day, and her appetite, which had always been robust, was disappearing. She was always in a sloppy sweatshirt and shorts, or jeans. Even when we went out, she did not wear her usual elegant and expensive clothing. Her face took on a bony appearance, and she was always pale. In addition to her worsening appearance, she was sleeping at least twelve hours a day. All thoughts of sending out resumes and talking to people about a job had vanished. I just kept hoping that one day, after one of those marathon sleeps, she would wake up and realize she had to somehow go forward. Her emotions were so bottled up it was hard to crack the gloom. I was not about to let this continue. I knew Maggie would never see a psychiatrist so that was a moot point. I also knew that this was taking a toll on me, and I simply had to try another approach to bring her back. I decided that if placating her was not the answer, then maybe the good old Pilsen method would work—a hard kick in the ass!

One day when I was off from work, I tackled the dreaded chore of mowing the lawn. Afterwards, I poured myself a glass of lemonade, taking it over to the TV where Maggie was watching her soap opera, *All My Children*.

"You are still watching that crap?" I joked. I always wondered why women enjoyed watching all the nonsense of a soap opera. It's always some guy cheating on his wife. I guess people enjoy watching other people suffer.

"So," I repeated. "You are going to spend the rest of your life watching this junk?"

She started boiling, but I did not give her a chance to respond.

"Look," I said, raising my voice. "Get off your ass! So you had a bad break. I am sorry but moping around in a daze is a waste. I'm getting sick and tired of it and sick and tired of your sorry ass cynicism."

I really blasted her, hurting inside as I was doing it. Really, I felt a sense of desperation at that point.

"You need some help here. There is nothing shameful about it. I know it's tough. I would not want to be in your shoes, but you have to do something." She had a cold stony look during my explosion, and after I had finished she erupted herself.

"Thanks for all the support," she shot back with a look of hate in her eyes. She then burst into tears and went into the bedroom to cry. I raced in to console her, but it was of no use.

"Get out of here!" she cried. That was the sorry end to the old Pilsen approach.

I will never know if my tirade was the cause, but there was a change in Maggie. Maybe it was just time working it out. She cried a lot more and for no reason. I would come home and find her in tears at the table.

"I'm used up," she would cry. "I'm done." For a period of a week or so, she cried on a regular basis. The worst was at night. She would go to bed and wake up an hour later crying. But she would not let me hug her. She would go to sleep, and in a few minutes, again, she would wake up crying. Sometimes she would get up, go into the kitchen, and cry. It was gut wrenching to watch. Needless to say, I did not sleep much myself. I don't know how I functioned at work during that period, but I did. It had to be adrenalin, and the best elixir of all, youth.

One evening I came home quite late from work and found Patty's car in the driveway. When I walked in the front door, she was sitting with Maggie, and Maggie was crying again. She had called Patty for a reason: a reason that she confided to me later. She was worried about hurting herself. Maggie was no longer sure she wanted to live. The depression had taken such a grip that she had entertained thoughts of ending her life, even though she admitted it was an act of madness. I cried myself this time and pleaded with her to get help. All the crying was taking a horrible mental and physical toll on her. I appealed to her years as a nurse.

"Look, you wouldn't want to get sick and wind up in the hospital. You know I love you and need you."

Anyone who even thinks of suicide, of course, is in deep trouble. I called Arlana for help, and she came over the very next morning. The only positive thing was that Maggie slowly realized what was happening. This time, she didn't fly into a rage when Arlana and I talked to her. She still cried, but you can't force a person to get help. All we could do was hope she would wake up from her nightmare. Patty also came over again to spend more time with Maggie. Deep down, I didn't really believe she would harm herself. Not only because it was insanity, but also because it was totally abhorrent to the psyche of a nurse. I did worry about her anorexia, though. If this lasted much longer, I feared she would get seriously ill or even die. Her eyes sunk in deeper every day and her weight loss was becoming more rapid.

As it turned out, Maggie was at her wit's end too. Logically she knew what we were telling her made sense. But her emotions had wiped out any reasonable analysis. Until she had cried it all out, there was nothing to do. The Maggie King that existed before the diagnosis would never exist again: seeing the faces of loved ones, working as a nurse, taking leisurely walks all alone, looking at food labels on jars, even planting flowers in a straight line—all were gone. A lot of the "taken for granted" things of life were quickly vanishing for her. While Maggie was always the first one to accept change, good or bad, this was different. This is what Maggie wrote years later about this awful period in her life:

>*"One of the least generative periods of my life occurred during the time that my vision was deteriorating. It was during that time that I became severely depressed. I was not only severely depressed, but frightened and confused and I also began to isolate myself from family and friends. The depression not only affected me mentally but was manifested by psychological changes, such as anorexia with weight loss, insomnia, lethargy and accompanied by episodic crying. I did not have a clue as to what was wrong with me and my world became more focused on just me. This was a very frightening experience for me and I was conscious of my non-generativity but continued to feel helpless and I did not know how to stop this terrifying process."*

Generativity means the power to originate, the power to move forward in life, to be a positive force. That was the theme of Maggie's essay. Her teacher scribbled a note next to the above paragraph saying: "You know your depression was behind your behavior. I am not so sure you failed in generativity during that period." The teacher was right. How could you not think of yourself and how could you not have self-pity after such a shocking diagnosis? The question always is how do you finally snap out of it? There is no timetable on that. It's almost as if you know you are going into an abyss, but you still have to go there before you can get back to the bright lights. Maggie had to become a mess first, and she did. It is a test of true character to emerge from this emotional pit.

One hot summer day in August of 1990, she woke up after her usual night of insomnia and crying. She did not eat anything at breakfast, and she looked pale, even more than she had been in the past month and a half. I asked her why she didn't eat, and she just mumbled she wasn't hungry. She sat for a few minutes at the kitchen table then went back to bed. I went to my room to read the newspaper and to pencil in the baseball statistics that I kept everyday to stay abreast for my job. This usually took about an hour or so. When I finished, Maggie was still in the bedroom, so I peeked in. Her eyes were wide open, and they were so full of fear that I laid down beside her and hugged her. I did not say a word. It was like a repeat of our adolescent days on May Street when she finally opened up on her own.

"Richie," she said, "my stomach is killing me." I immediately told her she needed to see a doctor, but she refused and instead went to get the Pepto Bismol. She took a shot glass full of the pink liquid and hoped for relief. It didn't work.

While I went for a jog outside, she stayed in bed feeling awful. I called the office and told them I would be in late. Then I called Arlana at work and told her what was going on. She did not hesitate a second, telling me to take Maggie to the emergency room at Hinsdale Hospital. Maggie's awful physical appearance of recent months sent warning bells off in Arlana's mind. I told Maggie what Arlana said, yet it still took two more hours to convince her to go to the hospital. The fact that she finally agreed to go spoke volumes about how serious the pain must have been.

Skinny, pale, and now seriously ill, Maggie looked like a ghost attached to my arm as we entered the emergency room. It took a while for a doctor to see us. When the doctor did arrive, he immediately realized by her appearance she must have been dehydrated. He also recognized that she had not been eating.

They gave Maggie an IV for nutrition and wheeled her into a corner room. She was scheduled for tests of her stomach and X-rays later in the evening. I was in a bind because I had to go to work. Being in a deadline business, you cannot push back the clock. Thank goodness, Arlana was off duty by now and on her way. I held Maggie's hand for as long as I could. She was not saying a word. It was almost as if she expected to hear that she was dying. I got the sense she would have accepted it. Talk about horror!

When I finally had to go, I kissed her, told her Arlana would be there in a few minutes, and I would see her at home that night after they kicked her out of the hospital. She didn't seem to care if I stayed or not, or even if Arlana was coming. Why I left her at the hospital I will never know. It's one of those stupid things you do in broadcasting, thinking the world will end if you can't deliver the news to your audience. It was just plain dumb on my part. I will always regret it.

I really did not expect to see Maggie at home that night. I fully expected her to be admitted and for the doctors to find an ulcer, cancer, or something horrible in her stomach. As I left the E.R., I glanced back and took a final look at her. With Maggie's white complexion and light hair, she seemed to blend into the sheets and the white walls. She was a ghost-like image, with her eyes transfixed in a witless gaze. I cried after leaving the room, thinking this was the beginning of the end, but it was actually the end and the beginning.

I barely made it to my radio broadcast and as soon as the show was over, I quickly called the hospital. Arlana told me Maggie was having tests taken that would take a few hours. It was 8 p. m. when Arlana finally called me with the latest update. Believe it or not, Maggie was being released. The nutrition from the IV's had perked her up, and the test results would not be available for a few days. Being a nurse with a nose for news, Arlana did find out from someone in the hospital that apparently there was nothing of major consequence from the exams. It was a minor miracle.

When I got home that night, I found Maggie sitting up in bed. For the first time in weeks, she looked somewhat at peace. In her eyes, I once again saw the old softness that had been missing. As she gave me a hug, it was like old times. A warm smile of relief greeted my advance, and I knew she was finally coming to her senses. Tears welled up in my eyes.

"I was scared shitless," she told me. What had happened was, Maggie had finally hit rock bottom. She told me she felt she was about to lose everything: her health, her life, and me. The lack of sleep and lack of food fed into her depression like gasoline on a fire. She had stared at the end of her life, as she had known it. Perhaps her feeling is summed up best by a line that James A. Michener used in the book *Centennial*. "When a man loses everything, only then does he know the value of all things."

As we lay in embrace, she talked to me without bitterness or cynicism. Arlana had been a huge factor because she was able to find out immediately that there was nothing drastically wrong. It made Maggie grateful. She was looking forward to getting the final test results in a few days, so she would know how to handle her stomach problem. I made Maggie a cup of tea and some toast (a remedy my mother always swore by for a sore stomach), and she was able to keep it down. She almost fell asleep in my arms, but I was able to kiss her and roll her over before she dozed off. This time she was able to sleep for a long spell without crying. We were not out of the woods by any means, but on a bright summer day when darkness was closing in, we had taken a huge step on the road back to happiness.

10
Parting the Sea

Two days later, we went to see the doctor at Hinsdale Hospital to get the test results. While Maggie was still somewhat exhausted and pale, her demeanor had improved with each passing day. The intense bitterness that marked the past four months had begun to fade. When the doctor said she simply had a nervous stomach, which was basically a bad case of gastritis, it made her feel even better. The doctor asked the reason for her lack of eating. When she told him, he suggested counseling. Maggie listened but I knew she would never go for it. I also knew something else: she didn't need it. I knew she was on her way back.

"I dodged a bullet," she said on the way home. We talked about what needed to be done. She felt she needed time to regroup and get her head on straight. I suggested perhaps she should go away with me, or Arlana, but she wanted to be alone for awhile. Traveling on a plane was out of the question and staying by herself in a cottage or a hotel room was also pretty much impossible. After some thought, however, I came up with a solution.

"Why don't you stay with my mother for a week? It gets you out of the house, and since my mother doesn't know the extent of the problem, you can hang around with her and go shopping or whatever." Maggie quickly agreed, but she did not want Arlana or me visiting her at night.

"Just tell your mother you are working all week." I knew this was a first step for Maggie. It was part of a process to move her towards steadily regaining her courage and physical strength.

The following week she left for the South Side of Chicago. My mother still lived in Brighton Park. Compared to the cement sidewalks of Pilsen, Brighton Park was a touch of suburbia. It was a very pleasant place. Maggie spent a week with my mother and enhanced her recovery from the grips of depression. Maggie's expertise was shopping, and my mother was a willing pupil, learning a way of buying that was totally foreign to her. She was raised during the Great Depression. Her mission was to save money on any kind of bargain, and when she did, it actually gave my mother an adrenalin rush. Consequently, she was amazed by Maggie's freewheeling ways and total disregard for how much things cost. One day, when Maggie was in the next room and could not hear us speaking on the phone, my mother whispered softly and somewhat shockingly, "You know, Rich, when Maggie shops she never looks at the price!" Price was the first thing my mother took into account, but for Maggie, it was the last. If she liked it, she bought it. Price was of no consequence.

I was happy to hear that Maggie was shopping again. It was a sign she was recovering. She returned home much better than when she had left, but she was still not back to her old cheery self. Though she had overcome the feeling that her life was over, it was not immediately replaced with her old glow of happiness. Thankfully, the depression was replaced with more rational thought, but there remained a sense of sadness about her. There was still a myriad of obstacles ahead.

She talked about getting a job again and even made inquiries at more clinics in the area. It was no use. Even when we thought about jobs less demanding than nursing, we came up empty. She could not work as a checkout person in a supermarket; she could not baby sit; she could not handle office work; she could not teach. The list seemed endless. I thought she would never work the rest of her life when, suddenly and surprisingly, I found *myself* out of a job!

I was in the last year of my contract at Channel 2, a CBS station in Chicago. I had risen through the ranks from radio news writer to News Producer to Managing Editor to Assistant News Director. Then I made the jump to Sports Producer and Sports Announcer in radio and, finally, made the big jump to TV Sports Reporter—Channel 2 sports director, Johnny Morris, the ex-Chicago Bears wide receiver, had hired me for the job. By that time, I had been with CBS for twenty years.

Having made the jump to television reporting, I had also made it to the big money in broadcasting. Besides my TV work, I had a very successful sports radio talk program on the air at the same time. I knew I would have been extremely lucky to avoid getting the axe at some point in such a volatile business, but it was still a shock when Johnny told me the station was looking for a new direction. They would not be renewing my contract when it was up.

Then I knew exactly how Maggie felt when that clinic in Hinsdale changed its mind and fired her before she even started. I felt totally useless, and my self-esteem took a huge dip. In short, I was devastated. My whole life, I had worked hard to reach a certain lifestyle. Suddenly, it is ripped right from under me. Everything looked gloomy. It goes without saying that you can live on less money, but it's hard to scramble for work, to send resumes out, and hope that somehow you will make enough money to maintain the lifestyle you enjoyed. After working so hard, I felt cheated. Even though I had come from a humble background, the prospect of returning to it was depressing.

There simply are not that many sports anchor/reporter jobs in any city, even a major market. In Chicago, you have a total of twelve sports anchor reporter positions. Besides mine, only one was available at the time. That was at WGN-TV, but the News Director there didn't want me. He did tell me I was a great reporter and journalist, but he was looking for a person who could anchor a show and said I did not have enough experience in that area.

Maggie did not believe it when I told her I was out of a job.

"You're a great reporter," she said. "How could they fire you?" She never quite understood that my business is madness. You are hired on a whim and fired on a whim. If new management doesn't like your face, or if a focus group that management has hired for consultation doesn't like your face, you could be as good as Edward R. Murrow and it wouldn't matter. Maggie gave me a hug, and the emotion welled up. It had been one blow after the other in rapid fire order: Maggie's diminishing eyesight, then the diagnosis of Usher syndrome, her depression, and both of us now had lost our jobs. As we hugged, we both broke down in tears.

"We have taken some shots," I mumbled.

We had a trip planned for Florida that spring, so we decided to make the journey despite our bleak-looking future. My contract with Channel 2 had a few months to go. So while the money was still coming in, it was a good time to take a vacation. The White Sox used to hold their spring training in Sarasota, Florida. It's in a gorgeous area on the Gulf Coast. I covered the team there and fell in love with the place. Eventually, Maggie and I vacationed there and stayed at various resorts along Lido Beach. This time, however, Maggie's favorite word applied to our week in the sunshine—bittersweet. One morning, I was jogging along the beach with my heart full of fear about the future. A million thoughts raced through my mind. Our lives as we had known them appeared to be ending. Maggie had severe medical and emotional problems. I was facing the prospect of a drastic reduction in pay, perhaps making only 20 percent of what I made at Channel 2. How could all of this have happened so rapidly? As I jogged, I came across a group of people having a picnic and heard a song blaring from their portable stereo. It was by Bob Seger, and it seemed appropriate to our lives. It was called *Against the Wind* and like Seger, Maggie and I were running against what were now the ill winds of life. Everything was going against us. Another part of the song also came through. The line was: "We were young and strong and running against the wind." That seemed to revive me, the words "young and strong." I was still only forty-two and Maggie was forty. As I ran along the sand, I convinced myself we could still survive "against the wind." Somehow, we would get through this if we just worked hard and forged ahead. That's the advantage of youth—no matter what ills befall you, time is still on your side. I did not know back then that such fortitude gets tougher to find as the years go by, and the youth is beaten out of you by life's endless challenges.

When we got back to Chicago, the wind had changed, at least for me. I received a job offer from a cable TV sports station. I would be co-anchor of their 10 p.m. sports round up. I would be taking a $10,000 pay cut, which was okay. The offer came in on Friday. The General Manager said he would tie up some loose ends over the weekend, and we would hammer out the final deal on Monday. When I came home that Friday night, WGN-TV Sports Director Dan Roan called and told me the news director had changed his mind. He wanted to meet with me on Monday. Just like that, I had two job offers.

I went to WGN-TV on Monday for a meeting. The news director was now anxious to sign me. Why? Because his hot prospect in Miami had turned down the job, and he was running out of time to fill the position. I also felt that the WGN-TV General Manager at the time, Dennis FitzSimons, had put in a good word for me. When I met with the news director and told him about my cable TV offer, he began to squirm.

"Oh, we can do better for you," he said. In our business, when another station wants you, your value automatically goes up. I went from being an inexperienced anchor to hot property in a matter of a weekend. He made me a fantastic offer, 50 percent better than the cable TV deal and 40 percent better than what I was making at Channel 2. I also would not have to put up with some of the egos I had dealt with at CBS because Channel 9 was filled with down to earth people. They had very few inflated egos, and it reflected in their down-to-earth 9 o'clock news team of Allison Payne, Steve Sanders, Tom Skilling, and Roan. I found out they were as humble off the air as they were on the air.

I tried to conceal my excitement about WGN's interest in me and reacted rather coolly when the news director offered me the job.

"That sounds good to me," I said with a controlled smile. When I got to my car and was alone, I let out a yelp of joy. It felt like I had just won the lottery.

Now I could focus on trying to turn Maggie around. While she was out of her deep depression, things were still not going that well. She was restless and losing hope of ever finding a job, and she still had her moments of anger.

One night Arlana took her to a nighttime concert at a park in Hinsdale. The parking lot they used was a grass field. When the concert ended, Arlana did not want to risk walking Maggie over the uneven grassy terrain, so she told her to stand by a tree and wait while she went to get the car. It all seemed like a good idea, but when taking care of a blind or sight-impaired person, sometimes the best of plans blows up. First, Arlana had trouble finding her car in the lot, and it was a good ten or fifteen minutes before she could locate it. Maggie was stuck under a tree unable to see much of anything in the dark because of her night blindness. But she could hear people brushing by her and cars stream by. She began worrying about Arlana, knowing there was nothing she could do even if something had gone wrong. In short, she was terrified. Maggie let Arlana have it when she finally picked her up, even threatening never to see her again. I knew what Arlana was going through because I had made similar "mistakes" and faced Maggie's wicked tongue. She still had a ton of fear locked inside, which exploded now and then. The two people she loved the most were always standing right next to the grenade.

I continued to work on Maggie to seek help. She needed to find out what jobs were available for a hearing and sight-impaired person. I kept telling her to call the State of Illinois or DuPage County or somewhere to see what kind of programs they had to offer. She did not want to hear the suggestions.

"It's all political BS," she said. "Besides, I can still see and hear. They are not going to help me!" She had a point. She was still somewhat in no man's land. That's how it stood for the next few weeks until I took matters into my own hands.

Without telling Maggie, I called the State of Illinois' Assistance Program for the Disabled. I was connected to a counselor and explained Maggie's problems. The counselor told me help was possible, but Maggie had to be evaluated. That required a trip to the town of Wheaton, Illinois, which was about a forty-minute drive from our house. Maggie would also have to undergo two hours of testing. The counselor told me that after the evaluation was over they would contact us to see what agency best suited Maggie's situation.

I confessed my "discretion" to Maggie about seeking help one morning after breakfast and braced myself for the expected response.

"You called without me knowing?" Maggie fumed. Then quickly added, "Oh well, it doesn't matter anyway. I won't be going."

I felt like flying off the handle and exploding. But this time, I kept my cool. There is a song by a group called Mike and the Mechanics that says, "When you talk in anger, you talk in defense." Both parties retreat into their positions that become like granite. This time I just stayed calm and pleaded with her.

"Just try it," I said. "That's all. If it's bullshit, it's bullshit. We come home. But just try."

We went back and forth for quite some time. It was proof that Maggie's depression was indeed waning because she softened and slowly came around. At last, she agreed to go.

Just because Maggie agreed to make the trip does not mean she did not complain about it. On the morning we left, traffic was awful. The usual forty-five minute ride took us an hour and a half. Maggie was quick to point out it was a bad idea.

The facility was packed when we finally got there. State social service agencies get short-changed all the time. If it's a government-backed pet project like bomb-building, the tax money is always there. In social programs, however, it always appears they operate on a shoestring with a small overworked staff and long lines of clients everywhere. Over the years, it seems to have gotten worse. As kids we made fun of the people waiting in line for bread in the old Soviet Union and ridiculed their system.

Today, our social service lines are just about as long, if not longer.

Maggie had to sign a batch of forms then take a long test. Usually taking tests upset her. She always feared her sight was not strong enough to pass it. This test had no pressure. It was designed to determine whether she was, in fact, legally blind and eligible for assistance. The whole thing took about two and a half hours, and when I saw her afterwards I expected her to be boiling over in anger. The exact opposite was the case. She was okay and even suggested it might have been a good idea to come.

"Well," she said, "we'll see what they come up with." That amounted to high praise for me. On the way back, Maggie said one of the women who spoke to her had mentioned an agency for the blind called The Department of Rehabilitation Services (DORS). She didn't get carried away, but I noticed a glimmer of hope in her eyes.

A week or so later, she got a letter from the State of Illinois and a call from a counselor. They had, in fact, recommended she set up a meeting with DORS. What she had termed "political BS" may have saved her life. In another of her college essays, she wrote about this turning point:

> "After a long adjustment and grieving process, I was fortunate to encounter the services of professionals who specialize in vocational rehabilitation. The expertise of the staff at this agency provided emotional and vocational counseling during a very difficult transition period. In addition to counseling, the agency was a pivotal point in my introduction resources, information networking, advocacy and empowerment; therefore, the social service agency was a strong influence which empowered me to move forward, both in my career and in my life."

Empowerment, of course, means independence. Maggie was trying to be her own person again and rid herself of the shackles that had robbed her of freedom. After reading the letter and hearing from the counselor, Maggie's adrenalin picked up. She was much more active, was sleeping fewer hours, and her entire demeanor started drifting back to the person she had been before her eyes became a major problem.

They gave Maggie an advisor with offices in Oak Brook, Illinois, just ten minutes from our house. His name was Don Davia, and he was a truly amazing man. He was small, about five feet eight inches and very thin, but he had a booming voice and a fiery disposition. He was like a character from our old neighborhood, literally barking out his words in a blunt manner. Because of the high volume of his voice, Maggie had no trouble understanding him. He joked about his tiny office and ripped the state for not giving him enough money. I laughed to myself because he sounded like a hard-bitten "pissed-off" administrator. Davia was completely blind but there was no pause in his step. He used his white cane aggressively, hammering the thing against walls, chairs, cabinets, or whatever was in front of him. He told us to take a seat while he found his desk and sat down on top of it, not in the chair. He took command of the most amazing session I have ever seen, a session that saw two people almost totally connect within a scant half hour.

It was a wonderful thing to watch, and I will always be grateful I was in the room. I recall almost all of the dialogue. It is not exact but the paraphrasing is close because the meeting became quickly etched in my memory.

"So," Davia began, "Maggie, I read (in Braille, of course) that you have Usher Syndrome and are legally blind."

"Yes," she said nervously. "I was diagnosed about a year ago."

"I didn't hear a cane," Davia responded. "Why don't you have a cane?"

"Well," she replied, "I can still see a lot of things."

"You can't walk into this room without your husband, right?" Davia shot back.

"Yes," she conceded.

"Well then, that's your problem. When he is not around, or somebody else is not around, you can't do much of anything. Hell, you need a cane, and you need it tomorrow. Oh, I know nobody wants to take that step. I know it scares you, but when you get it you'll be thanking me. You know why? It will be like the parting of the Red Sea. When you walk down the street with a cane, people know you are blind, and they will get out of your way. Now you are trying to fake it, and I bet you're in hell." Maggie smiled and admitted she pretty much felt that way.

"It doesn't matter if you have some sight or not. You're legally blind, and you have to admit you can't get around by yourself. Believe me, once you master the cane you can go anywhere. I do. So get a cane, Maggie. I'll set you up tomorrow."

Davia seemed to know everything and everybody in the blind community. He knew mayors, congressmen, senators, and big shots in every field. In the course of the conversation, he dropped a few names and even called a couple of politicians SOB's for failing to support what he felt was much needed funding for his programs.

"I read where you were a nurse," Davia said. "You quit because of your eyes?"

"Yes," Maggie replied, "I had to."

"Well, what do you want to do now?" Davia asked.

"I want to get a job in a clinic, but I don't think I can even do that with my eyes."

"Well, how about teaching?" Davia said

"Teaching what?" Maggie replied.

"Do you have a degree?" Davia asked. Maggie told him she had about two years of college.

"Well, that's better than most. So go back to college, get a degree and teach something. Hell, with your background as a nurse, you would make a great social worker."

"How can I go back to school?" she asked.

"How?" he growled back "There are blind people with masters' degrees, and you are sitting here with at least some sight and telling me you can't graduate from college!"

Davia then went into a long list of agencies that could help, from special equipment to enhance her sight to tutors who could help her with her classes, to note takers who volunteered their time. You could sense Maggie getting more excited by the minute.

"Look," he concluded, "you can't do a lot of things you could do before. You can do other things and maybe even better things. Look at me. I can advise you because I am blind and know what it's like. So can you. Get the degree, but first of all get a cane. No, I'll tell you what I'll do. I will send you a cane. I'll send you two of them because I have busted a few in my time. Call me in a week, come in, and we'll begin giving you lessons on how to use it. In the meantime, play around with the thing at home and get used to it. It's your best friend."

Davia told Maggie he would be her counselor and advisor until she found a job. Anything she needed would be just a phone call away. He was extremely good at what he did. He was also Maggie's kind of person, direct and loud. The most poignant element of the meeting was the connection. Maggie was hearing from a guy who was blind, a comrade. As loving and well-intentioned as I had been, it simply was not the same. I was a sighted person. I could not reach Maggie the way Davia could reach her. I had never thought of it until that moment, as deep as our love had become, there was now a new element that would be there for the rest of our lives. I welcomed it because Maggie was returning to life, getting back in that wonderfully forward-looking lifestyle (generative) that she'd had in the past. It didn't matter that I could no longer share a big part of her life. On our wedding day, I had vowed to make her happy, even if that meant giving up a part of her.

Maggie left the meeting with Davia, and for the first time in a long time, she was extremely chatty.

"Wow, what a guy!" she laughed. "He knocked my socks off." Then she got serious for a moment and said half-sadly.

"Boy, Richie, I'm going to get a cane. I never thought …" I quickly cut her off.

"Listen," I said, "it's the best thing. I know what you're thinking. I don't like the idea of you with a cane anymore than you do, but Don was pretty positive about it."

The more we talked about it in the car, the more Maggie warmed to the idea. Especially important was Davia's comment that the cane would give her freedom. Maggie's eyes burned with anticipation. She had a chance to get part of her life back, to regain a degree of independence.

True to his word, Davia sent the canes to our house within two days. They came in small white boxes. Each cane is collapsible into three parts with a tight rubber wire holding it together down the center of the tube. Maggie's excitement from two days before vanished. It was a scary prospect because a cane officially stamps you as blind. She really did not know how her family and friends would react. After she took the canes out of their boxes and used one in the house, she got very quiet. Since she wore her emotions on her sleeve, I had to think of something to keep the momentum going.

"I can tell you don't like it," I said. " What if you don't use it all the time?"

"What do you mean?" she asked.

"Well," I said, "you have to learn to use the thing, but right now when you are with me, or Arlana, you get by pretty well. So when we go out or go to Ron and Gail's house or Andi and Jim, leave the cane at home."

The suggestion was a big hit.

"That way," she said, "I can ease into it."

Feeling better, she walked around for hours with the cane. I realized with each obstacle that the psychological challenges Maggie faced were as big as the physical challenges.

About a week later, she had a lesson on how to use the cane. Arlana took her to Davia's office. That night she showed me how it's done. "It's all in the wrist," she laughed as she moved the cane from side to side on the floor. Davia also told her something that would be invaluable for both of us the rest of our time together. Maggie showed me the way to properly escort blind people when they are not using the cane. You don't grab them by the hand or by the back or by the shoulder. You do it in the formal way you see at weddings: you drop your arm to your side then extend your hand straight forward, as if a dish towel could be draped across your forearm. The blind person then takes hold of your arm just above the elbow. That way they can better adjust to quick starts, stops, or turns. It also looks much nicer. Once Maggie learned this, she had little patience for people who did not follow her instructions. I became an expert, and she was always very complimentary. I got a kick out of helping her. My aim was to be the best guide in the world.

Soon Maggie became comfortable practicing outside. Arlana once took her to downtown Hinsdale for her first big test, and Maggie had fun with it. After her depression lifted, she could joke about her blindness. When it looked like nobody was around, she gave Arlana the cane to use, just for fun. Arlana was having a good old time laughing, joking, and walking with the cane. Suddenly, a lady turned the corner and was walking right at them. Arlana did not have time to think. She greeted the woman, looked her in the eye, and said, "Oh, hi." The lady gave a quizzical response then gave Arlana a dirty look and walked on without saying a word. Maggie laughed herself silly when she realized what had happened. Arlana quickly gave the cane back to Maggie.

While she did practice a lot in the first few months after she got the cane, she did not use it by herself that much. As unlucky as she had been to get such a long shot disease, she was still somewhat lucky in that she had some sight to make the transition. Her next step was a visit to the Wheaton Eye Clinic, again set up by Davia. For Maggie, it was a revelation.

Maggie insisted on using her cane when she went to the clinic. Why? Because she knew it didn't matter when she was with people who had eye problems themselves. It was becoming her world. The receptionist wore dark glasses and was also legally blind. She put Maggie at ease from the start. The clinic was actually a two-story house that had been converted into a store for visual aids as well as a testing area. It was immaculate and extremely bright. Even for a sighted person it was a pleasing environment. Every corner seemed well-lit. The receptionist quickly explained that there were specially powered lights that were tinted to give it such a clear look.

We were met by an escort and given a tour of the place. When

Maggie walked in the huge living room area, she found a candy store full of special glasses, machines, magnifying glasses, and special devices for the sight-impaired. We were first shown a huge selection of sunglasses. Some were yellow-tinted, some were real dark and almost all were wrap-a-rounds because light seeping into the side of the glasses might cut down on the clarity for people who need all the help they can get. Maggie tried on a bunch of sunglasses, and she was really charged up. "This one is a little better," she chuckled, as she went through one pair after another.

They also showed her lamps with high-powered bulbs that helped you see better; clocks with huge numbers so there was no squinting to see what time it was; special large print cooking devices; enlarged playing cards; and on and on. One thing Maggie liked a lot, and used the rest of her life, was a special card for signing your name. It's hard for people who cannot see properly to locate the line on any document and then write their name in a straight line. The card, the size of a credit card, was black and rectangular and had a slit at the bottom just long enough for a signature. You placed the bottom line of the slit over the signing line of the document. That way, the black area on the card provided a perfect contrast to the white surface where you made your signature. Maggie almost flipped out when she saw it. She used it the rest of her life, and people would always marvel when they saw it.

The device that really made her eyes pop out, and changed her life drastically, was the VTech, which is a giant TV screen that enlarges print. The biggest one is the size of a small console television. The screen of the TV is 32 inches and is connected to a table that has a white iron slab that moves on tracks. The demonstrator switched it on then placed a book facing up on top of the slab. A camera catches the letters and presto—the page comes up right on the TV screen. The print is enlarged and very easy to see. You simply move the book on the slab and read it off the screen.

"Wow!" Maggie gasped. "I can't believe it. This is great!" She no longer would have to struggle to read. She simply could not take her eyes off the VTech. The demonstrator pointed out that you could change the backgrounds: black print on white or white print on black. It depended on the type of eye problem you had to deal with. Pictures could be placed on the machine, and they were also large and very clear to see.

Maggie did not want to leave the area. She checked out all the VTech's and came back to the big one. There was no question in my mind; I would buy her the VTech. We must have spent a good hour and a half at the clinic. Maggie was talking to people who were experiencing the same problems, and she was getting all kinds of tips. It was heartening. As she talked, I could see that spark return to her eyes. She was totally pumped.

On the way out, she bought a pair of sunglasses, an oven timer and, of course, the special card to sign her name. I also ordered a VTech. As she left, she vowed to call the receptionist to volunteer her time for some upcoming events at the clinic. She also used her cane on the way out, and she used it with confidence. There was no reluctance, it was almost as if she now suddenly liked the idea of using it. Maggie left the building a different person than when she went in.

On the ride home, all she talked about was the future. "Wow, Richie, with the VTech I can go back to school and get a degree. Then I can become a counselor or a social worker. Then with my background as a nurse, I can really help people and make a decent living doing it." She went on and on. Needless to say, I fed into all of it. I told her that with the VTech maybe she could read for the rest of her life. It was back to the days of being optimistic. Her whole mental outlook had changed. It reminded me of a line once used by one of my idols, Edward R Murrow. Maggie began to think again about "living a life, not an apology." The self-pity was almost totally gone and once again seemed to reinforce my belief that money can buy happiness. All the stuff we saw was the result of technology—material research. The material things in that room led to emotional happiness in the form of freedom to live somewhat independently.

Maggie, it turns out, did not share my theory about "buying" happiness. She had a somewhat different view of technology and wrote about it in a college essay for her philosophy class. The subject was how the great French philosopher, Descartes, would look at the modern world. The essay reveals a lot about her and a lot about her belief in people and machines.

"As I thought about Descartes grand vision of a better world, I realized I did not have to look very far for proof. There were an "infinite number of devices" right under my nose! I have my tape recorder to record lectures, I have a pocket recorder for my audio books, and I have an FM system that allows me to hear any lecture right into my hearing aids. In addition, I have a computer at home, with software to enlarge the characters on my screen and a closed circuit television (VTech) to enlarge all printed material. I consider myself very fortunate to be living in the twentieth century. Descartes, the mathematician, would be exultant over the 'usefulness' that has resulted from his scientific method.

How would Descartes the philosopher feel about it? Would he be as pleased with the final results? I think that the man, who was so capable of deep introspection, would have been very disappointed. It appears that people are not only being isolated from each other, but from themselves.

On a personal level, I can look into my own experience as a registered nurse. In the past 25 years of medicine, I have been witness to the tremendous growth in medical technology. I can remember working in intensive care, learning to manipulate more and more machinery and I could not help but think how easy it was to forget the main purpose of technology, the patient! It took constant vigilance to keep my priorities in perspective; and it made me wonder, as a technologically advancing society, are we continually distancing ourselves from one another, as well as ourselves."

A good example of how technology has overtaken reason is in the cable news business. The lifeblood of cable news is the "breaking story" where many times anchors and reporters are spewing out useless or outright wrong information about an unfolding story. The news comes before the explanation of the news, and that is extremely dangerous. I recall shortly after the events of 9-11, a small plane crashed into an office building in Italy. The Cable news station went crazy with it as if it had been the work of terrorists.

The New York Stock Exchange tumbled. A few hours into it, they discovered it had just been an accident, not a terrorist attack. Before satellite transmission, reporters would have had the time to sift through the facts before the story had been sent over the news wires. The late Howard K. Smith, a broadcast legend who worked with Murrow, wrote an autobiography with the best title I have ever seen. It's called *Events Leading Up To My Death*, and it summed up the debate between technology and humanity Maggie had addressed. Smith said that in each decade of his seventy year life there had been marvelous technological advances, but he also observed that when it came to morality and civil behavior, the United States had digressed in each passing decade. Howard K. Smith and Maggie were on the same page.

As Maggie continued her rebound, she was also looking forward to a special wedding. Arlana had finally decided to try married life, and her future husband was one of Maggie's old friends. She had introduced Arlana to George Fako, who grew up just a few doors away from Maggie on May Street. George is as true blue as you can be. He is a caring and a very giving man. They made a great couple, and Maggie and I were thrilled. She was the maid of honor, and she and Arlana were both gorgeous. There is a fantastic picture of the four of us at the wedding at the end of the book. I chuckle every time I see it. I still recall Maggie heading for Mario Tricoci's for a complete hair and make-up treatment the morning of the ceremony. She came back looking like a movie star and was beaming.

"This is one of the best days in my life," she said. It was hard to believe that just a few months before she resembled a dehydrated ghost.

Things happened rapidly. Within three weeks, the VTech came to our house, and Maggie did not waste time. She got her transcripts from UIC and found that she had two years of college credits. She would need two more years for her degree, so she called DePaul and Loyola to get information on their programs, and she quickly set up classes. Since public transportation in the suburbs is non-existent, George, Arlana, or I took Maggie to classes. It turned out they were at the Loyola campus in west suburban Maywood, just a few miles from our house. I would take Maggie to the door, but then she would get out on her own and use the cane to get to class. In the fall of 1992, she took her first class. She wanted to get acclimated to the VTech and perfect her use of the cane. "When I get rolling," she said, "I'll take two classes in the next semester and then maybe three." She figured it would take her three or four years to get her degree.

Maggie also formed more and more connections with people in the blind community. She joined a support group that met in downtown Chicago every Monday night. They would set up excursions, dinners, dances, and all kinds of special events. Taking Maggie there, I began to question why we still lived in the suburbs. The city is a much better place to live for someone with a cane, and I began to really think about making the move.

Maggie enjoyed life as a student while also honing her skills as one of the great spenders of all time. She wanted to remodel more rooms, beginning with the bathroom, the living room, the dining room. Then she had plans for the whole house. She said it needed a massive overhaul, but I was not about to get sucked into that again. We had done the same thing at our first house, and I was tired of having workers traipse around the place on a monthly basis. I put my foot down, but somehow, my wallet still wound up bleeding.

"Look," I told Maggie, "we are not going to do this again. If you want to remodel every room, we are going to save some money in the next three years, then have it all done at once while we go on a vacation. Or, if you want, we can buy a brand new house, or condo, that needs no work, right now."

Maggie's eyes lit up like a Christmas tree.

"Oh," she said cheerily, "the condo idea is a great one." She was never one to pass up an adventure. We found the home of our dreams in the town of Westchester, closer to Chicago, but still in the western suburbs.

It was a beautiful two-story townhouse that was just two years old. The floors were all hardwood, something Maggie had always wanted. It had three bedrooms and a loft, which she quickly claimed for her VTech, her computer, and all the rest of what she called her "toys." It also had a family room and a huge basement.

After we moved in, we found ourselves sorely lacking in furniture, and it was a problem that Maggie looked forward to solving. She quickly befriended our next-door neighbors, who happened to know an interior decorator. This was perfect for a person who could not see very well. Maggie convinced me to hire the designer, and it was the best decision I ever made. Maggie had an absolute ball riding around with Joyce to stores of all kinds and putting together her new doll house. She even went down to Merchandise Mart in downtown Chicago. Every few days a new piece of furniture would arrive, and it was all quality stuff at quality prices. I really didn't care too much about the money by then. Maggie was her old self, and she also regained the 'goofiness' that she had lost in her depression. Sofas, rugs, chairs, and stereo equipment—it all came in. Maggie even ordered a gorgeous chandelier for the dining room. When it was all over, we had a place that belonged in a home decorating magazine. We were also only ten minutes from Arlana and George.

Maggie was taking classes at Loyola. She was also meeting people at the Wheaton Eye Clinic and other blind services. She was volunteering her time for fund raising events, and she was cooking up a storm. Our sex life, which naturally suffered during her depression, came back to life. To borrow the old FDR campaign song from 1933, "Happy Days" were here again.

Every week Maggie would have someone over for dinner and go all out. She loved to make pasta, Italian sausage, seafood, vegetarian dishes; she was cooking them all and getting tips from everybody. She also got me into health food, and we bought a blender to grind carrots, spinach, and apples into juice. One day, in fact, I was at the health food store in nearby LaGrange when I saw a guy at the juice counter drinking some green stuff in a shot glass. He told me it was wheat grass. "What does it do?" I asked. "Well," he said, "you see this hair? (It was jet black.) Well, it was all gray before I started drinking this stuff! It takes years off your life." Gullible as always, I bought some wheat grass and took it home to blend. Maggie took one sip and started laughing. "It tastes like poison," she said, spitting it out in the sink. My brother-in-law took a sip of it and almost threw up. Nobody believed the "hair" story, and Maggie pointed out that I didn't even have gray hair. After about a month, I gave up on wheat grass.

One cool spring morning, I went out to pick up the newspaper dressed only in pants and a tee shirt. It was about thirty-eight degrees, and I made the mistake of locking myself out of the house. As I began to freeze, I raced to the back of the building where our bedroom was located and knocked on the window. When Maggie had her hearing aids out, she could not hear a bomb go off. So as she slept away, I raced back to the front of the house getting colder by the minute. I made the ill-advised decision to break in the garage door with my shoulder. It got me a pinched nerve in my neck, and I was barely able to avoid surgery after my front deltoid muscle atrophied. Living with a person who is hard of hearing, I had to be extremely careful. I learned to anticipate the unexpected and avoid putting myself in a bind.

As for Maggie's eyes, they were hanging in there. She was using the cane more often, but she still had a small degree of central vision. The VTech and the enhanced lettering on her computer made life a lot easier. In her first two classes, she received "A's" on almost every paper she handed in. She was coping well and never mentioned any concern about her diagnosis, but it came out in other ways. One way was her spending habits. I knew the reason she loved furnishing the house with expensive things. She wanted to buy them while she could still see them. The long-term future was not very promising, so she had to enjoy it all while she still had the chance.

I seldom stopped her from signing checks or using credit cards. My heart was too soft.

All the stuff she bought had to have a lot of color because it was more discernible to her failing eyes. She and Joyce bought some abstract art that looked like junk to me. One painting appeared to show an old washboard, a screwdriver, and a hammer painted in wild colors. It should have been entitled: "Hardware Store." I never liked it but didn't say a word. If she was having fun, what difference does my opinion on art make?

In early 1993 Maggie met Ted. One of the people at her support group told Maggie that Ted was extremely depressed after a diagnosis similar to Maggie's. He was also in his early forties. She met him at a picnic, and she made it her project to get him back on track. It helped a lot, of course, that Maggie was a beautiful blonde. That would get any guy back on track. She talked about him all the time and also talked to him on the phone everyday. She was relentless about saving him from his malaise, and she did not do it gently. I would hear Maggie ripping into Ted on the phone, calling him a phony or a liar or worse. She could do it because she knew he would listen—they shared the same illness. It was exactly what Davia had done for her. The badgering worked wonders for Ted. She used to tell me how good looking he was, but I was never jealous, although it did cross my mind that he was part of Maggie's new life. There was no question; she was happy in the world of the blind and sight-impaired. I never stopped her from seeing any of her new friends, even if it was at the expense of time she could have spent with me. Her happiness was all that mattered.

One weekend, Maggie invited Ted to stay with us, and it was eventful. On the first night, I was working so George and Arlana took Maggie and Ted out for dinner. When Ted had to visit the washroom, they convinced him to leave his cane at the table and have George escort him to the washroom, taking him by the arm. George said it was the longest walk of his life. Ted, by now, had reacquired his sense of humor and told George, "I love you," as they walked to the bathroom.

The next morning, at breakfast, I was serving Ted a plate of scrambled eggs. "Thanks, Maggie," he said, as I gave him the plate. Maggie, who was seated across the table, burst into laughter and chided Ted for his confusion. They both had a good laugh. There was never a fear of making fun of one another or cracking a joke about the blind. The difference was this: *they* could laugh at themselves, but never once did *I* ever joke about blindness or deafness with any of Maggie's friends. When we were alone I could laugh with her about anything, but with her friends, I never once made wisecracks. It was a wise rule to follow.

A few weeks later, I also learned just how well Maggie could use her cane. We made a trip to Las Vegas with George and Arlana. Maggie asked Arlana to make the plane reservations, which she got for a low rate, but with a catch, it was not a direct flight. We had to change planes in Dallas, both coming and going. Maggie gave Arlana hell for it, calling her a "cheap Bohemian." The trip to Vegas was fine, but on the way back we had a problem.

When we got to Dallas, we had an hour and a half layover, so we decided to get something to eat. As it turned out, the service at the restaurant was horribly slow. By the time we were served, we were pushing close to the time of our flight. Arlana kept warning everybody we had to eat fast. We were all nervous wrecks by the time the food finally arrived. George was especially nervous. He had ordered a hamburger and took a huge first bite, as if he were a starving escaped convict on the run. Ketchup went streaming down his face, and I began to laugh, telling him that Arlana had put the fear of God in him. Maggie was cracking up. We wolfed down our food and made a mad rush down the terminal for the gate, which was a long way off.

Maggie simply took out her cane, grabbed my arm, and we rolled! It was faster than if I had been walking by myself. I felt like I was on a moving sidewalk. Anyone who might have dared to stand in our way would have been crushed. Davia was right, people parted out of the way as if it was the Red Sea. Maggie wielded the cane to perfection, and we made the flight easily, although George had a horrible case of indigestion on the plane.

Maggie was getting a full head of steam once again and she was now well-connected to the deaf-blind community. She quickly gathered a group of new friends, and I learned they were just about the nicest human beings you could imagine. They were appreciative of everything. I once escorted Maggie to a function at the Chicago Lighthouse for the Blind, an organization on the West Side of Chicago. One of her friends, Wayne, needed a lift home, and I was more than happy to oblige. He lived in one of the toughest areas of Chicago. After we dropped him off, Maggie told me Wayne lived with his aging father, and they barely made ends meet. Any assistance he got from The Lighthouse was crucial. Wayne was such a nice kid that my heart went out to him. It's tough being blind or sight-impaired when you have money, it's tougher when you are extremely poor. I could just imagine Wayne trying to survive with more odds against him than Maggie.

We always embraced people. Maggie was not outgoing when she was young, but she became that way over the years. She lived with a man who loved to befriend people on the spot. Maggie always told me I was too outgoing, willing to discuss almost anything, from sex to philosophy, with people I barely knew. I told her what you give, you get. It's amazing, after you get by the small talk with people, you learn a lot of things.

Maggie used to wonder why I always talked to the female security guard at her school in Maywood. Maggie would come down from class, and the security guard and I would be talking about religion, racial issues, or sports. One evening, she even told me about her sex life.

"That's pretty personal stuff," Maggie barked.

I explained that maybe the woman was looking for help. The sharing of any topic or idea, when done with taste and respect, can only be a plus, in my opinion. I wish more people were open, but sadly, most people sit behind a computer or if they do talk, everybody is afraid they may say something that will offend. Sometimes, I think we are becoming "humanoids," a term Paddy Chayefsky used in the classic movie *Network*. We seem to be, at times, a nation that has lost its individuality, incapable of any conversation except the mundane. Most young people have little historical perspective beyond their own lives. Maggie stopped wondering why I talked to the security guard when I told her that because of the friendship I developed, we saved $3 every time I picked her up. When I told the guard I parked my car in a paid lot, she said quickly: "Oh, don't do that. Just park in front, and we'll keep an eye on it." Being open can also have monetary benefits.

Maggie was always very intelligent. In our earlier discussions with Andi, Jim, Ron, and Gail, she always had a lot to offer. Now that she was back in school, she was really becoming well-read on a variety of topics.

She was now paying more attention to current affairs, politics, and history. She read more books. After reading Robert F. Kennedy's book, *Thirteen Days: A Memoir of the Cuban Missile Crisis*, she had a deeper appreciation of the gravity of that confrontation. As a teenager, she hadn't paid that much attention. I had a hard time convincing her we had come close to nuclear war and blowing up the world. She and Arlana used to laugh at me, but after she read the book, she just shook her head.

"By God, you were right," she said. She asked a lot of questions about history, and about the news stories of the day. I gladly filled her in. Having minored in history, I devoured every book I could. I gave her the book *The Captains and The Kings* by Taylor Caldwell. It was a fascinating novel based on the Kennedy family. It was my favorite. Maggie also loved it, and I loved the change in her. The philosopher Nietzsche once wrote about what I felt is the most important ingredient to a successful marriage. "When marrying, one should ask oneself this question: do you believe that you will be able to converse with this woman in your old age? Everything else in marriage is transitory, but the most time during the association belongs to conversation."

Maggie and I debated just about everything. Our dinners were always fascinating. If I won an argument one night, she would go back and read more on the issue and fire something back at me. Or she would come back all excited and point something out that she felt backed up her case. This is how it would be the rest of our lives together. I looked forward to every day, every dinner, and sometimes I would deliberately say something outlandish to get a rise out of her.

To add to her feminist base, she became a strong advocate for legislation that would make life easier for the handicapped. She was liberal in a lot of ways, but on personal life issues, she was conservative. She was Pro-life in the abortion debate and winced in displeasure when she heard about one of our friends getting a divorce. She always felt it was better to stick it out. She was also a protector of the environment and an admirer of Native Americans. She loved the Indians' respect for the land. She did not care for Ronald Reagan but adored Bill Clinton. She defended him even through the Monica Lewinsky mess, which brought up an obvious contradiction in her beliefs. "If I had done that," I pointed out, "you would have kicked me out in a heartbeat."

As it turned out, I met Bill Clinton by sheer luck one night. I was doing a report from Washington D.C. for WGN-TV the night Michael Jordan became an owner of the Washington Wizards basketball team. After our live shot for the 9 o'clock news, I was surprised when a Secret Service agent stuck his head out from behind a curtain and said, "Does anybody want to meet the President?" My cameraman and I rushed in for the opportunity, and I got to shake the President's hand. Since I was not a big fan, I brought Maggie into my greeting: "Mr. President, my wife Maggie thinks you're the greatest."

"Thank you, sir," he said.

Maggie cracked up laughing when I told her the story.

Then there was the night Maggie and I went to see her favorite team, the Chicago White Sox. Growing up in the shadows of the old Comiskey Park, Maggie and her girlfriends became baseball groupies for a couple of summers during their teen years. Pitcher Gary Peters was Maggie's favorite player.

When the new ballpark opened in 1991 (now called US Cellular Field), I managed, through connections, to buy two season tickets very close to the field. I explained that Maggie was legally blind, so Rob Gallas, the Marketing Director and my friend, set me up with two box seats in the 4th row right by the first base on deck circle. The first year we went was 1991; and back then, Maggie at least could still see the pitcher and batter, while I had to give her a play-by-play when the ball was hit to the infielders or outfielders.

Over the next few years, she even lost sight of the pitcher and batter. About all she really saw was the big brightly lit scoreboard in center field.

On the night in question, I took Maggie to see the White Sox play the Texas Rangers, and the Sox were trailing the entire game. Maggie got sad as they began to lose, so I tried to cheer her up.

"Look," I said, "even if the Sox lose, you still have me."

"That's not enough!" she shot back and burst into laughter.

Then suddenly in the 9th inning the Sox rallied. They were down by three runs but loaded the bases. Everybody was standing when Robin Ventura came to the plate and laid into a pitch, sending the ball into the night sky and over the wall in right center field.

"It's gonna be a grand slam!" I yelled into Maggie's ear. The look on her face, as the famous commercial later would say, was priceless. It was one of total excitement and happiness. The Sox won in the most dramatic fashion, and she had been there to experience the feeling. Whenever someone asks why a blind person would want to pay money to see a ball game, remember this story. Just being there is good enough. To absorb the sound, smells, and the excitement means everything.

Going to ball games or other public places is never easy for the blind. Maggie would never use a public rest room unless she really was in dire need. Sometimes when she did, she would come out frustrated that the place was too dark, and she could not find the toilets. Many times, I would ask a woman going into the rest room to help her. Other times, when there was no one around I would knock on the door myself to make sure the stalls were unoccupied then go in with her. She always joked I would be arrested someday, but I never came close to being caught.

Overall our lives had once again fallen into a happy rhythm. Even though I always worried about Maggie's eyes and hoped they would not get worse, I was no longer concerned about her depression. It was long gone. The new technology she enjoyed, the new friends, school, and activities all gave her a zest for life that was perhaps even greater than she had before. We also became Godparents. Jim and Andi adopted a child in January, 1993. Then in February, Maggie came home beaming one day with even more good news.

11

The Miracle Worker

"Richie," she said excitedly, "I have just been given the chance of a lifetime."

Maggie had been invited to an internship at the Helen Keller Center at Sands Point, New York. It was a eight-week program that would enable her to learn how to help deaf and blind people. She explained that the program would go a long way towards reaching her goal as a social worker. She would be learning from professionals. The Center was in a beautiful country like setting of Long Island and, of course, was fully equipped for the hearing and sight-impaired. Besides the learning experience, she was looking on the internship as somewhat of a retreat.

She also read the books about Helen Keller and saw the movie, *The Miracle Worker*, with Patty Duke and Ann Bancroft. Despite being deaf and blind, Helen Keller's life was saved by a courageous instructor who taught her to communicate at the age of seven. Helen later graduated from college with honors and became an activist and author. It was exactly the path that Maggie wanted to take.

I readily embraced Maggie's enthusiasm for the trip, but I automatically assumed she would want me to go with her for the start of the journey then pick her up at the end of it. She grabbed my hand and with a tender voice she told me: "Richie, I hope you don't mind if I go alone. This is something I have to do by myself."

The thought of her getting off the plane and getting around in New York scared me to death. I had been there many times and anyone who has been there knows the pace of the city. Don't get me wrong! I love New York, but the people there would just as soon run you over as not. Besides the plane flight, she would have to make her way to Long Island on a train. What if she got lost? What if she fell into a construction site? What if she got mugged? The pitfalls seemed endless, but I did not express any reservations outwardly. Despite all the progress she had made since her diagnosis of Usher Syndrome, and her slow drift into the world of the deaf and blind, I guess I still thought she belonged in my world. However, my world was no longer *our* world. I would have to swallow my fear and let her go.

Another sad element to the trip was the fact that we would be separated for so long. In the past, it had been a few days and at the most a week. Now she was talking about a month and a half. That was a long time. She was not happy about that element herself, but she said the opportunity was simply too good to pass up. She could hardly wait to go. The internship was to begin the first week of May and end in the middle of June. She even talked about possibly extending her stay. I quickly realized I would be playing a lot more golf than I expected that summer. While I was really happy for her, deep down inside I was petrified. It was, again, one of those times when I simply had to fake it. I bit the bullet and put Maggie's needs first. She needed all the support I could give her. The last thing she needed was anybody dampening her enthusiasm. If I had to lie about my feelings, so be it. I recall reading a passage about Franklin Roosevelt in which he said he was quite prepared to lie if it led to positive results for the common good. Telling the truth is usually the best policy, but not always.

When Arlana found out about the trip, she had the same fears that I felt inside. To Maggie, she also faked it, telling her it would be a great trip. To me, Arlana's face was wrinkled in deep concern.

"How the hell is she going to do it?" she asked. I just laughed because I had the exact same words locked in my brain. I told Arlana we had to suck it up and hope for the best.

The prospect of Maggie leaving in June cast a shadow over my spring. When we went out to dinner, I held her tighter, and whenever I hugged her, it was longer than the previous embrace. Every kiss was special. In the back of my mind, I feared some calamity would befall her. But for Maggie, it was a no-brainer, at least on the surface. All she talked about was the Helen Keller trip. They had a special jogging track for the blind where you grab a railing and are able to run or walk without aid. They had this and they had that; the list was endless. You could tell she was thrilled at the chance to go there.

I bought the airline tickets and informed the carrier she was legally blind. As the time for her to leave moved closer and closer, I struggled more each night with my ability to sleep. My best dream was that the trip would somehow be cancelled. My nightmares had Maggie getting run over by a bus or getting attacked by some heartless thug. Those nightmares never left me, and believe it or not, continue even now years after her trip. I have not slept well since the spring of 1993. Almost every night is a struggle. When a person begins to worry on a daily basis for years, it's hard to shake and becomes a way of life.

The truth was, Maggie's life was about to change dramatically. In the days before her departure for New York, I tried to stay busy to keep my mind off my increasing concern. Maggie, in the meantime, was a whirlwind of activity. She was buying clothes for the trip, calling friends and relatives, and getting ready for her adventure. I did not dare talk to her seriously about her departure. I did not want to start crying in front of her.

Maggie and I had an aversion to saying serious good byes. For us, it was always a joke, a kiss, "enjoy yourself," and "I'll see you soon." I never discussed the fears I had about her safety, and she never expressed a concern to me. We were always protecting each other, but the question was, protecting each other from what? Well, at the time I could not quite put my finger on it, but now I know what it was. We were protecting each other from the pain and sadness of possibly not seeing one another again. We loved each other so deeply and connected so deeply in love that we never wanted to even consider the fact that it would end some day. We gave each other space, for sure, but at the end of that space we were always together. The anticipation of the happy reunion made the time apart fly by. The fear that something bad might happen during a trip was always there, but it was never allowed to manifest itself. The word 'goodbye' was in our vocabulary but never applied to our own lives. Permanently parting was something neither of us was prepared to endure.

The night before she left, Maggie went to bed early. Outwardly I joked about the trip and how I would improve my golf game by ten shots. I told her she would likely find a young stud to play around with in New York to pass the time. I suggested that the time would fly by and before you knew it, she would be home in July and back to the boring routine in Westchester.

One of the hardest things I had to do the night before her trip was go through my usual ritual of "tucking" her into bed.

She insisted on this every night that I was home, and we both looked forward to it. It was our signature moment and over the years it took on a quality of tenderness and bliss that bordered on heavenly. I would cuddle next to her for awhile as we talked and laughed about the day's events. As she got tired, I would take her covers and tuck them under her neck so she was nice and warm. Then I would drape my entire body on top of her, locking her gently under my frame. When her body was totally engulfed under mine, I would hold her tight and kiss her face, lips and neck, and we would talk and laugh some more until she finally faded off to sleep.

On this particular evening, I do not know how I was able to hold back my tears. I had her in my arms so safe and secure. I did not want to release her for a journey into a world so cruel and unpredictable. I wanted to be at her side to fight off the demons, but this time I could not. I had to let her go to New York by herself. She eventually got drowsy and looked up into what for her was total darkness. I can still see those weary but magical eyes and hear that sweet soft voice whisper in peaceful fatigue.

"I love you so, Richie."

"I love you so," I whispered back. "I'll see you in the morning for the big send-off."

I hugged her one last time then quickly jumped out of bed as Maggie turned on her side. I knew she would be sound asleep in less than five minutes. As for me, I was a basket case. I walked quickly to my rocking chair in the family room and sat there as tears rolled down my cheeks. I knew Maggie could not hear me cry; still, I muffled the sound. I sat there crying for a long time before flicking on the TV for relief. When I finally went to bed, I slept fitfully.

One of the devices Maggie bought at the Wheaton Eye Clinic

was an alarm clock for the hearing and sight-impaired. It emitted an ear-shattering alarm that would wake up the dead. It also had a wire attached to it. The wire was connected to a small saucer shaped disc that was tucked under Maggie's pillow for vibration. I called the thing "the bomb." When it went off, it felt as if a guided missile had hit the bedroom. "The Bomb" exploded at 6 a.m. the next morning. That was the end of my fitful sleep.

"Stay in bed," Maggie said. "I just have to get up early to finish packing."

My eyes had popped open so wide from the alarm that there was no way I would be going back to sleep. I stumbled up to throw some water on my face and saw red blotches of fatigue covering the whites of my eyes.

I was grateful I had the day off from work. Once I had finished taking Maggie to the airport, I planned on crashing for a long afternoon nap. Maggie's flight was at midday so we had a normal amount of time for breakfast. She was still making muffins.

"I made a bunch of them," she said. They are in the freezer, and they should last you for a week." I read the papers as usual and did my baseball statistics as Maggie made her final preparations for the flight.

Arlana was taking us to the airport, and she arrived all chipper and excited, lying through her teeth.

"This is the day, New York, New York," she sang, as she was dying inside. Maggie, as usual, had over packed. I could never get her out of the habit. Her suitcases were bulging. As we drove to the airport, everybody appeared in a positive frame of mind. With my bloodshot eyes, I was just happy I didn't have to drive. We parked the car and walked Maggie to the terminal. I bought her a cup of coffee, then we waited for the moment she would board the plane. It was the moment of a lifetime.

The gate attendant made the announcement that all people in need of special assistance should board the plane. Maggie was the first one of the group to go in. I gave her a peck on the cheek and held her hand briefly before she left with the stewardess. Maggie used her cane despite the escort. She was barely out of sight when I broke down in tears right there at the gate.

"Let's get out of here," I told Arlana.

As we walked toward the parking garage, I could not stop crying. I was grateful I had taken sunglasses. Arlana looked stunned. While she was sad, she was not in tears. I knew she wondered why I was so devastated, but I felt a sense of destiny when Maggie walked away. I was crying because I knew I had lost a big part of her as Maggie walked through that gate. It's true she had gained a degree of independence with the cane up to that point, but when she left on her own on such a long journey without me, I knew the so-called "normal" years of our lives were over. I was mourning the movies we would never again see together, the freewheeling vacations when she could walk alone on the beach and swim in the ocean or walk up to the bar and order herself a drink. I mourned the loss of the evening walks when she could still see my face. I mourned all the simple things we take for granted, playing softball at a picnic, watching airplanes go by, riding a horse, or simply glancing at a menu in a restaurant. All these things were part of the past now. They, no doubt, were the same things Maggie mourned when she was diagnosed. It hit me how horrible she must have felt to lose all of that. It also hit me how courageous she was to move forward and literally risk her own safety to gain independence. I knew then why she insisted I not go with her. What I didn't know was how Maggie felt when *she* boarded that plane. I found out many years later.

Maggie never talked about her emotions of that day. She did call me that evening when she finally arrived at the Helen Keller Center. She told me she had some minor problems getting to Penn Station, but once she got to Port Washington, they had sent a cab to pick her up and take her to the Center. She sounded tired, but she also sounded very, very happy.

"I'm glad I made it," she said. "The rest should be easy."

I discovered the full range of her emotions about that day when I was reading one of her college papers preparing for this book almost eleven years after that touching moment at the airport. As I read, I understood why Maggie and I were so connected. It turns out we had the same feelings and once again were protecting each other from sadness. Here is what she wrote in her college essay:

> "The final stage of my reintegration occurred after my training in orientation and mobility. Mastering the skills of mobility is one thing; actively using them independently was another matter entirely. The turning point for me was the opportunity to obtain vocational counseling at the Helen Keller Center in New York City. It was a golden opportunity to explore my potentials for work with the deaf-blind; however, it required my leaving home for two months and traveling alone for the first time in many years. My husband unselfishly gave his consent and enthusiasm even though, for him, it meant more inconveniences and loneliness. I will never forget the day I departed for New York. I remember being scared and excited at the same time. I did not look back as I boarded the plane, for fear of weakening my resolve. I will also never forget the soaring elation as I journeyed forward into

my passage, traveling alone. The spirituality that graced me on this journey fostered a strength and courage that would serve me well. The letting go of dependence enabled me to experience new opportunities and fostered a greater sense of well being."

I knew at the time that letting Maggie go it alone was the only option. As painful as it was, I was glad I never once considered talking her out of it. The trip was the final turning point in her emotional battle to cope with her diagnosis. She won the battle by walking onto that airplane. A simple act for most people, but for Maggie, it must have felt like walking through a minefield. Nevertheless, she had made it to safety. The seat of the airplane was actually her seat of freedom and hope for a new life.

As for my life without her, it got off to a bad start and stayed that way. I came home from the airport and tried to sleep but the emotion of the day would not allow it. I spent the day in a stupor in front of the TV. The next day, I woke up with a sore throat, the forerunner of a bad case of bronchitis. I think I was sick the entire time she was gone. About three days after she left, I did get some unexpected good news. WGN-TV was sending me to cover the Chicago Bulls NBA playoff series against the Knicks in New York. I would have a chance to visit Maggie! When she called and I told her, she was ecstatic. "It's a great place," she said. "You'll love it."

The following week, I found myself in the Big Apple and on the off day between games, I went to Penn Station and took the train to Port Washington then a cab to Sands Point and the Helen Keller Center. I was still sick as a dog, suffering from a painful cough, but adrenalin was carrying me through. When I arrived at the gate, I could see the impressive building in the background amid the fading afternoon sunlight. Tall trees surrounded the huge structure, and there was a big, perfectly landscaped lawn. It was like an old country estate from a bygone era. Maggie and one of the counselors greeted me at the gate. While I was really happy to see Maggie, I also had a strange feeling that I was intruding on her new life. I hugged and kissed her, and we talked to the counselor for awhile. Maggie asked for the name of a nearby Italian restaurant, which we went to for dinner. I brought Maggie flowers, and we took them with us to find out if she could see them better in a brighter environment.

Once I left the gate of the Center, and we were at the restaurant, I felt more at ease talking to Maggie. She was in fantastic spirits, but she said she had lost some weight most likely from not eating because of the excitement over the trip. We both ordered huge pasta plates and Maggie, as usual, cleaned up the entire dish. She would always take a piece of bread and wipe the final traces of marinara sauce from the plate and devour it. Maggie asked about things at home, but the main conversations concerned the Helen Keller Center. She was beaming about the place. She was learning so much and also helping people.

"I'll tell you, Richie. Even though my eyes are screwed up, I am one of the more fortunate people." She could not wait to show me around. She did, by the way, see the flowers a little better at the restaurant. At least, she said she did.

When we got back to the Center, we sat on a swing in the front yard and talked. I told her about my bronchitis, saying I obviously fell to pieces after she left. She laughed, but deep down I knew she loved being appreciated and wanted. I told her the latest on Andi, Jim, Ron, and Gail. We talked about my mother, and around dusk, she gave me a tour of the inside of the building. The advent of darkness had given the big estate a scary feeling.

Suddenly, I felt like I was in an ancient European castle in the middle of nowhere. There were very few lights on the outside, and once we went inside, things did not improve all that much. There was some light, but the hallway was dingy, and I wondered how Maggie could see at all.

As we walked, I was stunned and frightened by the sounds of muffled groans and screams. They emanated from the rooms of the clients. This was, after all, the Helen Keller Center and some residents could not see, hear, or talk. All three senses were gone. They could only communicate with whatever sound they could muster from their throats—or through sign language or touch. Maggie was correct in saying she was one of the more fortunate people in the building. By the sounds, you would think some of the clients were being tortured. It was the exact opposite. They were getting help and great care, and the Center was giving them a new life.

We passed a few people in the hall. One woman had a shawl draped over her hair, but I could see her whole head was disfigured, and her face was painfully contorted with one eye on her forehead while the other appeared to be on her cheek. There appeared to be bumps all over her face. It was stunningly heart wrenching. She walked hunched over to one side, and she also groaned as she shuffled past us.

The whole tour petrified me. The groans seemed to echo in the halls and get louder as we walked. I wondered what new horror I would see around each corner. Maggie kept telling me how great the place was while pointing out the cafeteria, meeting areas, work rooms and the rest. I believe she heard the groans but never mentioned anything about them. The hair on the back of my neck curled up as the groans grew louder. I thought to myself this is how it must have sounded in the torture chambers during the Inquisition. To Maggie it was no big deal. She truly loved being there. I could tell she was genuinely happy, and I knew Maggie better than anyone.

When we got to her room, it was also very dark. She flicked on a light, and I saw a place that was efficient but very Spartan. No TV, a small bed, a chair and a desk for work. It was a typical dorm room. Maggie put the flowers on her desk and told me she would get a vase from somebody after I left. The time was slipping by, and I was burning out rapidly, so she escorted me back outside.

I was never so glad to leave a building in my life. On the way out, I saw two more people walking down the hall muttering incoherently. Finally outside, I sat with Maggie on the swing for a few more minutes and really don't recall what we talked about. I do recall that every bone in my body wanted to take her back on the train with me to the Plaza Hotel in Manhattan, where the room was first class, the dining was elegant, the wine was rich, and there was gaiety in the air. I wanted to dance with her as we had in Jamaica and Hawaii and all the other wonderful places we had been. I longed to see her long blond hair fly in disarray as she swirled around the dance floor. I wanted things to be as they were before the awful diagnosis, the depression, and the white cane. I don't know how I managed to keep my feelings bottled up, but I did. If being at Helen Keller was what Maggie wanted, then I had no right to question her happiness. I agreed with everything she told me that night.

"Oh, it's a fantastic place," I lied, "and it's a great experience for you. I hope you can stay a few extra weeks as you requested." It was her world, and I was not about to reveal my reservations.

As usual, our parting was awash in optimism. She gave me some T-shirts to take home to George and Arlana. I started to complain about covering the Bulls and their unpredictable coach, Phil Jackson. He had a bad habit of fooling reporters by taking his team on a ferryboat ride instead of practice. Our camera crews had to follow the team bus to get the story, or we were out of luck. Maggie told me to take care of my bronchitis and said she would write Arlana to keep an eye on me. I gave her a final kiss and a short hug, using all my might to hold back any tears. She and the staffer closed the gate, and there was a cab waiting to take me back to the train station at Port Washington.

It was late when I sat down on the train back to Manhattan. My car was pretty much deserted. I felt like the depressed character in the Twilight Zone who was looking out a dark window to find peace and happiness of bygone times in a quaint village called Willoughby. Sick, tired, and lonely, I thought of my new life all the way back to Manhattan. It would be a new challenge meeting people who have had bad luck and struggle everyday. The last two weeks—leaving Maggie at the airport and the visit to the Helen Keller Center—had convinced me that there would be an element of sadness in almost every day of the rest of my life. It breaks your heart to see people struggling to see, to hear, to walk, or even to speak. It breaks your heart even more when you love someone beset with those problems. I had to learn to live with a new set of standards. I had to learn to talk to Maggie and her friends just as I would want to be talked to in that situation, as a fellow human being. I realized it would not be an easy thing to do after hearing mournful groans from people with disfigured heads and faces. We all hope to avoid seeing such tragedy in our lives, but I had to understand it and not just give lip service to the basic truth that we are all human beings— whatever our configuration.

While I eventually did face it, on that particular night I could not. I stumbled and coughed my way back to the Plaza, which had an excellent bar off the lobby. The place was alive with people who were drinking, talking, laughing, seeing, and hearing. I took a seat at the bar and poured down more than a few vodka tonics. Within an hour, I was pretty much wasted. I stumbled to my feet, signed the tab, then took a drink to my room. Getting drunk was the only way I could have slept at all that night, and while I knew the worst thing you can do with bronchitis is drink booze, I really had no choice. To know that Maggie was sleeping in the darkness at Sands Point while she should have been in my arms in a beautiful hotel room was eating me alive. The booze did manage to numb at least some of the pain from one of the lowest points in my life.

There was no numbing the pain the next day, however. I paid a heavy price for the vodka tonics. A hangover is a horrible feeling by itself, but when combined with bronchitis, fatigue, and a full day of work, you have the definition of hell. The ear-shattering noise of Madison Square Garden amid an NBA playoff game made my aching head pound even more. I was never so glad to see a workday end.

A few days after I got back to Chicago, I told Arlana about the trip. After a few minutes she asked me how Maggie looked. I told her she looked fine even though she had lost a few pounds. Arlana then gave me a letter that Maggie had sent to her. Maggie never wrote to me, which tells you the power of her love for Arlana. Up to this point in the book, most of the words from Maggie have been from her formal college essays. They are excellent sources for how she felt about the issues in her life. These letters to Arlana reveal Maggie's informal way of talking. They are the _real_ Maggie. They reflect a wonderful down to earth quality that made her special. I still cherish reading them. They were written on the stationery from her room, and they were written with a large black felt tip pen. Her handwriting had to be big so she could read it.

5/24/93

Hi Bags,

Loved your card! I thought I would write you and save you some money. Richie just left and is <u>very, very</u> tired! We had a nice meal in Port Washington (town in which Sands Point is located). After dinner, we sat on the swing bench on the estate. Thanks for sending my junk. When I call next time, I will be requesting more. I miss your funny face. Do you miss my funny ways?

Today's activity here was cooking, which I missed. But when I returned there was a beautiful fruit salad. Delicious, too! A real nice volunteer named Mark helped the clients make it. By the time I got back there was food all over the lounge. What a mess! Then one of the clients went kind of crazy. I heard it was her typical routine. She was looking for more food—she even began digging into the garbage!

Yesterday afternoon another client who screams and lays on the couch all day went nuts in the bathroom. I found him kicking his legs and licking the washroom sink. Unfortunately, I was the lucky one to find him in the <u>women's</u> bathroom! He was hunched over the bathroom sink, and I couldn't tell at that point if he was a man or woman. So I made sure he was breathing and called one of the aides.

Another client is leaving Friday for his home in Hawaii.

He walks around all day saying: "Oh shit, oh shit, oh shit."
I never left my family! I think he had Tourettes Syndrome,
but nobody seems to know what it is.

Can you believe I am going to LA (for a deaf/blind
conference)! Actually the university is 35 miles from LA,
but they say it is beautiful. As for tomorrow they say we
can do whatever we want. I want to go sightseeing. I want
to see if there are any vineyards relatively close. Tell George
to give me his selections.

Have I mentioned my classes? Oh yeah, the real reason
I am here. I was introduced to an ancient calculator called
ABACUS. It is Japanese and you calculate with beads.
They still use it in Japan. It's great for visually impaired
people because you can feel the beads. Fun, huh? I know
you will want me to teach it to you.

I think I'll close for now. It's 11 p.m. and I have to
get up at 7 a.m. I forgot to mention that Rich brought me
some flowers. They brighten my room. When I get some
pictures I'll send them to you. I hope you and Georgie will
like your surprises. Remind Rich if he forgets to give them
to you … goodbye old pal and don't be yelling at Georgie?

Love,

Mags

This letter was typical Maggie. When I read it, I was very
happy. Being a nurse, Maggie was quite at home with the clients
at the Helen Keller Center. Groans, screams, and strange behavior
did not frighten her. The letter made that quite obvious. Her
desire to learn things, to sightsee and everything else confirmed
my observation during my visit that she was enjoying her time in
New York. Despite my depression over seeing her in the Center,

I was glad I went. It was an education on how to deal with the enormous problems that a serious debilitating disease can bring into your life. Just make the best of what you have, that's all you can do.

Arlana then told me she also would be visiting Helen Keller in two weeks. Maggie would have more company from home and even better company because Arlana planned on taking Maggie to Manhattan to shop. In the course of the next few weeks, Maggie called me asking for more money. She laughed and said that she was taking the opportunity to shop in the shopping Mecca of the world. I gladly sent the money but only later did I learn the money was not really for shopping. Arlana then received a second letter from Maggie, and looking back on it, alarm bells clearly were going off. We just could not hear them at the time.

5/30/93

Hi Bags,

It's me again! Have I mentioned food lately? I don't usually weigh myself, but its part of the routine here. I lost 10 pounds. It's not that I don't eat. Three meals a day plus snacks, but I am doing so much physical activity that it's falling off. If you are complaining about being a "fathead," book a room here. Let me put it this way—I really can't decide whether Auntie I's cooking is better or not. I think she is probably better.

I'm really writing to send you the enclosed schedule and give you my list. You pick up the train at Penn Station and go to the end of the line (Port Washington). A cab ride to Helen Keller is five minutes and will cost $6.00 *plus tip. If you come from Manhattan, it will cost you $80 plus! Take the train. They run every 20 minutes.*

Please bring me the following:

A beach towel. My sign language book — it's on the top shelf in my computer room about eye level. It's a soft back paper book in black. Have Rich give you my small transistor radio and two batteries. If you pass any food on the way, bring it, or else I may resort to cannibalism! See you later.

Mags

It did not concern me at the time that Maggie was losing weight. Whenever I am on the road, I don't eat as much. So when Arlana told that me Maggie was getting skinny I just laughed.

I had arranged through a friend at work to get Arlana booked at the Regal Royale in New York. She did take the train to Long Island and arrived at the Helen Keller Center on a Friday afternoon. Maggie gave her the same tour I received, and Arlana also left with the same impression. She wondered how Maggie could enjoy being there. Arlana was happy to be taking her back to Manhattan, and they had a wonderful weekend. They ate at Tavern on the Green, toured the UN building, Radio City Music Hall, took the ferry to the Statue of Liberty, and shopped until they were exhausted. They even booked a Broadway play to see Lynn Redgrave perform. Arlana said Maggie was joking, smiling, and laughing the entire time. As it turned out, she had been blocking something that she had kept secret, even from Arlana.

On the last day of her weekend with Arlana, Maggie simply could not eat her breakfast. She ordered a big omelet with toast, juice, and coffee. She said she was not hungry. Anyone who knew Maggie and her voracious appetite knew something was drastically wrong. At first Maggie was very quiet when Arlana asked her about the sudden loss of appetite. It was understandable. Maggie had waited until the last possible minute to tell Arlana some bad news. She first wanted to enjoy the weekend. How she could block such things out was hard to understand, but that was Maggie.

When they arrived back at the hotel room, she confessed that she had developed a lump in her right breast. Being a nurse, Arlana wanted to check it out for herself immediately. Maggie said it did not look good. When Arlana felt it, she was also alarmed but, of course, did not show it.

"You know, sometimes these things are cysts," Arlana pointed out.

Maggie said she had already been to a doctor, and he said it was suspicious. That is why she had called me for extra money. The doctor had scheduled an ultrasound test for the next week. All the signs pointed to breast cancer, especially the sudden loss of weight. Arlana tried to be as upbeat as possible, but the joyous trip ended with a thud. Arlana took Maggie back to the Helen Keller Center and tried her best to maintain a positive outlook, but it was pretty much impossible. As usual, Maggie left strict instructions not to tell me anything.

"Maybe this ultrasound will give us some good news, and he won't have to know anything about this," Maggie said.

In a kind of macabre irony, Arlana's trip on the train from Port Washington to Manhattan was a carbon copy of the one I had suffered two weeks before. She was in tears and worried sick. The only thing that sustained her was the outside chance that the lump somehow was not cancer. Arlana knew that sometimes people get lucky. Now she was hoping her best friend would get a similar break. She was also thinking about how much bad luck one person could have. Just a year and a half after the diagnosis of Usher Syndrome and potential blindness, Maggie now faced the prospect of having to battle breast cancer.

When Arlana came back home we got together for dinner. I wanted to hear about the trip to New York. She told me about everything, except the cancer. It was a great burden on her, but she was not one to back away from adversity. She was as courageous as Maggie, but the truth would eventually have to come out.

It was a warm Friday afternoon, and I was at home when Arlana called about 2 o'clock. I had taken the day off from work and was in great spirits looking forward to a weekend of golf. I could tell Arlana was fumbling for words right from the beginning of the call.

"Hi, it's me," she said. "Look, I am coming over in a few minutes. I have to tell you something. Maggie is coming home from New York early."

When I asked why, Arlana simply said that she was on her way to our condo and would explain when she got there. In the ensuing five minutes, my mind was racing. I envisioned some sort of accident where Maggie had broken a leg or worse. Or maybe there was some incident with one of the clients and Maggie was hurt. Even rape crossed my mind. It's a horrible spot to be in. The five-minute drive seemed like fifty minutes to me. I braced for what I knew was bad news.

When Arlana told me Maggie had a lump in her breast, and it appeared to be cancer, I just leaned over in my chair, covered my face with both hands and took a deep breath. A ripple of total fear raced through me from head to toe. After all the worry and concern over the deafness and blindness, I was stunned with the news that Maggie now faced breast cancer. Arlana did her best to say the lump was small and these things can be taken care of without any danger to life. None of that worked. When I heard the word cancer, the next word that came to my mind was death. It was that simple. My mind and body went numb, and the only emotion I had was terror. All rational thought dissipated in a matter of seconds. It took me a long time to recover and begin asking questions. Slowly, I got my feet under me as Arlana and I began to develop a game plan.

Just as with the eye disease, I knew my role: to get her through this with total support and care. That was the only thing I could do. Arlana then told me something that will stick with me forever.

"Maggie did not want to tell you because she was hoping it was a false alarm. Once she knew she had to tell you, all she has been talking about is being with you.

"'Rich will make me feel better were her exact words. She can't wait to see you."

Maggie had protected me for as long as she could. How many lonely nights she had in that dingy dorm room in New York, God alone knows. It had to take enormous strength to battle those emotions by herself. She could have told me from the outset, and at least gotten some moral support, but she did not think of herself first, she thought of me. She lied to protect me, as I had lied to protect her. I was not at all angry at her or Arlana for the secrecy. I knew Maggie's reasoning, and I admired it. There is no greater virtue in life than giving, and giving even when it hurts is an even greater virtue. To me, it defines true love, and the reason we are on this planet. Maggie did what she had to do.

There was little time to digest what had just hit me because Maggie was arriving the same evening at 7 p.m. at O'Hare

Airport. In a way, it was a blessing that I had very little time to think about our reunion. It reduced the time to think about how I would react when I saw her. I did not want to cry. The fact that she had not yet undergone the biopsy was a plus. Until it was official, there was room to be optimistic that perhaps she would still get a break.

Arlana sent George to a Subway Sandwich shop for a vegetarian delight sandwich, one of Maggie's favorites. We figured she would be hungry after the flight. We parked the car at one of the airport garages then walked to the terminal to await her arrival. As the time grew closer, I became a bit apprehensive about how it would all go, but then the inexplicable nature of love took over. When I saw her walking toward me, I almost forgot the bad news I had learned just a few hours before. She was thin, for sure. She was tired, and she was walking very slowly with the cane, but she was my Maggie, and she was back in my arms.

Suddenly, I did not have to act optimistic—I really was optimistic. Just holding her again gave me such happiness and peace that I felt we could beat anything. The fear was pushed aside, and it seemed her mere physical presence filled me with a new confidence. I believe she felt the same way. It is an unbelievably beautiful sensation, like being lost in a bad dream then waking up in your warm and peaceful bed. She was my total joy in life, and she was back. It was as if the cancer did not exist. There is a Spanish song that contains the words: "Porque yo se, mi amor, que sin tu amor no vale nada." It means that without Maggie's love there is no value to my life. Maggie would scoff at such sentimentality, but it was the truth for me. She was all I had.

Maggie devoured the sandwich as soon as we got in the car, and everyone was upbeat. The breast cancer was never discussed on the way home. We waited until Maggie and I got back to the condo, which must have seemed like a mansion to her after five weeks in that dorm room. She was extremely tired and did not stay up long. We both talked about getting the biopsy done as soon as possible and getting on with the fight. We were hopeful that if any cancer was there, it would be curable. Maggie was somewhat buoyed by the fact that she noticed the lump early. "I was taking a shower near the end of my first week in New York when I felt it," she told me. "I just hope all women feel their breasts for lumps every time they are washing up."

Being a nurse, Maggie knew the importance of always checking for lumps on her breasts. When she told me to touch it, I was even more optimistic. The lump seemed so small! Then again, what did I know about breast cancer?

It did not take long for Maggie to head for the bed. She said she was exhausted almost on a daily basis, but she did giggle and grin when I tucked her in. She had really missed our nightly ritual of hugs and kisses. She was asleep in two minutes after she hit the sheets. I shut the light off and left the room. Strangely, the initial shock and fear of the afternoon had been replaced by a feeling of contentment. Having her back meant everything. She never once mentioned the fact she initially failed to tell me about the breast cancer. We both knew why she hadn't. It's the kind of unspoken connection that only evolves in the course of a lifelong love.

12
From Hell and Back

Maggie slept for almost ten hours, and when she woke up she had her freshness back. Her complexion was more pale than usual, but her energy level, at least in the morning, was normal. So was her appetite. We went to a nearby pancake house where she devoured scrambled eggs, hash browns, toast, juice, and coffee. She left not a scrap on the plate. Next we went about the business of trying to schedule the biopsy and had an immediate setback. Since it was the July 4th holiday weekend, our family doctor was on vacation. We were told we had to wait for him to come back in two weeks to schedule the procedure. That simply would not do for me.

I hated to use my status as a TV personality to pull strings, but for Maggie, I did not have to bat an eyelash before doing it. I knew that my boss, Dan Roan, had a family doctor at a different hospital, and I quickly called Dan to tell him what happened. He graciously agreed to help and the same day, his doctor called me. We scheduled a biopsy for the next day. Maggie was greatly relieved. Neither of us wanted to wait two weeks. Why some doctors are willing to wait is another matter. I will spare you most of my anger about the insensitivity of some doctors, and the heartless bureaucracy that sometimes exists in patient care, but I will tell you that if it is a member of the doctor's family, there is no waiting. This was cancer, not a sprained ankle. I saw senseless medical delays time after time for the rest of Maggie's life. I will end my soapbox on medical care, but my final analysis is that we direly need a national medical health plan. The medical system in this country is in crisis, from outrageous cost to patient care and people are suffering for it. Maggie felt the same way, and she had served the industry for twenty years.

The biopsy took place the next day, and when Maggie came out, the doctor had some decent news. He said while the lump appeared to be cancer, Maggie had caught it in time. However, he cautioned, anything he did tell us at that point was very premature and that the biopsy would answer any questions. At least he had the kindness to tell us something. Doctors know just by sight of a biopsy how things shape up. When I cornered him privately, he told me even more.

"She will likely need a lumpectomy, not a mastectomy, and we will have to take a few lymph nodes out that may affect the strength of her right arm. Still, she will be able to use it almost normally."

As bad as that sounded, I felt like I had just hit the jackpot— a lumpectomy, that's all. But I failed to ask a whole bunch of questions I should have asked. Maggie knew the score much better. When I told her about the diagnosis, she simply said, "Let's just wait until the biopsy. Don't get carried away." I was an amateur among the pros.

The biopsy results would take a couple of days, but I was so optimistic I no longer carried any trace of doom. The only disconcerting thing was Maggie's complexion. It would change hour by hour. She would look okay in the morning, and then by noon she would be as white as a ghost. Later on in the day, a bit of her color would come back only to disappear again. I noticed the same thing in my father the year before he died. When I went to visit him he would look normal one week then horrible the next. Eventually, of course, he looked bad all the time when the cancer consumed his body. I learned from that point on how important it is to watch a person's complexion. I even paid close attention to my own.

Three days after the biopsy, we got a call to come to the doctor's office.

Even though we had some preliminary information, the morning before we got the biopsy results was filled with tension. Maggie did not eat breakfast, and my appetite was not that good either. Maggie knew that anything we had heard previously could be wiped out by this definitive test. Arlana arrived to drive us to the doctor's office. The wait to see the doctor was interminable. When we finally got in, he wasted no time. He said it was cancer, but he thought that it had been detected in time. The tumor was two centimeters, and it would be taken out with a lumpectomy. There was no danger Maggie would lose her breast. The cure rate was very good but would go up or down depending on whether the cancer had spread to the lymph nodes, several of which would have to be removed during the surgery. Then he gave us the bad news that I had failed to even think about earlier. The doctor said she would need nine treatments of radiation and chemotherapy. She would temporarily lose her hair, would suffer from nausea, perhaps get rashes, and would also get progressively more tired as the chemo treatments continued. She could try to maintain some of her normal activities, but the doctor advised it would not be easy.

I could tell Maggie was devastated. Amid the good news about the cure rate was the sentence of what amounted to a year of suffering. Being a nurse sometimes is a curse. She knew well the pain she would have to go through, but that was not the big reason for her gloom. She was supposed to start taking classes full-time at Loyola in the fall, and now that was all gone. It would be a wasted year just when she had regained her footing after the devastating diagnosis of impending blindness. She did not display any emotion in the doctor's office, but in the car on the way home, she exploded.

Arlana and I tried to stress the positive, but Maggie cut us off before we could get started.

"Both of you, shut up," she said. "I don't want to talk about it. Just shut up." We did and the ride home was made in complete silence. She just stared straight ahead with a cold painful look in her eyes. After Arlana dropped us off, Maggie just sat on the couch. I could think of nothing to say, so I just sat next to her and held her. She quickly broke into a sustained cry.

"I can't even start school, Richie," she mumbled amid the tears. I just held her tighter and cried a little bit myself. We stayed locked in tears for a long time. When she finally began to talk, she again cursed her bad luck. I just listened and held her.

She quickly regained some of her equilibrium. I stressed that at least they had found the cancer in time and that the recovery rate was good, but she also cautioned me.

"They won't know anything until they see the lymph nodes." She was way ahead of me. "Don't bet I won't lose my breast. When they go in there, they might change their minds and decide to remove it."

The lack of food and the emotion of the day had exhausted her. She went to the bedroom and took a long nap. I took the opportunity to head to the nearby Oak Brook shopping mall. I figured she needed some kind of lift, so I bought her a thermos for coffee, a suitcase for school papers, a bunch of notebooks, other school supplies, and a portable reading lamp. When she awoke I gave her the surprises.

"Before you know it, you will need these," I joked, and she seemed to respond. Amazingly, her depression over the cancer seemed to last only a few hours.

"I'll be damned if this gets me down after what I have been through," she asserted.

It's not that adversity had become easier, but when you go through one shock, you can handle a second one with more fight. The human spirit is amazingly resilient. Her appetite returned, and we went out for a wonderful dinner. To this day, I am still astounded at how rapidly she shook off her depression about the cancer. There is only one word to describe Maggie—tough. In one day she had all her fight back. If it were me, I would have been in the tank for months.

The surgery was scheduled for the following week, and one aspect of Maggie's behavior surprised me. She insisted on making love almost everyday. It was a bit hard for me, considering all the sobering news, but it was obvious Maggie felt she might lose her breast. If that was the case, she wanted to enjoy her final week with everything intact. I kept trying to tell her it would only be a lumpectomy, but she was not buying it. For me, making love under such circumstances required an enormous degree of concentration. It is easy to tell somebody else to be positive but not so easy to follow your own advice.

The night before the surgery, she gave me two instructions. They seemed a bit odd, but I just figured she was understandably shaken by the fear that such moments create.

"Tell the doctor that if he feels it's necessary to cut off the whole breast just do it. I'm ready for it. Secondly, I hate being in the hospital, so tell him I want to be released right after the surgery. Arlana can take care of me at home." Why she didn't tell the doctor these things herself, I will never know.

The next day when the doctor came in to see me after Maggie had been prepped for surgery, I gave him Maggie's suggestions. He actually laughed out loud when I told him.

"No, no," he assured me. "This is a lumpectomy. What are you talking about? As far as leaving tonight, if she wants to do it she can, but it would be a miracle. I guarantee you she won't want to leave the hospital."

The surgery was short and went well, but it was horrible to see Maggie as she was wheeled from intensive care into her room. She looked a step away from her last rites. She was in great pain until Arlana read her chart and found out they had given her the lowest dose of painkiller. Why? Who knows, but thank goodness Arlana got the nurse to give her a shot with more punch. Maggie fell into a peaceful sleep the rest of the night. She never had a chance to leave the hospital, as she had hoped. No wonder the doctor was laughing.

I arrived at the hospital at 8 a.m. the next morning. Maggie was wide awake and clamoring to go home. Shortly after I kissed and hugged her, she gave me my orders.

"Get me out of here."

It took half the day, but I did get her home that evening. She still had two drainage tubes connected to her breast and even though they were drained before she left the hospital, they were half filled again by the time we got home. Thank goodness Arlana was with us to change them.

Maggie recovered pretty well at home, but she was dreading the chemotherapy. We were all worried about the results from the lymph node tests. There would always be some new hurdle. Maggie had been through a lot already, but the battle against cancer was just beginning. A week later, we went to the doctor's office for the crucial word on the lymph nodes.

Lymph nodes carry the blood throughout the body. If they are infected with cancer, the chance of the disease spreading greatly increases. The way Maggie's luck was going I feared the worst and had already braced myself to ask a series of questions about her ability to survive. When we got called into the doctor's office, I walked Maggie in, and she took a seat by the doctor's desk. Arlana and I could sense the mood, and we liked it. Doctors have a way of looking much better when they are delivering good news. As Maggie sat down, the doctor walked behind her and happily uttered the good news.

"They are totally clean—all of them." Arlana and I could barely restrain ourselves from jumping up and down. Maggie just sat there. We were perplexed over her non-reaction.

The doctor then went into a long discourse about the surgery and the plan for chemo and radiation. His instructions lasted a good ten minutes when Maggie suddenly burst out with a question.

"That's all well and good," she said, "but what about the lymph nodes?" The doctor laughed and told her he had already given her the news.

"Totally clean!" Maggie said excitedly. "Great. I didn't hear you before." We all laughed, and Maggie's whole demeanor changed. The color returned to her face, and she sat higher in the chair. She now knew she had a great chance of beating her breast cancer. It was the first good news she had received in a long time. I really do believe she felt that it was a life and death moment for her. The doctor explained the chemo and radiation would start in a week. We left the office in great relief.

We walked to a nearby coffeehouse in Elmhurst for a bite to

eat. It was one of the happiest late breakfasts I have ever enjoyed. Maggie was ecstatic. She ordered a huge meal—eggs, pancakes, hash brown potatoes—the works, and she ate it all. Arlana and I then explained to her that we had heard the doctor give the "all clear" about the lymph nodes ten minutes before she asked her question.

"What?" she laughed. "And you let me hang in the wind?" She was not angry at all. At that moment, nothing could make her angry.

Dr. Patricia Madej, Maggie's oncologist at Hinsdale Hospital, who was outstanding throughout the entire ordeal, gave her a 90 percent chance of survival. She was thoroughly professional and down to earth.

But despite all the optimism, the harsh realities of chemotherapy soon emerged. Maggie began chemo treatments with a full head of steam, but there were severe side effects. The nausea was the worst, even though Maggie handled it pretty well. Still she had her mind set on scheduling a class at Loyola, but Arlana threw up a caution flag.

"Why don't you wait for the second treatment and see how it goes first?" she said. Arlana was right.

Maggie started losing her beautiful blonde hair after the second treatment. It was a tremendous psychological setback. She explained that it was like being stripped of her youth all at once. Arlana actually became physically sick herself when she saw Maggie's gorgeous hair falling out. Maggie purchased a wig but really hated wearing it. She preferred wearing handkerchiefs on her head when she went out. If researchers could somehow discover a chemo treatment that did not lead to hair loss, it would sure give cancer patients a huge psychological lift.

Maggie's second treatment further weakened her, and the

nausea was much worse. She broke out in a rash and was in bed for a week and a half. It was nearly impossible for her to eat. Arlana made her mashed potatoes, macaroni, and Jell-O. That's about all she could handle. As a result, she lost more weight. By the third treatment, she was totally wiped out. Everybody reacts differently to chemo. Maggie was having a tough time. Her white blood cell count was too low causing the fourth treatment to be postponed. That added emotional stress to her already weakened physical condition. I did my best to keep her upbeat.

I figured the best way to do that was to keep her smiling. I called her "my ghost." She had a white complexion even when healthy. Now she was even whiter. The teasing made her laugh. She would walk into a room announcing: "Your ghost is here!"

I also showered her with affection. I had my hands all over her when we were together. I made a lot of jokes about sex, and how when she was done with this mess, we would go on a vacation and lock ourselves in a room for a week. I took her for walks when she had the energy. Most of all, we talked in depth about her future. She loved to talk about getting a college degree and starting a new career. She never got tired of the subject. It always cheered her up. She had hope, and hope is everything.

I don't know how many nights it happened, but after I would tuck her in, my heart would break. The hardest thing to do in life is to watch someone you love suffer. I always thought it was crazy when people said, "I wish it were me instead." When I looked at Maggie in bed, so weak and frail, I understood those words. I loved her so much it was more painful for me to see her suffer than to suffer myself. Many nights I would do my best to act happy, but when I put her to bed then left the room to sit in my rocker in the family room, I would break down in quiet tears. She looked so bad I wondered if she would survive the cancer only to die from the chemotherapy. I also worried about the chemicals affecting her eyes. A myriad of negative visions constantly swept across my mind. I always slept fitfully.

The nine months of treatment seemed to drag on. Every time Maggie had the chemo, we worried about the blood count. It upset her when there were postponements and fortunately, there were no more. By the last treatment, Maggie was barely able to function. She was sick and exhausted but happy it was finally over. When we got back from the hospital, she told me how grateful she felt to not have to face another hellish chemo session.

On the week after Maggie received her last treatment, I got a call from my mother. She was in tears telling me that my brother, Don, had been diagnosed with lung cancer. It was hardly a surprise, but it was still a shock. He was a life long smoker and even though he tried every possible way to quit, he simply could not. My mother even offered him money if he stopped smoking, but all she got back was a cold stare. Don and I were very close when we were kids, but sadly we drifted apart in our adult years. I saw him a few times each year on holidays and other special occasions, but we were really two different people. He was a lot tougher and more blue-collar. I think he viewed me as a college hotshot. Despite our differences, we loved each other and just like Maggie, he fought his cancer with tremendous resolve. He always talked about what he would do with his life after he had beaten his cancer.

Tragically, in his case, it was the chemo and not the cancer that killed him. The doctors had to give him such a large dose that his immune system broke down. From that, he developed an uncontrollable infection. He went into a coma and that was the end. The horrific decline and his death took only a few months. He was only fifty-one years old. My sister-in-law, Peggy, called me late on a Friday afternoon to tell me the sad news. I had the horrible responsibility of driving to my mother's house to tell her. It was the longest drive of my life. On top of all the emotional strain of Maggie's eye disease and cancer—now this!

As you know, Maggie and I didn't have children, so I pass no judgment on parents. Mothers and fathers love all their children, but it's a simple fact that they have their favorites. I knew all my life that Don was my mother's favorite. When I was younger, it bothered me, but as I grew up, I learned to accept it. He was the first-born and after the father, the first-born is the leader of the family. I understood it and accepted my place. It was the old time tradition of Eastern European families. To be totally honest, however, the love Maggie had for me made up for everything else, and I held no grudges.

When I rang the doorbell at my mother's house, I anticipated what would happen. I actually feared her having a heart attack. After seeing the sad look on my face and hearing the words, "Don is dead," she simply collapsed in my arms, screaming, "No, no, no!" I carried her to the couch where I held her tight and just let her cry out loud in indescribable agony. We both cried for a long time. She just kept repeating the word "no" over and over again. It took a long time for her to recover and regain some semblance of composure. I stayed with her that night making phone calls to relatives and making sure she did not have any medical problems. For a seventy-two year old woman thankfully, she was in great physical shape, but my biggest fear was that Don's death would so devastate her that she would die in a short period of time. I can't imagine what it feels like to bury a child. It seems to me there can be nothing worse. Thank goodness, my mother was able to survive, and I have done my best to take care of her since Don's death. Not a day goes by when I do not talk to her, and I drive to her house every Sunday morning for pancakes.

Maggie, in the meantime, was regaining her physical strength from her year of chemo. Most importantly, from a psychological standpoint, her hair was growing back. Amazingly, it was thicker and darker than it was before. Maggie could not wait for her hair to grow long so she could go to the hairdresser and get back her own light blonde look.

As it turned out, Maggie's strength returned a lot quicker than her hair. It took a few months for the chemo drugs to work their way out of her system. Once she was able to eat, she rapidly regained much of her lost weight. She had already planned on going to school for the winter term, which required taking classes at the downtown campus. In the meantime, she stayed active with her volunteer work and returned to her weekly sessions with her support group for the blind in downtown Chicago.

In late September, about two months after her last chemo treatment, Maggie and I began a new ritual of taking nighttime walks. She had just bought her 150th new coffee maker and brewed a pot of decaf after dinner. On my days off or even if I arrived home early from work, we would reheat the coffee, pour some into a couple of mugs, and take it with us for a walk around 10 p.m., just before bedtime. We would enjoy the ritual the rest of our lives with increasing contentment.

13
Bearing Crutches

Interwoven with the concrete streets and sidewalks of our townhouse development was a wonderful forest area where Maggie and I walked arm-in-arm. We talked about everything, especially what Maggie had just been through, and I noticed a change in her. She did not lose her fiery zest for life, but I noticed that she had mellowed a great deal. I now saw a person who appreciated life even more than she had before her breast cancer and was less concerned with the mundane aggravations of living. A shoe out of place, a dirty sink, or even a delay in her school plans no longer pushed her temper button. She spoke more philosophically about life and tried to put all that had happened into perspective. Over a two-year period, Maggie was diagnosed with progressive blindness and knew she faced a good chance of going deaf. We both lost our jobs, and then came the breast cancer along with the death of my brother.

There was an old saying her grandmother used when something bad happened to someone. "God only gives crutches to those who can bear them," she would say. According to that logic, some coward who could not handle the adversities of life would get a free pass on pain and hold parties on his yacht screwing an endless procession of hot babes, while other unfortunates have to suffer just because they can "bear the crutches." Maggie enjoyed a good laugh when I pointed out the absurdity of her grandma's logic.

"If there were any two people who did not need adversity to appreciate life," she said, "it would be us."

From the night of our marriage in 1970, we vowed to live passionately and appreciate every moment, and the more I thought about it, there was an element of the crutch theory that made sense. Every evening that we strolled together and every day that passed after her breast surgery, we were falling more deeply in love. We learned that the scope of love is boundless. In our case, the setbacks served to deepen our connection. When you already love a person deeply, it's amazing to discover that you still have more to give and more to receive. Maggie believed strongly in a spiritual connection, an out of body love that lasts forever, and I could feel this in our nightly walks. There was a glow of wellbeing in the pit of my stomach. I was totally happy in the moment and nothing else seemed to matter. This is how it was for the rest of our lives and even though I did not share her spiritual beliefs, I allowed her spiritual joy and contentment to engulf me. I felt like I was the luckiest man alive.

During one evening walk, I asked how she handled the chemotherapy. Some days and nights were awful. The powerful drugs created such dreadful nightmares that, on several occasions, I would hear her screaming as she slept. After I would wake her, she would shake in fear and thank me profusely for ending her horrible dream. She told me the nightmares always involved a different scenario but the theme was always the same, she would always be aware she was about to die. We talked about her mother and how she simply gave up on chemotherapy and accepted death.

"I can understand how she felt," Maggie said. "One third of

your cells are probably dead anyway during chemo. The misery is so great that even the survival instinct is challenged."

Such talk chilled me to the core, but it was also enlightening to hear Maggie explain her feelings. She had stared death in the face and through countless nightmares had actually experienced it graphically. So while the coward who can't handle adversity enjoys his parties on his yacht, he may never experience the deep appreciation and joy for life that Maggie possessed. The people who receive "crutches" in life perhaps can reach greater highs. You can flip the argument either way but all I know is what I saw. Maggie radiated happiness.

When I took Maggie to downtown Chicago to her support group meetings, I used to park the car and walk around for an hour while Maggie enjoyed her two-hour sessions. I had worked downtown most of my career and loved the city. The diversity of people and the bright lights were more to my liking than the suburbs, which basically closed down after 6 p.m. Since so many of Maggie's deaf and blind activities were in Chicago, and since she would be attending classes for the next two or three years downtown, I thought it would be a good idea to move to the area. I knew it would be a huge undertaking, but in the long run it would be a lot better for her and for me. When I raised the idea to Maggie on the way back to Westchester, she almost jumped out of her seat.

"Oh, can we Richie? That's a great idea!"

Maggie loved to move more than any person I have ever known. I hated it, but Maggie thrived on packing boxes, calling gas and electric companies, calling the post office and sending out change of address cards—these were all exciting things to her. I used to say she had a moving sickness, but part of it was her desire to keep an active life. She wanted to take in as many new experiences as she could and enjoy as many new places as she could while she still had some vision.

When she raised the idea of moving with Arlana, Maggie took a step back. Arlana was greatly disappointed because it would mean a much greater separation. Arlana lived literally five minutes away from us. A forty-minute drive downtown was a huge difference, so Maggie put moving to the city on the back burner.

As it turned out, going to school in the city from the suburbs was more difficult than she could have imagined. When Arlana and I could not take her, Maggie was forced to ride a commuter train. That required her getting a taxi from our home in Westchester to the train station, getting off the train in the south Loop and getting another taxi to Loyola, which was located in the Streeterville area in the section of Chicago known as "The Magnificent Mile." It was a lot of work for a person still learning to perfect the use of a cane. Since she also could not hear very well, she would at times miss her stop in Western Springs and would call Arlana or me from a station two or three stops down the line. She always felt embarrassed and angry about it. Even when she got off the train okay, she still had to navigate her way to taxi stands and that was especially difficult in Westchester.

One night she came home from school crying. She had fallen off the train platform at Union Station in downtown Chicago, walking right off the edge. I can only imagine her fear. She did not know if she was falling seven feet or seventy feet. Fortunately, it was just a seven foot drop onto the track, but she could have been paralyzed or broken a bone. Somehow, she landed right on her tailbone, and thankfully, railroad personnel and bystanders raced to help. She was hurt physically, but it was far more damaging to her psyche. I held her tight all night, never let her out of my sight, and told her everything would be okay. I tried to console her by explaining it would take time to master using her cane and accidents were inevitable but would disappear for the most part later on. I iced down her sore tailbone, gave her a Tylenol, made a cup of tea for her, and then we talked in the bedroom. Gradually, she regained her edge and was able to crack a few jokes about the toughness of her butt.

Living with a blind person, I learned to appreciate how much courage it took to simply perform the normal tasks of everyday life. Things we take for granted, like walking down a busy street, were dangerous for Maggie. From the moment she left the door of our house, the potential for serious harm to her body or even death had to be in the back of her mind. Yet, she never let this fear, if it in fact existed, stop her.

This determination allowed her to adapt to using a cane, but the bottom line was she had to use it as frequently as possible to really master it. It was quickly becoming apparent that our only course of action was to move downtown where she could gain a greater degree of independence by using her cane not just part of the time but all the time. Soon, we began our search in earnest.

We looked at several high-rise buildings in the Gold Coast/Streeterville area and quickly settled for one at Michigan Avenue and Chestnut Street. We paid top dollar for a small three-bedroom condo with roughly a third of the space we had in Westchester. Painfully, we gave away half of the furniture Maggie had purchased for our home, with Maggie's family benefiting the most. What was left, we squeezed into our new condo on the 34th floor.

The location was perfect for Maggie because it was on the same street as Loyola where she would be attending classes for the next couple of years. I knew our new place was greatly overpriced, but it was worth it to make things easier.

The whole move exhausted me. It was a complete change of lifestyle, but I quickly learned to love it. Chicago is simply the best of the big cities. I have spent a lot of time in a lot of cities all across the country. Chicago, with its scenic lake front and Mayor Richard M. Daley's beautification program, is clearly the best. It has all the great cultural elements of a big city; yet, it is neat and tidy. I could not believe we were living in such a choice area of one of the greatest cities in the world, especially since we had grown up looking at raw garbage in the alleys of Pilsen.

Maggie, however, did not have a very good start downtown. Michigan Avenue is always filled with people and is sometimes so packed you have trouble finding a lane to walk. For sighted people, it is merely an annoyance, but for Maggie, it was a major problem. On her first day of school, she went out the front door of our building, walking east on Chestnut toward the lake then took a right onto busy Michigan Avenue for a block before she got to Pearson Street and the Loyola campus. She came back depressed the first day because she was banging into people left and right. Some people downtown were in such a hurry, they don't even stop for a blind person with a cane. The parting of the Red Sea theory did not work well on Michigan Avenue.

The next morning when she left for school, I followed her, without her knowledge. I just wanted to see what she was talking about. Yes, it was an ordeal. She turned the corner on Michigan Avenue and bumped into a few people. A toy store had a display on the sidewalk featuring some stuffed dogs and cats. Maggie managed to knock a few over with her cane then stepped on a few more with her feet. She had no idea what they were. When she got to the stoplight, she had trouble knowing when to cross. Some people jumped the gun and walked before the light turned red, and others disobeyed the lights that allowed cars to make left hand turns. It took Maggie forever to get to school.

I quickly realized there was a solution. The back door of our building opened onto a side street where there were far fewer people. Maggie did not like the idea at first.

"How can I get out the back door?" she grumbled.

The next day, I took her down the elevator and instead of going out onto Chestnut, she went the other way—down the sidewalk at the entrance to our parking garage then onto Pearson Street where she easily made it to a stop sign and across the street through the school door. She was ecstatic, while I felt like Einstein.

Slowly but surely, Maggie gained more confidence with the cane. The bolder she got, the more I worried, recalling the dangerous fall at the train station. So when she would tell me she was going for a walk to practice with the cane, I would follow her. She never knew I was there. Many days, I would be right behind her, then race ahead at the end and meet her back in the apartment. Maggie's self-training was an amazing thing to watch. She began to walk faster and faster with the cane. She learned the patterns of the people walking in the downtown area and learned their behavior at traffic lights. She also memorized the streets and counted the blocks to and from our condo to her destinations. Within a few months, she had made major progress with the cane, with that came the exhilarating feeling of independence. She was free to move around and would be for the rest of her life. Using her newfound freedom, she tackled college life with zeal.

It was enormous fun watching Maggie go to school. I had a blast helping her with papers and going to the library with her, feeling like I was back in college myself. We were living a lifestyle we never dreamed of in our youth in Pilsen. We dined at the great restaurants of Chicago at every opportunity. They were literally just a few blocks away. Our evening walks were now a magical delight amid the sparkling lights of the big city, with Starbucks decaf in our hands instead of "laboring" over a pot of our own. If ever there was a good life; that was it. We also resumed our vacations. They would never be the same, of course, but in a way they were even better.

There were times when I could sense Maggie getting down a bit, but the episodes were minimal. She had a way of filtering out the negatives and just admitting the positives into life. Almost every day was fantastic. We took golf trips to the state of Michigan with Andi, Jim, and their young son, Jamie. Though Maggie could not golf, she brought her Braille books and audio books and had a great time just riding in the golf cart with me and inhaling the crisp clean evergreen air of Michigan. When we stopped to eat at the 9th hole, it was a real treat. It's a small thing but a hot dog, hamburger, or in Maggie's case a cheese sandwich on the golf course have their place among the pleasures of life. I also learned something about myself on these trips.

I am, without doubt, one of the worst golfers in the world. Even though I love the game, I always wound up throwing a club or swearing at myself over what amounted to a series of inept shots. Amazingly, I had no temper problems at all when Maggie was in the golf cart with me. Not once. If I did hit a bad shot, I would go back to the cart and grab her thigh with my hand and say, "I'm so glad you're here, I don't even care if I am horse shit."

She would laugh and hug me. Maggie was a reminder of the real importance of life. I fully realized how ludicrous it is to blow up over a silly game where you hit a white ball around and chase it all day long. What is funny is that when I played golf without Maggie, I would resort to an occasional temper outburst again.

There was no question she was magical for me.

At the end of her first full year at Loyola, Maggie was on the Dean's List, getting straight A's. I told her we would celebrate with a trip to Puerto Rico for New Year's Eve. She had been through a lot and in the process your sex life gets pushed aside. The trip to Puerto Rico restored it. We were back in old form. Getting away from home amid the palm trees and sandy beaches is always a turn-on. We took a couple of salsa classes at the resort. I have to admit, it was not easy for the teacher or for me to teach the moves to a blind person, but we managed. Maggie was able to pick up most of the steps, barely avoiding collision after collision thanks to my last second guidance. She did even better on the dance floor at the hotel. With the big New Year's Eve dance party scheduled for the weekend, I took Maggie to downtown San Juan for a shopping spree. Having seen all the provocative low cut dresses worn by the lovely ladies at the hotel, I told Maggie I would pick out a good one for her. It was the lowest cut gown she had ever worn in her life, and in the back, the material hugged her butt. She was a knockout even if she was apprehensive. "Can I wear this thing in public?" she laughed.

She wore it on New Year's Eve, and she was stunning. We danced the night away, then at midnight all the hotel guests walked out into the pool area carrying a glass of champagne to watch the New Year's fireworks and share a kiss. It does not get more romantic. As it turned out, Maggie's dress was one of the more conservative gowns of the evening. Some of the women had dresses that plunged almost to the navel in front and to the tailbone in the back. It was an extremely sensuous trip.

At that point in our lives, however, sex took a backseat in our relationship. The longer we were together the more the true meaning of love took over. Young people, and especially young men, have a hard time understanding this, but you actually get more of a high from the love than from the lovemaking. Maggie wrote a poignant college paper on the subject, and this is a good time to share it:

> *"The reflection of sexuality brings immediately to my mind images of my mother. Although there were no explicit lessons, the interactions that went on daily between my mother, family, and friends provided positive demonstrations of the various relationships between men and women and boys and girls. The myriad of relationships were a formative base for my own sexuality. There was a pervasive attitude of caring and sharing with people of all ages and gender, which was evidenced by my mother's constant touching and hugging.*
>
> *I remember one particular afternoon I came home from school and sitting at the kitchen table was a struggling college student enrolled at the University of Illinois. This total stranger was devouring a sandwich that my mother had prepared, and my mother was busy ironing a suit as they chatted. Later, we were to learn that my mother had met him at the local laundromat as he was searching for a place to have his suit pressed. I can also remember my father lecturing my mother on the dangers of letting strange people into the house. Undaunted, my mother was able to expose her vulnerability, and as a result, she gained the trust and respect of a young man. I suspect the young man, like me, has neither forgotten the encounter nor the memory of my mother.*
>
> *Such experiences occurred often and are the central force that helped me develop positive feeling about my*

own sexual identity. This positive experience gave me the understanding of a sexuality that transcends the physical realm. I was extremely lucky to find a mate who shares this understanding of sexuality. A poignant example occurred after a diagnosis of breast cancer in 1993. My husband and I were faced with the disfigurement of surgery, baldness after chemotherapy, and the emotional trauma that such an ordeal entails. The many years of positive reinforcement equipped me with a strong confidence in the person that I am and helped to lessen the burden of the physical ravages. I was not happy about these changes that occurred; however, I understood that these changes did not alter my essence. In addition, my husband, sharing this definition and understanding of sexuality, never faltered in the intimacy that is vital in a successful sexual relationship. Despite my unhappiness with being bald (my self image was temporarily bruised) my husband never ceased to make me feel loved and beautiful.

Young people can be hypnotized into believing that romance is supposed to be an ever-present occurrence and this delusion can only lead to hurt and disappointment. If I had been deluded into believing that romantic love is the most essential part of a loving relationship, I would not have fared as well in my battle against breast cancer. Similarly, my husband understood the love that was part of a lifetime commitment and not a romantic love that faded with the bridal bouquet."

All this did not mean we gave up on lovemaking. We still had a bang up time in Puerto Rico, no pun intended. I didn't know it at the time, but that was our last really intense carnal fling. It was one final week where we reached back into our youth for a sustained period of ecstasy. I do not write this with sadness because we had both evolved into a state where our love alone gave us enormous ecstasy—a different kind, and in all truth an even better kind. Our love was approaching the kind of deep spiritual connection that Maggie had read about in one of her favorite books, *The Celestine Prophecy*. To her, there was an afterlife, and if you reached an intense state of love in the physical life, it would carry over after you died. That was the theme of the *Celestine Prophecy*.

"So," I asked her during one of our typical dinner debates, "are we all going to be together after we die?"

"Sure," she said, "but not in our bodies."

"You will know it's me; I will know it's you, and we will be happy?" I pressed on.

"Sure," she replied.

"It makes no sense to me," I shot back. "When your brain dies how can you be anything? Don't you just fall into a dreamless sleep?"

"No, you are a spirit."

The debate got really intense.

"So, you will see your mother and father?" I asked.

"Yes," she said. "Of course"

"Well," I replied, "how about people like Caesar, Napoleon, and Hitler. Will I see them? What about the guy who was cheating on his wife and screwing his secretary in the physical life? When all three of them die, are they going to see each other? Will his wife's spirit kick his spiritual ass when she sees him?"

"You are fried!" she laughed. "You can't think totally in human terms about this."

"That's all I am," I replied. "I only know what I see. If there is a Supreme Force, isn't it cruel to give us this brainpower and the knowledge we are going to die while not telling us the reason why we are here?"

"There will never be any proof of a God, but there will be signs," she said.

"Well, I'll make a deal with you, whichever of us dies first has to give a sign to the one left behind." I said.

"Okay," she laughed, "you have a deal."

I have to admit that while it may be coincidence, or wishful thinking, I do believe I received a sign from my father after he died. He had a box of medals, dog tags, spent bullets, and other memorabilia from his combat in World War II. He even took a Nazi medal with an engraved Swastika off a dead German Soldier. In the months after he passed away, my mother and I could not locate the medals anywhere, despite looking all over the house. My father died in August. Strangely, when I came to see my mother on Christmas Eve, I had the inspiration to look for the medals again. Surprisingly, I found them in the first place I looked—down in my dad's tool shed in the basement. I found them within two minutes at almost the exact time we would have exchanged Christmas gifts if he had been alive. Was it a coincidence? Perhaps, but it sure seemed like a whole lot more.

Maggie and I enjoyed our many debates. Going to school gave her a greater interest in politics and world affairs. We had great discussions about the Middle East, about the environment, and about issues such as the homeless. One day coming back from dinner three different panhandlers approached us asking for money. The last guy put me over the top. He was a young man who looked totally fit and capable of working.

"Look, you're the third guy who's hit us up," I barked. "Get a job. It pays more than panhandling."

After we passed the guy, Maggie exploded and ripped into me.

"You don't tell people that," she said. "A lot of these people are legitimately in need." She had done a college paper on the homeless. While many were suffering from drug and alcohol problems, and many more had mental disorders, Maggie learned that about 30 percent or so are people who really could not make ends meet and wound up on the street or in shelters.

"So, keep your mouth shut," she growled. I have never again said anything negative to a panhandler, and quite often, I do offer them a dollar. Maggie served as my Guardian angel.

Maggie's school years were wonderful. She was totally happy with her new life and already helping people by doing volunteer work for The Lighthouse for the Blind on the West Side of Chicago. In the meantime, we were having a blast. She was full of fun again and the goofiness came back into our lives. We were having lunch on our vacation in Puerto Rico in a noisy restaurant. The background noise was so loud Maggie could not hear me all that well, even with her special FM system, which connected directly to her hearing aids.

"What kind of lemonade do they have?" she asked.

"Raspberry or regular," I replied.

"What?" she asked.

"Raspberry or regular," I repeated.

"Get the crap out of your mouth. I still can't hear."

"Raspberry or regular," I replied, in a voice that could now be heard over the entire restaurant. Everybody stopped to look at me, and the Spanish-speaking waitress came over, hesitated just a bit then asked, "She no speak the English?"

On a plane flight, the same kind of thing happened.

"What's on the food menu?" she asked. This was back when they had decent food on planes, not just snack boxes.

"Chicken or pasta," I replied.

"What?" she said.

"Chicken or pasta," I repeated.

Then I almost shouted it out on the third try.

"CHICKEN OR PASTA," I bellowed. By this time everybody on the plane was looking at me. They must have thought we were having a big fight.

Another time, she didn't like the menu at all on the flight. They had two meat dishes, which was of course the kiss of death for a vegetarian.

"Shit," she said, "I can't eat meat." Then she had an idea.

"You know, they have to have some cheese on the plane for the meals, right? How about asking for some cheese?"

"Sure. I'll tell you what," I said, "I'll just ask the pilot to grill you a cheese sandwich with one hand while he flies the plane with the other."

She socked me in the arm for that one.

In Florida, Maggie argued that you could actually taste the difference between the type of limes from the Florida Keys and limes from other parts of the country. Her theory being that the Key Lime pie made in the Florida Keys was the best in the world. We argued for a half hour, but it ended with her saying, "Yeah, I really can taste the difference in the limes in Key Lime pie." I just shook my head. Perhaps the loss of two of her senses made her sense of taste more acute.

She also insisted she could taste the difference in coffees. When she would ask Arlana or me to order a decaf soy latte from Starbucks, she would always say, "Make sure they use Americano brand coffee." Arlana and I would both tell her what the waitress told us, "They didn't have anything called Americano decaf."

"Then its crap," Maggie would say.

"You mean to tell me that with the soy and the sugar in the mixture, you can actually taste the difference if it's Americano?"

"Sure," she insisted. Arlana and I got to the point of telling her it *was* Americano, when it really was just regular old Starbucks' decaf. Maggie drank it, but she was always suspicious we were not telling the truth.

"I know you're bullshitting me," she would say.

She also got involved in exotic vegetarian foods she read about in obscure books. Countless times she would make me ask about foods that dumbfounded store employees. At times the store manager was even called in, and he would scratch his head.

"This is a horse shit store," Maggie would whisper, after we left without finding her goods. One time, I put my foot down and refused to embarrass myself.

"Ask the guy where the Ghee is," Maggie asked.

"What?" I laughed.

"Ghee," she said, and spelled it out. "G-H-E-E. It's a vegetarian butter substitute."

"Sounds like some illegal weed that you smoke," I replied.

"I am not asking about Ghee. What's wrong with Fleischmann's anyway?"

One Christmas, I was surprised by a pop-up Santa as I walked in the door. Controlled-remotely, the plastic Santa Claus popped up after you passed through a sensor. A greeting could also be pre-recorded on an audiotape. So, when I passed the thing, it popped up then Maggie's voice rang out: "Merry Christmas, Richie, Ho! Ho! Ho!" It scared the devil out of me.

She bought endless devices like that and her spending habits, already robust, skyrocketed.

One night I came home late from a long day at work and was starving.

Maggie had already gone to bed. To my delight I spotted a delicious looking cinnamon roll in the kitchen. It had the brown sugar topping just oozing off onto the plate it was on. It looked wonderful in the dim light under the kitchen cabinet. I made myself a cup of tea and could not wait to dig into my treat. Just after I put the water in the microwave, I was shocked when I got a closer look at the cinnamon roll. It was not a delicious pastry after all. It was actually a wax candle! The darn thing looked realistic. There is nothing worse than anticipating a culinary delight than finding out it's wax. I was crushed and had to settle for a dry piece of toast with jelly on it. I have kept that cinnamon candle to this day, and almost every time I look at it, I laugh.

One would need two volumes to describe Maggie King spending stories. She was the greatest consumer this nation has ever seen. I once told her that Alan Greenspan should mention her when he testified before Congress.

"Oh, yes," he could say. "We expect a good season again from Maggie King, which should fuel an upturn in the economy." She bought just about everything you could imagine. Her favorite TV program was *The Shopping Channel*. She received more advertising magazines than any person alive. Occasionally, she and Arlana went on binges in stores and malls whenever they had a chance.

Maggie bought all kinds of exercise devices: the butt buster, ab-cruncher, thigh master, etc. You name it; she got it. She bought a Pilates machine, she belonged to exercise clubs, and she bought all sorts of exercise tapes from Kathy Smith to some guy named Gilad. Her room and the closet in her room were full of them. As for cookbooks, she had a library that rivaled Julia Child's. She bought racks of clothes and dressed like a model in a fashion magazine. Sometimes women in the building would stop us in the elevator to compliment her clothes. Her shoe rack rivaled that of

Imelda Marcos, and she loved every minute of it, admitting she was doing it all while she could still see.

"You are spoiling me rotten, Richie, and I love it!" she told me countless times. I simply could not say "no" to her. Occasionally I would get upset, but she knew that would blow off in a few hours.

One day after I got her usual astronomical credit card bill from American Express, I showed it to her with a pained face and told her it had to stop.

"Why does this have to be so much every stinking month?" I moaned.

"You're absolutely right," she said. "I am a sick woman. Take this card and hide it from me. I don't want to see it."

Never one to look a gift horse in the mouth, I grabbed the card and buried it in the deepest part of a big drawer in my desk. A month later, I was startled when I opened the Amex bill and found the same hefty $2,000 charges.

"What happened?" I asked Maggie.

"How could you buy all this stuff?"

She put on her best sheepish smile and sad face and told me she had memorized the number and the expiration date on the card! I laughed and threw my hands up in the air then gave her back the card. What was the use?

Not a day seemed to go by without at least one delivery of a package to our door. Maggie's eyes would light up as I handed her the latest goods. Sometimes she went to the door and got the package herself. The guy who brought them to our door was named Jeff. He was very thin and wiry, and Maggie never saw him all that well in the hallway. One day, in the bright sunshine in front of the building, I saw Jeff passing by and said "Hi." Maggie finally got a good look at him and said: "Is that Jeff? I didn't realize he was so thin."

"Well," I replied, "he was 200 pounds before you moved into the building. Maggie laughed but once again nailed me in the arm.

Amid what was one of the happiest periods of our lives, there were also some scares. One morning she woke up with red blotches all over her body. Her right arm, the one where the lymph nodes were removed, swelled up almost double its normal size. She looked awful, and my thoughts immediately jumped to the worst possible conclusion. Maggie was scared witless herself. She had no idea what it was nor did Arlana. We went to the emergency room at Northwestern Hospital where she was taken in for an extensive series of tests. We were there half the day waiting and getting carted in and out of rooms for exams. When I was alone waiting for her, I was extremely depressed. I thought she would be admitted, then we would be told the worst. Happily, it turned out she just had the flu. Her arm swelled up because the lymph nodes had been taken out. Their removal affected her whole body. It was quite a relief to get some good news.

Since her diagnosis with Usher Syndrome, and since the breast cancer, I worried about Maggie on a daily basis. Despite all the good times, I could not quite put the worry behind me. The slightest ache and the slightest pain were causes for concern. I always thought the cancer was coming back. When she passed the five-year mark after her breast cancer, we went to dinner to celebrate. The success rate increases after five years. It was all well and good, but Arlana and I kept a close watch on Maggie, especially her complexion. Our fear never went away.

We also kept an eye on her deteriorating vision. It was a slow process, but she *was* going blind. Each month became more difficult. Even at home she would walk straight toward a wall. Often times, I had to yell at her to change direction. Sometimes, it was too late. She would crash into the wall and cut her head or bruise her arm or twist an ankle. Maggie always laughed it off and would claim, "I'm made of steel!"

I could never quite relax even while watching TV because if she knocked something over in her room, I got up to make sure she was okay. Many times, she would swear in frustration when she dropped something on the floor and could not find it, and I had to get up and find it for her. It was almost constant vigilance, but as strange as it sounds, I learned to enjoy it. To be able to help someone gives you a great sense of worth in yourself. It's gratifying to be needed and needed so much. To see her happy face after I solved one of her problems was a reward in itself. But at times, it was also exhausting. Being a caretaker is rough especially when you are tired to the bone and don't feel like getting off your soft sofa. When you do, it makes you feel great inside.

Maggie was amazing in the things she could do without vision. There were many obstacles, for sure, but she overcame all of them. The VTech was her best friend, but it was a slow process. You had to place a book under the machine then slowly move it across the projector so it showed up in big print on the TV screen. Yet night after night, Maggie worked tiredlessly in her room, reading, and writing with the VTech. What takes sighted people fifteen minutes to read took Maggie thirty. She was grateful for the sight she had. In class, she had note takers next to her at lectures and teachers wore a microphone around their necks so that Maggie could hear them on her special FM receiver connected to her hearing aids. It was cutting edge technology at the time and the damn thing always broke down. Since it was crucial to her, we had it repaired as quickly as possible. It was the same thing with the VTech. If there was a problem, it was like taking Maggie's life away. She was always in a panic to have it fixed as soon as possible.

She also became a master of the computer. There is a system called MAGIC, which enhances the print for sight-impaired people. It made the writing of essays and term papers so much easier for her. She and Ted would be on the phone for hours talking computer language that was totally foreign to me. I somehow longed for the old days of the typewriter. Maggie constantly made fun of me. "Old fart" was the comment she used most often.

The problem with computers is they are obsolete two years after they are made. Maggie would keep track of the latest technology and insist on a new computer every couple of years. The last one we had was really powerful. Maggie insisted on getting a two-way video-cam with the computer so she could see Ted on his screen in Florida. I told her it was a waste of money, but that argument never impressed Maggie. She got the two-way video cam anyway then spent three days on the phone with Ted getting it to work. Finally, they connected the contraption and Maggie put a goofy stocking cap on and had a ball kidding around with Ted on the other end. They used the thing once, and that was it. It never worked again.

Maggie's teachers always wrote glowing things about her school papers.

"Well written and very interesting," or "Wonderful essay," or "You have so much to offer as a social worker," and also "Outstanding and insightful." When she started school, she would ask me to read the papers and check them. I did offer her a few suggestions, but after the first few months I told her to forget even showing me. They were always so well thought-out and well edited that anything I could add would be nitpicking.

Maggie did have a lot to offer as a social worker. Coming from a poor neighborhood, being a nurse then overcoming severe depression after her diagnosis of Usher Syndrome, gave her an incredibly unique perspective. She outlined her goals in one of her essays starting with her fateful internship at the Helen Keller Center. I am printing a large part of what she wrote because it provides her own take on how best to help disabled people. Maggie was very high on the way they did things at Helen Keller.

"The objectives of the Helen Keller National Center are directed to meet the needs of the deaf blind community. These goals are clearly stated in their literature, available upon request. For each unique individual, the agency strives to provide the following:

a) Meaningful contact with the environment and effective means of communication,

b) Constructive participation in the home and the community,

c) Initial or enhanced employability, and

d) Any other development important to the optimum rehabilitation of the individual who is deaf blind. Thus, the agency employs a multidisciplinary team of professionals.

At HKNC I worked with highly skilled professionals and this helped me to confirm my decision to become a social worker. I experienced firsthand the care and concern of these dedicated people. It was also an excellent opportunity to do networking and learn about the many resources available in the deaf blind community. Thus I enrolled in the School of Social Work at Loyola University and decided to combine my experiential knowledge as a deaf blind individual and as a health care professional with a career in social work.

In addition to my professional experience, I have gained many insights as a survivor of breast cancer. Both of these roles, the nurse and the patient, have increased my understanding of a holistic approach to wellness and have sharpened my empathic skills.

My volunteer work at the Chicago Lighthouse for the Blind also has affirmed my decision to enter the social work profession. The staff at this agency exemplified the paradigms of what social services should be: that is, they are very positive role models in their performance and delivery of services to vulnerable and marginalized populations. As a result, the clientele that are served by the organization are the beneficiaries of an improved quality of life."

This paper pretty much sums up what Maggie was all about. She was intense in achieving her goals. I sometimes made fun of some of her papers. I always accused her of using too many "Ivy League" words: "multidisciplinary" could simply be "versatile." It's a much softer word and more understandable. This was a college paper, after all, and Maggie would shove it back into my face all the time. Then when she got her usual "A," she would laugh and say: "With your puny words, I would have gotten a "B" or a "C." She was probably right.

Watching her go through college made me long to return myself. It was such a rewarding experience and at age 48, I think I appreciated it more. She did need assistance. We had to hire a tutor for one of her math classes because she was petrified trying to see and understand equations, but she got through it fine. Sometimes, she would have to take a bus to the Lake Shore campus of Loyola, which was located just off Sheridan Road and, literally, right on the shoreline of Lake Michigan.

"If I take a wrong turn when I get off the bus, my hat may start floating before I realize I am submerged," she laughed. She was only half-joking. It was very dangerous for her in strange areas, and I worried about her each time she went to the north campus.

Arlana and George also gave Maggie lots of help in getting to places she needed to go for class interviews. She had a good support team, but it was Maggie herself who did the job. None of us could help her write the papers, take the tests, and get the great grades. She did it on her own as a member of the deaf blind community. She got better grades than a lot of sighted people. The formula was simple: dedication and hard work. Maggie had plenty of both.

She did have time for a lot of other interests. She was becoming an amateur nutrition expert. She would devour one book after the other. One of the biggest influences she had for a while came from a book called *Diet for a Poisoned Planet*. Maggie believed that the hormones they inject in cattle to make them bigger caused her breast cancer. She did not eat a single ounce of meat the rest of her life. I once drew her wrath for not catching bacon bits amid a vegetarian dish she had ordered at a restaurant. I pretty much agreed with her on the hormone issue, but I pointed out that one or two steaks a month were not going to hurt you. She would have none of it; meat was out of the question for her.

One day, she announced she had a brilliant cure for my high cholesterol. She had read in a book by Suzanne Somers that recommended an Atkins diet of high protein. It seemed to fly in the face of conventional wisdom. I could eat eggs? She suggested I try it for two months so I could get off the Zocor that had been prescribed for my condition. Maggie did not like pills—a strange irony for a nurse. So I went on this "diet," which allowed me skim milk with whole grain cereal, no sugar, wheat toast with no butter, fish or meat with vegetables only, no potatoes, and no rice. Gone were the vodka tonics, and for snacks, I ate whole grain pretzels or carrot sticks. It was such a pain in the butt that when we went to a restaurant I was often tempted to go off the wagon. Maggie would get that angry look and stare me down. "Stay with this and you'll see," she would say.

Well, I did see. After a few months, my cholesterol was down fifty points. My weight was also dramatically down. I went from 180 to 162 pounds causing my face to get hallow. At that weight, I looked bad on TV and people wondered if *I* had cancer. That was the end of the experiment. Off the diet, it was like heaven sinking my fork into a stack of pancakes again. However, I must admit, I did not feel bad physically. But the old Billy Crystal/Fernando Lamas line from Saturday Night Live clearly applied in this case. When you are on TV, it's not how you feel, its how you look—I looked bad. So the diet had to end.

As for Maggie, she looked fine as a vegetarian. Her face was full and her complexion was good. Even though I worried about a recurrence of the cancer, I hoped she had made it through the worst and would fully enjoy spending my money after I bit the dust and passed on.

Almost every day seemed to be full of fun and interesting insight with Maggie. It was interesting to watch people downtown react to us as we walked along. When she did not take her cane, all was normal. But when she used her cane, I could see just about everyone staring at her. When I thought about it, I realized that all her life, in varying degrees, people stared at her—in school with the hearing aids and now with a cane, as a blind woman. Being a minority, she related so much to African-Americans and

Latinos, as well as the homeless. In bygone days, families locked up the blind in their houses and would keep them off the streets, as if there was shame attached to the condition. So I guess that even now many people do not like seeing blind or handicapped people. One thing, I really grew to understand from living with Maggie is to treat people all the same. To this day, if I see someone in a wheelchair, I always look at him or her, say hello, and offer small talk. In return, I always receive a gracious response.

Near the end of her days as a student, Maggie wrote *Ode To Diversity* for one of her classes. The teacher was so impressed that she scribbled a note on the bottom asking Maggie to share the paper with her classmates. It is utopian for sure, but it asks us to find our better angels in ourselves. God knows the mass media does its best to bring out the worst. If people lived by Maggie's ode we would all be much better off. Maggie spelled out the word "heterogeneity" to come up with a code of conduct for each letter. I have included it in its entirety along with her teacher's response.

My Maggie

ODE TO CULTURAL DIVERSITY
by
Maggie King

Homogeneity is boring. Life is interesting, exciting when we share our differences. The more we learn about each other, the better our life will be.

Equality for all human beings: women, men and children. Equal access to all resources. Move marginalized people to the center.

Traditions of all cultures should be acknowledged with respect. We can learn from the values and belief systems of other cultures.

Ethnic cleansing cannot be tolerated. We must work globally to achieve equality and justice for all.

Race should not matter. It is only a microscopic part of who we really are.

Take time to understand the essence of each person you meet.

Order of priority: human decency before abusive power, injustice, material goods and money.

Ground rules: truth, justice, equality. Eliminate distortions of reality.

Egalitarian policies and practices must be employed in our institutions.

We must advocate for positive, nonviolent change.

Nurture the soul with faith, love and hope. Give of yourself. Help people who are less fortunate than you and you will rich in spirit.

Empowerment is the precursor to individual and collective achievement of goals. Advocate with people to attain their natural rights.

Information is the key to understanding and growth. Eradicate the myths that breed discrimination. Share your knowledge.

Tomorrow is too late. The time is <u>now</u>.

Your experience is unique and valuable. Together let us affirm and <u>celebrate</u> our diversity!

Maggie, This is wonderful. Would you like to share it by the class?

Maggie's experiences taught her to value diversity, and the seeds for her beliefs were sewn by her mother. Ann would have been beaming as Maggie graduated from Loyola in June of 1999. It was a lesson in diversity for me, as well, because I found myself as a minority on her graduation day. I was the only guy wearing a suit in a sea of caps and gowns. They had given me special permission to escort Maggie to the stage to receive her diploma. I wondered whether some people thought I could not wear a cap and gown because I had flunked.

The weather broke perfectly for her special day—sunshine and clear skies. I took her out for breakfast then to Mario Tricoci's for her usual big event makeover. She had her hair done, as a make-up specialist gave her the look of a Hollywood starlet. I often joked that I was afraid to touch her when she got back from the hair salon. I had never seen her so happy, and I was able to preserve it forever because I took extensive videotape of the day. The best shots occurred in the morning when I caught her walking out of the bedroom. She had a playful look of happiness as she swung her arms up and down in a goofy walk. When she finally discovered I had the camera, she laughed then walked over and made a funny face right in the lens. She then backed off and gave me that wonderful innocent smile that radiated beauty and goodness. I asked her about her cards of congratulations she had placed on the dining room table. She had about three dozen cards, and she proudly pointed some of them out.

The graduation ceremony itself took place at the Gentile Center on the north campus of Loyola. It felt great just to share her joy and George and Arlana also took plenty of pictures and videotape. Maggie insisted that her graduation celebration be limited. She did not want to invite her family. It was George, Arlana, my mother, and one more person, Maggie's good friend

Karen McCulloh, with whom she shared time in a support group then worked with on many volunteer projects. Karen had macular degeneration, and she became a big influence during Maggie's life.

After the ceremony, we all went out for an early dinner. When we finally were alone at home, Maggie and I talked about the future. I was fifty-two years old and Maggie was fifty. My idea was to make a lot of money in the next five years and retire from the business I was in. Maggie was going in the opposite direction. She was just starting a new career and was about to be hired by the Lighthouse for the Blind as their Chief Volunteer Officer. She was beaming about being back at work and had rejected a suggestion by one of her teachers that she immediately seek a Master's Degree. That would have meant two or three more years at school, and Maggie felt she didn't have the time to do it.

"I want to help people right away. A college degree is enough to do what I have to do."

As for my suggestion about my retirement, Maggie said I was nuts. She could not understand why I wanted to end my career early. Having fought her way back to a new life, she once again felt productive. She had worked so hard to get to a spot that I was willing to give up. She valued her new career. She valued her life. She valued each and every moment, and while some people may be faking it a bit, I can assure you that was not the case with Maggie. This was the real thing. A trip for cappuccino with her blind friends was a blissful occasion. A dinner at a fine restaurant was savored and talked about for days. Vacations, parties, shopping sprees—were all the source of genuine elation. It was as if she was celebrating the countdown to a new year on a daily basis. To borrow a phrase from an old Home Front World War II radio documentary, "the only thing that mattered for the moment *was* the moment." Over time, I came to understand the reason for her happiness even though I did not adopt it myself on a regular basis.

When she faced the loss of her life with cancer and was diagnosed with Usher Syndrome, it gave her a totally different view of life. Talk of the future and excessive worry over money was a waste of time. Planning for retirement seemed ludicrous. She was a fifty year-old woman living like a teenager. That explained her practical jokes, her goofiness, and her happiness over a biscotti and a cup of decaf. It's the kind of philosophy found in self-help books or seen in a movie, but watching it actually being lived out was fascinating.

The reason I could not totally adopt it myself was that I was going the other way. I was faking happiness and was in the first stages of "burn out." The years of worry and sweat had taken a toll on me. I would laugh about it at times with Maggie, but I never quite let her know the depth of my feelings. I simply could not because I felt she relied on me to be the rock of her life and I could not let her down. I was raised to be strong and accept responsibility and pain.

My father and the Roman Catholic Church drilled the sense of responsibility into me. Having questioned a lot of the Catholic Church's teachings in this book I have to admit that the discipline they emphasized was entirely beneficial in my case. Whether you agree or disagree, the Roman Catholic Church stands for something. The concept of punishment and reward is sorely missing in what has evolved into a no-fault society in the United States. It seems everyone has an excuse for everything. If there are no consequences for your actions then there is no moral value to anything. I made a vow on the altar of God to take care of Maggie for life and was bound by my conscience to obey it.

So when Maggie jumped me on the retirement issue, I backed off.

"Look, it's five years away. Let's forget it." She always felt she had talked me out of it. It always made her happy to think that she had.

While I was talking retirement Maggie was beginning a brand new job, a dream job for her. Even while at university, she had performed volunteer work for the Chicago Lighthouse for the Blind. It was founded in 1865 as a beacon of light for the disabled. This was a grass roots place serving the needs of the blind, the sight-impaired and the hearing-impaired. It provided a myriad of services: education, counseling, job placement, and recreation. The Lighthouse had a federal grant that enabled the blind and sight impaired workers to make clocks. It turned into a profitable business and gave many people the dignity of a job, and that's what Maggie was getting. Upon her graduation, she was named the Chief Volunteer Officer and also a counselor. It was a perfect match. The Lighthouse was good for Maggie, and Maggie was good for the Lighthouse. She brought with her not only the educational background needed, but more importantly, the life experiences that made what she did and what she said believable beyond question.

14
A Second Life

Two weeks after she graduated from Loyola, Maggie began her new career. From the start, she was well connected in the deaf blind community. She involved herself in support groups, did work for the Foundation for Fighting Blindness, did work for the American Cancer Society, and added friends on a daily basis. Her calendar was jammed. I once told her she seemed "connected to all living things," stealing a line from the leading character in one my favorite movies, *Network*. She would leave the house early and come home late. I never saw her so busy and so happy. When she was home, she was most often on the phone.

Her room was filled with all kinds of gadgets. One allowed her to receive telephone calls from her deaf friends. The device was connected to the phone, and she could type out questions and receive replies on a small screen that spelled things out. The technology was amazing. All her phones were equipped with sound enhancers, and she now owned two VTechs: a big one and a small one she could move around the room. She learned the computer backwards and forwards and memorized the icons on the screen so if she had trouble reading them she would simply count down or across the screen and click on it. She and her friend, Ted, were on the phone several times each night going over computer information and sharing ideas and laughs. I could tell Ted was a changed man. I think he relied on Maggie as his constant inspiration. She had changed his life, just as she would change others. Maggie's natural ability to bring out the best in others came out through her friendship with Arlana so many years before. Now in her second life, she fully realized this gift by serving the many individuals in need that reached out to the Lighthouse for help.

Maggie even wound up on the local news one night. CBS carried a movie in prime time about Helen Keller and the local affiliate, WBBM-TV, called the Lighthouse to ask them if there was a person they could interview for their 10 o'clock News program. They, of course, had to have someone who was not deaf. The Lighthouse gave them Maggie's name, and she was interviewed for a news feature that aired that evening.

Maggie hated the idea but could not turn it down because of the publicity it would bring to the Lighthouse for the Blind. They showed Maggie making her way to one of her meetings in the morning with her cane, but she was not a great interview because she did not like talking about herself and she did not feel she was worthy of the attention. She did not look comfortable on camera, and she joked afterward that she had a better appreciation for my job. The strange thing about being on TV is that the more animated you are, the better off you look. A normal speech pattern will make you look boring. You have to "pump up" the volume and pour out more electricity from your body. In person, Maggie was full of life and energy; however, TV can distort things.

The advent of her new job was the advent of three years of increasing happiness for us. Every day seemed full of work and fun. On the night before she was to report to work, we had our usual wonderful night out at one of our favorite restaurants,

Volare's. It had great fish and vegetarian pasta dishes and had a wide variety of offerings. We celebrated her new job in style with a glass of wine. When I toasted her, I grabbed her hand, kissed it and leaned as far as I could across the table toward her. I looked into her beautiful blue eyes and said in a loud voice, so she could hear me, "You made it. You made it all the way back. You are the best!"

Maggie was beaming. As we walked home after dinner, she looked at me sweetly and said, "I hope this never ends." We had said the same thing thirty years before when we formed our union as husband and wife. It is hard to describe the depth of our connection. The only thing that comes close is to say it was perpetual happiness.

Maggie began work early the next day. She had to get up at 5 a.m. and, of course, "the bomb" would jolt me as it clanged and vibrated the plaster off the walls. I always went to bed around 1 a.m., so I knew this would be a tough deal for me on a daily basis. I learned to live with it and tried to roll over and go back to sleep after she got up. Maggie always had everything organized. She had her outfit for the day all ready to go, having picked it out the night before. She would many times ask me if the colors matched. She had arranged for a special cab service to pick her up in front of the building. This would be her routine for the next three years. Her work hours were 6:30 a.m. until 3:30 p.m.

Sometimes she would be called to meetings in the suburbs. Arlana and I would take her when we could, but on several occasions, I had to call a limousine service. A couple of times they actually sent a big stretch limo. This huge thing came to the front of the building, and I would escort Maggie to the back seat.

"You realize," I joked, as I helped her into the car, "that some people in this building might think you're a call girl." She came back with a good line: "Oh no, that's impossible," she laughed. "No one would ever believe I am YOUR bimbo."

Maggie's new career took off like a rocket. Before receiving her degree, she had worked as a social worker in the low vision clinic, working and counseling people who are losing their vision. Within a few months, she was promoted to Manager of Volunteer Services. She had been volunteering for so many things for so many years that the job was a natural for her. She had connections, but she did not give up her old job. She still had a hand in information and referral and counseling, helping all kinds of people. Within a year at the Lighthouse, Maggie was honored as one of their outstanding employees. Jim Kesteloot, the Executive Director of the Lighthouse, had hired Maggie, and he saw her make a rapid advance.

"If I had to talk about her greatest quality, her greatest asset to people who are blind, it was her personality. She had great character and unbelievable stature. And poise beyond belief. She also had dignity. I have been blind almost my whole life and just being around her, she motivated me to raise and elevate my performance to her standards. If you talk about blindness for a minute, you lose your sight and you lose your job. You are running from doctor to doctor looking for answers to get your sight stabilized. You owe money, you can't drive a car anymore, you can't read, you have difficulty with simple travel, and you have to deal with the adjustment to that loss of sight and maybe depression. Then, if you add deafness to that, incredible isolation can occur. You get separated from others and that isolation can cause great problems. Maggie had a great rare quality. She was naturally therapeutic.

If a person was losing sight, you wanted that person to be around Maggie. She gave people faith and hope. She was somebody you wanted to be around because she made you feel like it was going to be okay. That you were going to get through this, and that you were going to make it."

When I heard these words from Jim, I thought of Maggie's humble beginnings in Pilsen. We had lived as underdogs in our youth, so we had to be tough to succeed. I felt an incredible sense of appreciation because I had seen her evolve literally from childhood. All love is great, but there is something special about a love that begins in the passion of youth and sustains and deepens into old age.

Maggie had transferred her love and caring as a nurse into love and caring for the disabled. I once came home around 11 p.m. one night after a long day at work and found Maggie sitting at the table talking to a woman who had just been diagnosed with Usher Syndrome and was talking about suicide. The lady was in her mid thirties and in deep depression. Maggie had befriended her and made it her mission to save her. Even I got involved. What's amazing about it is that as tired as I was, I always seemed to have enough energy to help people. I joined in on their conversation and watched as Maggie calmly coaxed this woman into thinking positively. She told her about what you can accomplish under any hardship, but it was not only her words that were important.

Many of her blind or sight-impaired friends, I believe, saw great possibilities for themselves just by seeing or hearing how Maggie operated, and what kind of life she was living. On this particular night, the woman was awed by our Gold Coast condo, the doorman, the valet garage service, the brand new Lexus I was driving as we gave her a lift home. The disabled are no different than the rest of us, they have dreams, too. Many are spiritual in nature, but many also crave material things. I think this woman felt that she could acquire what Maggie possessed. While she initially did not wipe out her depression, six months later Maggie was able to report that the woman was doing much better. She had gotten a job and was coming to grips with her life.

Maggie showed me a statistic one day about the divorce rate for the disabled. As you can imagine, it was astronomical. Eighty percent of the marriages broke up after one spouse was diagnosed with a disability or serious illness. She asked me if I ever thought about divorce.

"Not once," I replied. "How can you give up on someone you love? I really believe that when you are taking your last few breaths of life, you would look back with a deep regret, and wish you had stayed the course."

I gave up quite a bit being married to a disabled person, but on balance I got much more back. My happiness became seeing Maggie happy.

She was extremely happy almost all the time. I realized she was the happiest person I had ever met. I would look around at people who were totally healthy, and they were always complaining about something. Some people especially seemed to have no passion for life. A wave of cynicism has spread over the country. Bitching about things has become normal. Sarcasm is now a way of life in the United States. The media and entertainment industry feed this negativity by constantly celebrating nastiness and sex. It makes me laugh when the media invokes the First Amendment right to free speech every time they get challenged on decency issues. What I am about to say does not come from some outside observer of the media; it comes from a forty year insider. Too much of the news, talk radio, and entertainment industry peddles sex, violence, sarcasm, and the rest of the junk because they think it sells. It's not a First Amendment issue. It's about money, pure and simple. Most CEO's are decent church-going men or women with families. Yet many of them toss their values aside when it comes to the bottom line. If we are to have any return to civility, these men and women will have to come to their senses. They know how powerful they are, and they must use that power for more than just the balance sheet. If they have a conscience at all they will take all the Jerry Springer type garbage off the air. "It sells!" should no longer be their cop out reply. To paraphrase what Candy Spelling told Paris Hilton during her brushes with the law, we should "add more to [society] than new definitions for infamy."

To be part of Maggie's world was refreshing. Her world was all about overcoming cynicism and depression and most of the people she worked with and befriended were uplifting. Maggie and I always attended the annual golf outing for the Foundation for Fighting Blindness. I was the emcee of the event and also wound up as the auctioneer. Once, we received $5,000 for a ball autographed by Michael Jordan. The place was full of people committed to raising money for fighting blindness and finding a cure. While Maggie supported the cause, she never got carried away.

"I hope they find a cure," she said, "but it's not likely. You simply have to accept what you have today and live with it. Always looking for a cure can drive you nuts. I'll get excited when I see something big, until then I am happy doing my thing with the sight I have."

I am afraid I was one of the guys always looking for a cure. I would see something in the newspapers or on TV and get pumped up. When I would tell Maggie she would always laughed it off. I recall when Maggie and I attended a lecture from a prominent researcher in 1990. At that time, they were looking into inserting computer chips in the eye to cure blindness, cell replacement, and other hopeful remedies for restoring sight. During the question and answer session, I asked the doctor if he could put a number on the number of years it would take before we had a significant breakthrough, and "three to five years" was his answer. That was seventeen years ago! So it's great to have hope and the research may one day bear fruit, but Maggie's point was well taken, live in the moment.

Maggie made the most of her moments at work and away from it. I don't know how she kept up the pace. She exhausted me in the process. Maggie's hearing problem became more acute than her sight issues. She had trouble hearing phone calls even with an enhanced speaker. Many times, at night, she would grab a piece of paper and a pen and sit me down at her desk to listen to the messages she had received from work. Even I had a hard time understanding some of the people who called. What amazed me, though, is the number of requests she handled. One guy wanted to buy a guide dog for his mother, another guy had a question about free large print books, and some were medical questions about what doctors to see. During just one night, I handled twenty-three messages. The next night eighteen and on and on it went. If Maggie did not have the answers herself she had to find someone who did. That plus the volunteer work she handled made it a full day and night.

She also took on the role as editor of an international newsletter called "Usher around the World," written by and for people with Usher Syndrome. Maggie's mission was "to provide continued information, education, advocacy, and empowerment to people with the disease." The newsletter was originally based in Minnesota, but Maggie ran it right out of her home office on the computer. She gathered articles every week and even wrote some articles herself. What a blast it was for her! She was getting letters from London, Moscow, Berlin, and other cities all across the globe. Maggie was always fiddling with the bold print and the background colors so that people could read it better. It was a labor of love.

Then one day Maggie came home and told me she was in "politics." She had joined the staff of Illinois governor Jim Edgar, a Republican. Hardly the place for a Democrat! Thanks to the Lighthouse, Maggie had been appointed to the Blind Service Planning Council, a committee that worked to aid the governor on issues of the blind and visually-impaired people in Illinois. The Council made recommendations to the governor and his staff. I don't think Maggie ever met the governor, but she did meet some of his aids and learned a lot about fashioning legislation. It required making a trip to Springfield four times a year. She would go alone many times because Arlana and I had to work. She never had a major problem, and while it always concerned me, Maggie was far removed from any fear about travel. She relished it. I saved all the letters Maggie received from Governor Edgar (One is included at the end of this chapter). I used to kid her that it was a big step for a little girl from Pilsen. She was rubbing elbows with big shots in Springfield.

Maggie was also involved in conferences and meetings all across the country from New York to California. Sometimes Karen went with her and sometimes she went with people from the Lighthouse. Other times, Arlana would join her. Sometimes she went alone. Since I also traveled quite a bit for my job, our lives took on a similar rhythm. Each time we got back together, it was like a celebration of New Year's Eve. When she was home and

I would walk in the door from a trip, she would scream out my name. "RICHIEEEEE !" I would hold her and pick her up off the floor. The joy we felt is hard to describe. It was as if my heart was suddenly filled with happiness and contentment. No matter how difficult my trip had been all my gloom was erased in a single moment. If people think that's an exaggeration, then, I truly feel sorry for them. I wish everyone could feel the true joy we felt.

As the years went by, I dreaded leaving her and got depressed the day before I took a trip. Ironically, I did not feel depressed when she was going away. She was always so happy it was hard for me to think of myself.

Maggie was making new friends by the dozens. She went out with Marlene Fishman, the wife of her eye doctor. One of her support group members, Sue Cox was a regular, and the list went on and on. The closest "new" friendship she developed was with Karen McCulloh. Don Davia referred Maggie to Karen, who had also been a nurse. Karen had developed macular degeneration, hearing loss, and multiple sclerosis. She had the same maiden name as Maggie, Smith, and the same qualities Maggie possessed. Karen was extremely intelligent and a fighter. She was far more aggressive than Maggie in mixing it up with people for her cause. Like Maggie, she was also blunt and was not one to suffer fools.

When they first met, Maggie was still a bit depressed about her future. Karen told her there were about 500 different fields of nursing, and surely, there was one Maggie could explore. She lifted Maggie's spirits, and the two became very close sharing their joys and fears. Together, they became quite a force for the cause of the disabled—particularly disabled nurses.

Maggie and Karen spoke to nurses at hospitals all over Chicago. They taught a class at the Loyola University School of Nursing, Masters Level. It was called *Pioneering Health Care for Women with Disabilities*. They were not two women to make it a superficial textbook class. The message they sent out was from the heart—from their personal experiences as women with disabilities. Maggie and Karen, *combined*, had suffered retinitis pigmentosa (progressive blindness), macular degeneration (also progressive blindness), hearing loss, breast cancer, and multiple sclerosis. It was a resume no one would want, but they had it and were determined to use it for the good of others.

Karen and Maggie laid it on the line about what it's like to lose a job because of a physical problem. Not a great deal was known, particularly, about visual impairment. They conducted the class for five years, and at the end of each class asked the students if they would work with them to try to find work that disabled nurses could handle. The classes were usually silent. No one had been paying much attention to their former colleagues, but now Maggie and Karen had at least put the issue on the table.

As a result of the classes, Maggie and Karen got the nursing school at Rush Presbyterian Hospital to form a committee to examine the possibility of setting up a recruiting program for nurses with disabilities. It was a win-win situation. The disabled nurses who would get the jobs not only were earning a living again but gaining an enormous boost in their self esteem. The hospitals and patients also won because these new nurses brought with them a sense of appreciation and dedication even beyond the norm for the profession. Two determined women, given one bad break after the other, were able to forge ahead and achieve wonderful things.

If Maggie's fingers were on these keys—and how I wish they were—she would be saying to others in a similar situation, "If I can do it, you can do it."

Maggie received a letter of recognition from RUSH, which

she would have loved because she was said to be an articulate speaker. She worked hard over the years to minimize her speech impediment and it showed. She had rock hard determination.

Maggie's honorarium was always donated to the Lighthouse. We both had a policy of never taking money when it involved imparting knowledge to young people on a part-time basis. When I stood in front of a broadcast class for an hour, I felt guilty taking money. Maggie felt the same way.

Karen and Maggie traveled all over the country lobbying for the disabled. They went to Springfield, Illinois to lobby the Illinois Nurses Association to set up a committee to study the issue of how to get disabled nurses back in the workforce. They traveled to Washington to the Josephine G. Taylor Institute, sponsored by the American Foundation for the Blind, to push the issues of the disabled. Maggie and Karen were there twice, and the first time there were no considerations given to the hearing-impaired. Karen says Maggie had to give her FM system to the speakers at the various symposiums so she could hear what was going on. Maggie and Karen spoke up about the oversight, and the second time, special headsets were made available. They learned to push for everything. Karen told me that Maggie's influence was greater with male lobbyists for a rather obvious reason.

"Let's face it," Karen said, "when a woman is beautiful in this country, she has more of a chance to have an impact. Maggie was gorgeous. When we went into meetings, she learned to use her good looks. It helped her to be assertive for the cause."

Karen said Maggie was a hero among people with Usher Syndrome.

"She had the beauty, she had money, but she also had a big humble heart," Karen said. "She represented hope, and that's why people flocked around her like moths to a flame."

Karen said the program she and Maggie pioneered to put disabled nurses back to work has flourished.

"We now have committees in seventeen states and have placed dozens of disabled nurse in jobs. Sometimes, I look at Maggie's picture in my office and break down in tears. She should have been here to see this. She would have been thrilled."

Karen then told me a story that epitomizes the work and the fun they shared together. Their travels for the cause became their lives, and they enjoyed every second of it.

"We traveled independently, together, and we were at the Marriott Hotel in Washington; I was her sighted-guide sometimes, and she was mine. We always said between the two of us we had almost one good eye, and I always stood on her left so she could hear me. We would go through the lobby first thing in the morning. We were all dressed up for our day on the Hill. As always, Maggie was impeccably dressed. She would pack full weeks worth of clothes in one carry-on suitcase; I would need a couple. Maggie always got on my case for checking bags at the airport. She promised to give me lessons on how to pack. One morning, we rushed down to the lobby to get a cup of coffee. She was quite the coffee drinker. There we were; I was acting as her sighted-guide, and I had my cane out. She was carrying two cups of coffee, and we were walking towards the elevator. Now, in my low vision, I could see two people coming towards me, and I was thinking, surely, they will see the cane in my hand, and they will step aside. All of a sudden, we rammed right into something, and we did not know what we had hit. The coffee went flying out of

Maggie's hands, and all over our outfits. As usual, Maggie looked at me and said: 'You're a great sighted-guide. Who did we hit?'

'A mirror,' I replied.

It was a mirror, and we had walked into our own images. Maggie and I laughed and laughed, as we dripped with coffee. We had to go back upstairs and change, and we laughed some more. Here we were, these so-called 'leaders of the disabled,' dripping with coffee in the lobby of a major hotel. It's a sign of how happy and well-adjusted Maggie really was that she could laugh at herself."

Maggie also had many escapades walking around downtown. She developed a friendship with a lady named Cathy Klein, whom she had met at the Lighthouse. As it turned out, she lived in a condo just a few blocks from ours. Cathy and Maggie became legendary walking around fearlessly with their canes. Chicago had become a hot bed for movie-making, and Maggie told me that one day she and Cathy were storming their way along Michigan Avenue and walked right onto a movie set, during a take! Maggie said she heard the director yelling, "Cut! Cut!"

On another occasion, she and Cathy made their way into the middle lane of Lake Shore Drive, where a police car had to escort them to safety. If you know Chicago, you will realize that walking onto Lake Shore Drive is an invitation into the back of an ambulance at best, a hearse at worst. Maggie just laughed it off. She and Cathy would walk miles and miles all around Chicago's downtown and North Michigan Avenue areas. They sought out exotic coffee shops, looking for that perfect cappuccino. When Maggie took me to some of these places that she raved about, they wound up being just a step above a "dive."

"Well, it looked good to me," she would laugh and then add, "but I am as blind as a bat."

Maggie and Cathy also joined a ski club, and they went skiing twice a year. Each blind skier had a guide. Maggie talked endlessly about the exhilaration of coming down a hill. She never once exhibited any fear about plowing into a tree. In the back of my mind, there was always fear, but I did not utter a single word. I guess, if she and Cathy wound up in the middle of Lake Shore Drive with their canes and survived, skiing with guides could not be all that dangerous.

There were also local outings. One event took place at Navy Pier. I escorted Maggie and her friends and found myself walking with five blind people at once. Maggie grabbed my arm, the next person grabbed her arm, and it went on for five people. Now, there were a string of blind folks walking down the pier. I felt like the Pied Piper.

During the evening, Maggie insisted on taking a ride on the Ferris wheel. There is a huge one on the Pier, but it never stops. For sighted people, it's no problem to jump onto the gondola on the slow-moving ride, but I was worried about Maggie falling. So, I jumped in the car first, then picked Maggie up and lifted her into the car. It helps a lot to have considerable physical strength when caring for the blind.

I recall one night we went to dinner about four blocks from our condo. Rain had been threatening, so Maggie brought along an umbrella. It happened to be a night that I was dog-tired from a tough week on the job. As bad luck would have it, the storm hit just as we were returning home. Maggie was holding a "doggie bag" from the restaurant, and I had to hold her and the umbrella. Had it been a normal rain there would have been no problem. This was one of those showers accompanied by high winds that whip around Chicago all too often. I had to use every ounce of energy to hold Maggie steady, watch for cracks or potholes in the street, and hold the umbrella over her. It is interesting how you lose all concern about your own safety in such situations. I was getting pounded with rain, had to use all the power I had in my right arm to hold her steady as I was struggling to keep my feet moving in a straight line. It turned into a long walk home. I was never so glad to see a door in my life. When we got inside, I took a deep breath and laughed, but the truth is the entire episode left me physically and emotionally wiped out.

I learned a lot of secrets about caring for a blind and deaf person. The biggest thing is the proper extension of the arm. When you go into a revolving door always go first, then reach back and put the hand of the blind person on the door before you begin to rotate it. When they feel the door moving, they move. Maggie was always very complimentary of my technique. Also, when you pull out a chair in a restaurant, don't assume the blind person knows exactly where to sit. I would place Maggie's hand on the back of the chair to feel its location.

I also had to make sure there were no water glasses or other materials on the table that are unseen. I always took Maggie's hand and placed it on the water glass so she knew exactly where it was on the table. In the case of her deafness, I had to be certain she knew if a plate was hot. Just because I could hear the waiter say it does not mean she could also hear him. I always asked for the brightest table available because then she could see the outlines of some of the objects on the table.

It was constant awareness, and while I did get used to it, sometimes it would grind me down. When I was eating by myself I realized how easy it was, especially when I could relax and not worry about Maggie knocking over a glass of water. I learned not to take so many basic things for granted.

Besides losing her central vision cells, Maggie also had cataracts, a film over the eye. Usually, they are caused by advanced age, but in Maggie's case, the disease caused her cataracts, as if it had not caused enough damage. One day when I took Maggie to her ophthalmologist, Dr. James Noth, he had an idea.

"You may see a little better if I can take out that cataract on your good eye, the left one. I don't know how much, but your sight may improve at least temporarily." Maggie did not have to be coaxed.

"Go for it," she said.

The surgery turned out to be a major success. I was with her on the day of the operation then took her back the next day when the doctor took off her eye patch. It was one of the best days of my life. As we were walking back to the car, Maggie stopped, smiled in amazement then said, "I can see things more clearly." She saw a woman and told me the lady had red shoes.

"I can't believe it!" she said excitedly. My eyes welled up with tears. On the way home, it was like a carnival. Maggie saw the license plates on cars, telephone poles, billboards, and much, much more. Things she had not seen in years. We were both ecstatic, but the most dramatic moment came when we got home.

When we walked into the kitchen, she quickly flicked on the light. Her eyes opened widely as she stroked my face with her hands. She looked at my face, laughing and crying at the same time. "Richie, she gasped, "I can see all of your features again. You haven't changed. You don't have a lot of wrinkles."

I couldn't hold back my tears. I really did not know the full extent of her vision loss. She could see enlarged computer and TV screens, but the rest of the day she was looking at blurry forms and faces that were hard to distinguish. Now she could see them again. It was heart breaking. Can you imagine not being able to see the face of the person you love?

Over the next few weeks, we enjoyed every moment of her newfound sight. When we would go to dinner, I would quiz her, "What kind of shoes is that woman wearing?" She would laugh when she had the correct answer. It was wonderful, but it did not last that long. After a few weeks, Maggie could no longer see as well. I have no idea what happened nor did she. It appeared the newfound clarity had disappeared. Perhaps the progression of the disease in her eyes had brought back the cataracts. I don't know. She no longer talked about seeing things better, and I slowly dropped the issue. If she was depressed about it she never showed any outward signs and seemed to be as happy as before. I guess she figured it wouldn't last anyway. We would still have the same wonderful goofy times at dinner, and she would many times look up at me, on the way home, and say, "Richie, this is the best!"

How she could shake off such disappointments was hard to believe, but she did.

Each year the Lighthouse held a big gala dinner/dance to raise money. It was a huge affair attended by 400-500 people, many of the city's rich and famous were on hand. It was always held downtown, which was great for us. Maggie would use the occasion to buy a brand new outfit, and I don't mean just a dress. She would go shopping with Arlana on Oak Street taking in the fabulous posh dress shops, picking out a wonderfully expensive gown then adding earrings, shoes, and whatever else she felt like buying.

"Can't you wear one of those great dresses you already have in the closet?" I would ask. "Aren't they good enough? Do you have to buy a new one for each event you go to?"

"Are you crazy?" she asked. "You can't wear a dress that you wore somewhere else."

"You mean that some people might have seen you in that old dress and it would embarrass you if these exact same people would be at the gala? What are the odds of that happening?"

Maggie would just laugh.

I had to rent a tuxedo for the event. We looked like the kind of people you see in the newspaper gossip pages posing at charity events. Maggie did her usual pilgrimage to Mario Tricoci's for make-up and hair treatment on the day of the event. At the last one she attended in 2001, Maggie was absolutely gorgeous. Despite the operations, the slightly swollen right arm and her fifty-one years, she looked about the same as when she was in her thirties. Her face also showed few wrinkles. She had the same lean form as a result of her ongoing workouts. She wore a black silk gown that was sleeveless, tapering off at her neck. She showed just enough skin to be tasteful, as sexy as you can get. The top of the dress served as a gold choker that hugged her throat.

Marlene and Jerry Fishman were there, and Marlene snapped a picture of Maggie and me, catching Maggie at the perfect moment. Blind people, of course, have a hard time finding the exact location of a camera and many times they look strange in pictures. This time, I took Maggie's head with my hand and guided it right to the lens then quickly took my hand away before the picture was taken. The result was breathtaking. Marlene caught Maggie's eyes open and alive with happiness. It was the Maggie I saw every day. When I look at that picture, I can see the excitement of life in her eyes. As diseased as her eyes were on the outside, they were windows of beauty to her inner character. Her face was radiant, the shoulders sexy, and the gown that hugged her body highlighted her sensuality. It was the picture of a lifetime, and while I looked like a dork, I really didn't care. Nobody would be looking at me anyway. When we got the picture back, I told Maggie how amazing she looked, but I don't believe she was ever impressed. She put it under the VTech and nodded her head that it was great, but she did not have the same depth of feeling about it that I had.

As the gala continued, Maggie and I got a glass of wine and strolled around the lobby to look at the items in the silent auction. We put an $800 bid on a one-week stay at a condo in Vail, Colorado. The dinner itself was fine, but afterwards there was a dance band. The noise was deafening, and it was the worst thing possible for Maggie. Even with the FM system connected to her hearing aids, she could not understand me. Eventually, we had to go out into the lobby for some peace and quiet.

I could tell Maggie's hearing was failing rapidly, and I did not know how much longer she would be able to hear anything. The hearing aids used to allow her to hear just about everything. In the past few months however, I found myself repeating more things, and I noticed a slow deterioration in her speech pattern. She was sounding more and more like a person who had severe hearing loss or was totally deaf. The FM system was her best bet but that did not always work out either. I had a sinking feeling. We so loved our dinner conversations and all the rest of our discussions. It would be horrible to give them up or struggle through them. Sign language was out of the question because Maggie could not see well enough, and I felt yet another major component of her life slipping away. I envisioned a time when she would be totally deaf and blind. It was like looking up at the blade on a guillotine that you know is someday going to drop.

Over the years of struggle, I had never let down my guard with Maggie. I felt my role, my offering of love, was to be her rock. I was always reassuring her that all would be okay. We would get around any obstacle then if another one occurred, I told her we would get around that one also. While she was a confirmed optimist, there were still times when she would get down. I developed a second sense about her moods and knew when she needed a lift. Most times, it was simply a reassuring chat or a trip to a coffee shop that would end her blues. She always recovered rather quickly.

But all the concern and worry was beginning to take a toll on me. I was fifty-three years-old, still performing in a high energy profession, and caring for Maggie on a 24-hour basis. Sitting home at night, I was never free from worry. I had to make sure Maggie didn't bounce off a wall, didn't hurt herself trying to open a can, or get frustrated at not finding something in her room. The only time I felt relaxed was after I tucked her in, and she had gone to sleep. That was around 9 p.m. and I had three or four hours to finally unwind. Eventually, however, even that disappeared. I found I could not unwind, even then. I was always "on," always worried. Sleeping became even more fitful than it had been before.

This created problems at work. Going on the air for a five minute segment may not look like much to the viewer, but there are hundreds of thousands of people watching, and when you know your bosses are studying every show with a critical eye, there is always a huge adrenalin rush. I needed a lot of energy to get the job done, and I found myself running on fumes on some nights. I would hyperventilate during shows, a nightmare experience for a broadcaster. I somehow got through these episodes by taking pauses during the sports plays I was voicing over. Thank God I was not on camera when they happened. By controlling my breathing, I was able to regain my composure. This was not a case of nerves. After thirty years, I was not nervous. It was a case of too much worry and anxiety in my life. I was beginning to burn out.

It was the role of the caretaker that caused it. I had really become more of a caretaker than a husband to Maggie. This role did not diminish my love but instead increased it. I loved her even more than when I was just a husband. It seems to me that I was caring for Maggie as if she were a vulnerable child. It was a strange juxtaposition of emotions. I was her husband, her best friend, her lover, and her caretaker. The best advice I can give to someone in a similar situation is the first rule for the caretaker, which none of us really heed, is make sure you take care of yourself also. Take time to be by yourself and regroup. I was lucky in that Maggie got away a lot on her trips for work or pleasure, so I did have some time to myself, and it may have saved me. The constant twenty-four hour worry and work can eat you alive. You have to realize that if you go down you are useless to the person who needs you. I must admit, however, relaxing even for a while is easier said than done.

And, of course, Maggie herself had become a caretaker. She took every opportunity to help blind or visually-impaired people who were in trouble. There was a friend of hers who had been charged with sexual harassment. He had been accused of making sexual comments to two women while riding a bus.

"A blind guy charged with harassment?" I asked.

"Yes," Maggie said, "and I know this guy. It had to have been a misunderstanding."

Maggie went to the trial and was scheduled to appear as a character witness, but it never got that far. The judge dismissed the charges, but Maggie's friend and his family never forgot her kindness.

Maggie also had a friend from out of state that was having

trouble with her husband. Maggie had met her at one of her low-vision conferences, and they struck up a friendship. After her friend learned about Maggie's transition, she was greatly encouraged. Maggie even invited her and her husband to our condo for a weekend, but she made a point to tell me not to give anybody lectures about how well we had gotten through our crisis with blindness.

"Just enjoy the weekend," Maggie said. "If questions come up, we will answer them but don't assume our answers are the right ones. Everybody is different. We made it through our way, but that doesn't mean it's the right way for them."

The weekend was a lot of fun, and I think it did work to help Maggie's friend and her husband. We rented a four-seater bicycle at Navy Pier, walked around downtown, and treated them to dinner at one of our favorite restaurants. Maggie's friend had more sight than Maggie possessed, and it appeared to me that she was at the stage Maggie had passed five years before. She could move around pretty well, but she also knew what was coming, and she still was learning to get used to the cane. As for her husband, I could tell he was reluctant to talk about any of his wife's issues, so I followed Maggie's advice and said nothing. Finally, however, Maggie's friend did ask me how I coped with the advent of Maggie's blindness.

"It's a hard thing to face," I said. "I have no corner on answers, but the only thing I can tell you is that I love her. When you love a person, you can get through anything. Her death is the only real fear I could never overcome, but as long as she is breathing and is in no pain, I can live with blindness, deafness, whatever. I am not saying you never get depressed because that is obvious. What happens is basic. You use the adversity to strengthen the relationship." I didn't say it, but I thought of the Kennedy speech of 1960. You don't "shrink from the responsibility."

The night after the couple left, Maggie and I talked about the weekend. She felt we might have done some good, but she said, you never know.

"One weekend," she said, "is really not enough to make a huge impact."

She was sure about one thing about us.

"We have become one soul, Richie," she said, sweetly and happily. "We are like one person. It's the happiest feeling I have ever had, and it seems to get better by the day."

I felt the same way, and the profound element for me was that it was not just a physical attraction anymore. It was a feeling of warmth, not connected to the physical world. It was a scary feeling for an agnostic. I wondered whether there really was something to look forward to after we died.

STATE OF ILLINOIS

OFFICE OF THE GOVERNOR

SPRINGFIELD 62706

JIM EDGAR
GOVERNOR

January 6, 1999

Ms. Margaret King
111 E. Chestnut, #34C
Chicago, IL 60611

Dear Margaret:

As my final term as Governor comes to a close, I have spent a great deal of time thinking about all the things that we have been able to accomplish and all of the people who have helped me to accomplish those things.

I am especially indebted to those people, such as you, who have served the citizens of Illinois and my Administration by participating on a Board or Commission. You and hundreds of other Board and Commission members have shared your time, your knowledge and your talents to help make Illinois an even better place to call our home.

In my final days as Governor of Illinois, I want to take this opportunity to thank you so much for the work you have done, the assistance you have provided and the support you have given as we have worked together.

Best wishes for a happy and prosperous 1999. I believe our paths will cross many times in the future because of our shared interests. Again, thank you.

Sincerely,

Jim Edgar
GOVERNOR

JE:jmc

15
Helping Others, Again

Maggie quickly became a counselor for people recently diagnosed with eye problems. When a person came in who had just been diagnosed with a progressive eye disease, they sent that person to Maggie for a series of meetings. She never tired of helping people. Almost all of the people she saw became her friends. A typical case was Robert, who had Usher Syndrome.

Robert was down and out after being diagnosed. He entered a support group at the Lighthouse.

"All they kept telling me was, you have to meet Maggie King. So my first meeting there, I stuck in the corner before I finally heard a voice introducing herself to everyone as Mrs. King. I quickly took the chance to speak up. Are you Maggie King," I asked. She shot back in a loud and clear voice.

"I am, do you have a problem with that?" she quipped.

"We both laughed, and I knew I had found a friend with a sense of humor."

Maggie met Robert on a regular basis. They talked a lot about their similar problems, but they also talked politics, poetry and just about every other subject you could imagine. Robert quickly saw what most people saw in Maggie, a reason for hope.

"During my depression, I couldn't get satisfaction from my psychologists or my doctor," he said. "I received that from Maggie.

I never saw her spirits down, and she never had pity parties or ignored others due to her own health issues. It was Maggie who lifted my spirits to a new level!"

Maggie at first did not tell Robert she had also battled breast cancer. He found out one day when they were having lunch.

"Not many people can comprehend what it's like to be deaf and blind, but Maggie did. She also defeated cancer with an amazingly positive attitude. She broke down barriers with her kindness and generosity. I will forever be in her debt."

Robert not only emerged from his depression, but he also found a new career at the Lighthouse for the Blind. He is now their Manager of Sales for the Veterans Administration, selling deaf-blind items to the VA. His whole life is back on track.

She also kept up her daily calls and contacts with Ted who was now really coming into his own. Ted was dating again and shared his experiences with Maggie. I think she enjoyed the stories he told her. It was like a soap opera. Ted would meet a woman on a train and invite her to stay at his house for the night. "He's totally fried!" Maggie laughed. "He is boxing himself into a huge mess, and I told him so." I told her that she was thinking like a woman. "Look, his libido is back. Let him enjoy it."

One day, a couple told Marlene Fishman at a fund-raising dinner that their teenage son had just been diagnosed with progressive blindness. He was depressed and looking for answers. They asked Marlene if anyone could help him get through it. Instead of recommending a psychiatrist, Marlene sent him to see Maggie at the Lighthouse.

"About six months later," Marlene said, "the couple called to tell me that their son had made a big improvement and was now looking forward to going to college. They thanked me for sending him to see Maggie."

Maggie had been in a depression, she was going blind, and she had graduated with honors from college as a legally blind and deaf person. There could not have been a better person for the young man to talk to unless it was a psychiatrist with the same ailments. That would have cost his family $140 a pop.

Maggie also became treasurer for the Illinois Consortium for Leaders of Vision Support. It was yet another support group for the visually impaired. She participated in three support groups, but being in charge of the money for this one was a joke.

"I would never put you in charge of anything connected to money," I laughed. "I bet it won't take long for your consortium to be in debt." Maggie was also amused, and admitted she was ill suited for the job.

"The only thing I know about money is how to spend it," she said.

There was not a Saturday or Sunday during the summers that Maggie was not involved in a fund-raising event for cancer research or for some cause for the fight against eye disease. She was working seven days a week. In June of 2001, we cashed in on the vacation condo in Vail, Colorado purchased at the Lighthouse's silent auction the year before. I did not ski anymore, and Maggie wanted to go in the summer time anyway, so we selected a week in June to take off. This time it was just the two of us.

Maggie and I spent the entire vacation just basking in the sunshine by the pool. The weather was perfect and so was the setting. The West gives you a feeling of humility. The majestic mountains seem to reach into heaven itself. Maggie could not see all that much, but she did remember what those wide mountain ranges looked like. We had been to Colorado just a year after our honeymoon. Maggie had enjoyed horseback riding back then, but that was out of the question now.

Over dinner one night, I saluted her career.

"You have become quite a force," I said. "It's really amazing when you look at how it all began."

"I have been lucky," she replied. "You see so many people who have no chance, no money, and no backing. If not for places like the Lighthouse, they are lost. I am sick and tired of people cutting back on social services. The government wastes so much money it's unbelievable. If we can't help our own people in need, what good are we?"

"You sound like a New Dealer," I laughed.

The tone of what Maggie was saying was not one of bitterness; it was one of sadness. The once raging anger inside her was long gone.

"You have come a long way also, Richie," she added. "Imagine being a TV sportscaster in a major market for so long. That's something!"

"I don't feel that way," I replied. "My job does not help anybody. Reading a bunch of highlights and getting sound-bites from players is hardly in a league with what you are doing."

"No, you're all screwed up," she said. "When you did your radio talk show, people used to tell me how much they enjoyed it. People say the same thing when they watch you on TV. People have fun following sports. So why is it bad to be part of that? You are doing a service."

I disagreed, but she had a point. Whatever you do in life, if you do it with high standards, it has value.

Our week in Vail was a slice of heaven. The complex we stayed in had spacious grounds that were landscaped to near perfection with all types of beautiful trees, plants, and flowers. Maggie had become increasingly fond of flowers with each passing year as her eyesight deserted her. They were among the few things she could still see rather easily. Flowers had discernible sharp colors, and Maggie loved to walk along slowly and take them all in. We took leisurely strolls during the day and the evening. Our condo was fully equipped with a coffee maker, so we brewed our usual pot of decaf, and we each took a cup for our stroll into the cool evening air. Our light jackets and coffee took away the evening chill. I tried for the 1,000th time in our life to get Maggie to see the stars. On a wonderfully clear night, they were sparkling everywhere. As I had done so often in the past, I tilted her head this way and that hoping her limited vision would catch the sparkling light amid the blackness. It never happened. "I just can't see them, Richie," she said, and a small tear welled up in my eyes. Knowing how much she appreciated everything in life and knowing she had never seen the beauty of the constellations left a sick feeling in the pit of my stomach.

During the daytime, we also spent a lot of time at the pool. Since it was empty most of the time, Maggie was able to swim without worrying about bumping into somebody, and she was an excellent swimmer. Her fifty-two year old body was still trim and athletic. When we tried to go bowling one day later though, Maggie took just one shot and had to call it quits.

"My arm is gone," she laughed. "Maybe I will have to learn how to be a lefty." For a moment, my mind darted back to our teenage years when Maggie's right arm was so strong that a playful punch in the arm packed a considerable wallop. She once took the air out of me with a shot in the back. I again choked back a tear when she had to give up on the simple act of throwing a bowling ball.

On the final evening of our trip, we attended a free outdoor concert at a nearby park. It featured a lively early 40s-style "swing band." There was even a trio of singers in the band that imitated the great Andrew Sisters. Maggie and I loved the music of that era, even though it was almost ten years before we were born. Live music in general was always a treat for Maggie because it was loud, allowing the sound to filter well into her hearing aids. We took a seat in the back row, snuggled up close in our jackets and held hands, just as we had as kids on the front steps of Maggie's house in Pilsen so many years ago. The concert began during the final moments of daylight when the skies were still blue. Within a few minutes, it gave way to the soft summer glow of twilight. The setting sun had just enough radiance to shine its beam on Maggie's golden hair. It was as beautiful as it had been forty years before. As I looked at her, I did not see the face of a fifty-two year old woman. Maggie still retained the resilience of youth despite all the struggles on the road of life. Her eyes still sparkled with life, love, and happiness. It was a moment and a night I hoped would never end. I wanted to freeze the clock and let the band play on forever.

The concert ended all too soon, and we made our way back to the condo to pack for the return trip to Chicago. If I were granted one night of my life to live over, it would be that enchanted night I spent with my Maggie in June of 2001, listening to the music of a bygone era under the stars in Vail, Colorado. I had all the joy I ever wanted when Maggie was by my side. I had peace and contentment and no fears save one, the fear of losing her.

16
Lost For Eternity

When we got back to Chicago, Maggie plunged back into her hectic schedule. One afternoon, while I was working at WGN-TV, she called and told me she was home from work early. "I've got some kind of pain in my back," she said. "I had to come home and lay down."

She said she was going to call our doctor to get some muscle relaxing pills. I didn't like the sound of her call one bit. I worried about every pain Maggie had, but this was worse. I had a friend whose wife had died five years before from ovarian cancer. He said she woke up one morning with a sore back, and a year later she was dead. Ovarian cancer is a silent killer. Women don't feel the symptoms until it's too late.

The only encouragement I gave myself was that Maggie had been going to a so-called Early Detection Program for ovarian cancer at Northwestern Memorial Hospital. She was aware of the connection between breast and ovarian cancer and had been getting tested every six months. Maggie never told me she had any problem, but then again Maggie was always protecting me, so I dismissed that thought immediately.

She was hoping the pain would go away, but it didn't. She did go to our doctor and received pills to relax her muscles. I prayed she would wake up one morning and tell me the pills had kicked in and the pain was gone. It was not in the cards. Now she was having considerable trouble sleeping. I helped her prop extra pillows under her back. As the days went by and the pain persisted, my concern grew.

After a week, Arlana and I suspected the worst. We told Maggie she had to see the doctor again and get some answers. She did not want to go and tried to "gut it out" for another week.

Finally, Maggie could wait no longer. Arlana came over for dinner one night, and Maggie finally opened up. This time she had hidden the truth even from Arlana. She told us that six months earlier an ultrasound test at the ovarian cancer-screening program had detected "debris" near her left ovary. Why doctors use terms like "debris" or "mass," I will never know.

When any doctor uses those kinds of words you think it's cancer. Maggie said the "debris" was so small that the doctor decided to wait to see whether it showed up again on her next ultrasound. What may have confused him was that her blood tests were normal.

Arlana and I were shaken by the news. In the nine years since her breast cancer, we worried about every single ailment that came up. Even a prolonged flu was cause for major alarm. This was our worst nightmare. Even though Maggie talked like it was not that big a deal, Arlana and I felt a horrible uneasiness. We could only hope that Maggie would be right: somehow it would be a minor problem.

Arlana got Maggie to agree to return to her doctor at the Northwestern Hospital testing center. She made an appointment immediately and was examined within a week. More tests were conducted while Maggie suffered from increasing back pain. Now she was having trouble sitting down as well, and things got bad in a hurry.

The hospital told us that the tests would determine whether Maggie had to have surgery, but after a week we got no response. One morning, Arlana and Maggie got into a big fight over the lack of progress in her treatment.

"Where are the test results?" Arlana demanded.

"They were supposed to call me yesterday, but I received no news," Maggie replied.

"What?" Arlana snapped. "Exactly who has the results?"

Maggie told her the results should have arrived at the office of the surgeon who would make the decision to operate or not.

"Give me her number," Arlana demanded.

"Screw you," Maggie replied. "When she calls, she calls. I am not going to bother her."

Arlana did an end run and called me at work. I hit the ceiling. Without Maggie's knowledge, Arlana and I went to work. We called the Northwestern Hospital Ovarian Center and learned they had sent the test results to the doctor's office the day before.

"So, she has the stuff," Arlana spat out.

We then called the doctor's office and were told the doctor had not received the information yet. When it came to Maggie's health I did not care who I offended, so I ripped into the nurse.

"Well, you tell the doctor that if she doesn't have the time to find out the results of a test that could determine possible surgery for a woman who already has suffered breast cancer then she will be hearing from me in person, and it won't be pleasant."

An hour later, the doctor called Maggie and told her to come in for a meeting the following day.

Maggie laughed when Arlana and I told her we had spent hours on the phone badgering nurses and receptionists.

"You two are fried," she said.

Arlana and I were a bit crazed, but when you love someone so deeply, you find your cool exterior can melt away pretty quickly. If you have to step on toes in the name of love you do it.

I don't exactly know why Maggie was so cavalier about finding answers. Maybe she was masking a deep concern. On the outside, she was talking tough. She never verbalized any real fear simply saying she was glad she had joined the early detection program.

"Whatever is in there," she said, "it has to be small. Thank God I went to the testing program even though it was a pain in the butt to go."

At the outset, it appeared Maggie had been right. When we went to the surgeon's office she reviewed all of Maggie's tests. I had never seen a doctor more optimistic. She described it as a small mass and repeated over and over again that it was not cancer. It would be a routine hysterectomy.

The blood tests were totally normal, and we were told that was a key element. Arlana and I walked out of the office beaming, but Maggie was quick to jump us.

"I told you guys everything would be okay, didn't I?" she laughed. She called us "the panic couple."

The surgery was scheduled for two weeks later. In the meantime, Maggie went back to work. Still, I watched her closely. Her complexion continued to be quite good, she was not losing weight, and her energy level was fine. All that, plus the doctor's report, was beginning to reassure me that she would be okay. The only nagging problem was her back. The pain simply would not go away, even though she took Advil on a regular basis. She could not wait for the surgery so that she could sleep in peace once again.

Having been through so many obstacles in our lives, we took this latest setback as just another hurdle. Unlike the breast cancer, there were a lot of encouraging signs this time. The mood was quite upbeat. Maggie, in fact, was glad she was having her reproductive organs taken out.

"I wish I had done this a few years ago," she said. "For older women, all those organs are just potential trouble. Now I won't have to worry."

Except for the back pain, life went on as normal. Maggie's appetite was outstanding, as was her appetite for spending money. The packages kept coming to our door. As the day of the surgery approached, Maggie's mood got even better. She figured she would be laid up for just a few weeks but would be able to work on the computer and stay in touch with people.

It was a beautiful warm summer morning in late July of 2001 when Arlana and I took Maggie to the hospital for the surgery. Maggie walked to the hospital with Arlana on one arm and me on the other resembling three warriors about to do battle again. We were all in a very positive frame of mind, joking around about all the time we had spent in doctor's offices and hospitals. Maggie knew she would be in the hospital for a few days, so I kidded her about the night of her breast cancer surgery when she wanted to get out on the same night.

"I could have made it," she joked, "but you guys never woke me up. You're wimps."

We took Maggie to the prep room then left her with the doctors so they could apply her epidural anesthetic. When we were let back in, I did not relish the sight of Maggie all wrapped up in what looked like a straight jacket. She had been through so much she did not deserve any more of this type of nonsense. The doctor then met us in the room and was so upbeat that it took my gloom away. "This is going to be a routine deal," she said. "Don't worry about a thing."

The operation was scheduled for two hours and Arlana and I left to get some breakfast. We did not linger over our food very long, coming back in a half hour. I had learned from my father's episode that there is always concern waiting out a surgery, even if things are supposed to go well. While Arlana and I were characteristically nervous, we had no deep-seated fears. The evidence suggested a routine operation. Right on schedule, two hours into the surgery, the doctor came out. But we were stunned to see she had a look of doom on her face and seemed to be walking on her ankles. It scared me to death. When she asked the other people to clear out the waiting room so she could talk to us, my knees became weak.

The doctor sat on the couch. I sat next to her. Arlana was in a chair in front of the doctor whose eyes seemed glazed with tears.

"I'm really shocked to tell you that I found two tumors in Maggie. One was near the omentum, which was causing her back pain, the other was in her uterus but it was a lot smaller. It is cancer."

If I had not been sitting down, I would have fainted. I placed my hands over my eyes, looked down at the floor, and began to breathe deeply. I was trying hard not to collapse. The doctor grabbed my shoulder, trying to console me.

"Now, Mr. King, I know this is tough, but we have to take it one day at a time," she said.

I said nothing, but I knew Maggie was gone. "One day at a time" means terminal, and as much as the doctor tried to encourage us, deep down I knew I would have to endure the unendurable. I just didn't know how soon. Arlana and I were both so shocked we could barely ask questions. The doctor admitted being totally caught off guard. Everything looked normal. All the blood tests and the ultrasounds meant nothing. The only good news was that the tumors had been removed and were small. The doctor told us Maggie would be in surgery for two more hours then in intensive care for another two hours. The doctor assured us she would tell Maggie about the surgery and about the outlook.

We finally mumbled a few questions at the doctor, but she really had no answers pending the appointment of an oncologist. Any talk about possible cure, recovery, or treatment would have to wait. The doctor returned to finish the surgery.

I really don't know how I got up, but I did. Arlana and I went for a walk at Lake Shore Park, which was near the condo.

"I can't believe what I just heard," Arlana said, with tears in her eyes.

"I think she's gone, Arlana," I replied and broke down in tears as we walked. We sat on a park bench and didn't say all that much. We were both numb.

"How in the hell do we handle this one?" I cried.

We sat there for an hour re-grouping and trying to get our wind back.

We each resembled an exhausted boxer getting pummeled in the ring groping for the ropes to regain his balance and just hoping to survive. The whole conversation with the doctor was surreal, like a horrible nightmare that had left us dazed and grief stricken. Somehow, we re-gained some equilibrium.

"Maybe we can catch a break," I said. "Maybe we are reading this all wrong. There is no sense in giving up. Let's just dig in again. You know she is going to battle this thing with all she has, so that's the only course to take."

We snapped out of it and went back to the condo to make some calls telling people the bad news. Arlana called Patty and some of Maggie's friends, and I informed my mother about the news. To all the people we called, we were upbeat stressing the tumors were taken out, and there was a good chance Maggie would be okay. It really is a study in human survival how a person can rationalize any news. You always opt for the best-case scenario. By the time we went back to the hospital, we had convinced ourselves and were ready for the fight again.

As it turned out, Maggie's assigned oncologist fed into our optimism. We met her before Maggie came back to the room. Unlike the surgeon, she was upbeat and full of news about the operation. It turned out that the tumor on Maggie's right ovary had attached itself to a mesh lining that was connected to a membrane called the omentum. The tumor was pulling that mesh and Maggie felt the pain. She would feel it no longer. As for the tumor in the uterus, it was described as very small and buried in the lining. The oncologist said that there was hope that chemotherapy could take care of any cancer cells that had spread, but she did not give us any odds. The full report on the operation would not come in for a week or so.

Arlana and I felt better with every word. Maybe this would be like the breast cancer and Maggie would once again prevail. We had a lot going for us, with the biggest force being Maggie herself. She was as tough as they come, and we knew she would not back away from the battle. By the time we finally saw Maggie, the shock of what happened four hours before had somewhat subsided.

She was pretty drugged up when they wheeled her in the room. I kissed her and held her hand for a while and she smiled. Then she quickly fell asleep. She looked at peace. It was evening by now. Arlana and I were just about wiped out, but we did not want to leave until Maggie woke up and was able to talk to us. She slowly emerged from her sleep around 11 p.m. It was not a dramatic scene at all. Maggie said she knew what was going on and looked ready for the battle.

"At least I will be able to sleep without that damn pain in my back," she said.

Arlana and I filled her in on our conversation with the oncologist, since she seemed eager for the news. If she had any fear or depression about the day, she never showed it. Arlana and I stayed until about 1 a.m., when Maggie dozed off to sleep again. Arlana left the hospital first while I stayed a few more minutes just to hold Maggie's hand. My courage was waning as the exhaustion of a harrowing day set in. I kissed her on the forehead and left. There is something about the night that feeds into fear, and as I walked home all the doom and gloom re-emerged.

The next day, we returned to the hospital somewhat refreshed, ready for the task at hand. Maggie was weak but upbeat. Her first order of business was getting out of the hospital, which was a place she loved to work, but hated as a patient. There was a bloating in her stomach that we asked the doctor about on the first day then again on the next, but the doctor said it was just gas and swelling from the operation. Finally, on the third day, we got an apology. Maggie had a hernia because they had failed to sew her up properly.

"We can fix that in a few months," the doctor said. "It is just a minor operation."

I bit my tongue, but I was livid inside. Just how much was this woman supposed to take? First, we were told it was a routine hysterectomy. Then the hernia was supposed to be swelling. The only thing that kept me from exploding was I did not want to embarrass Maggie who liked all the doctors very much, especially her oncologist.

She diagnosed Maggie as having Stage One ovarian cancer.

In the brochures they offered at the hospital, this stage had an 80 percent success rate. Hope can give you patience, so I refrained from any nastiness.

After a week in the hospital, we took Maggie home where she improved rapidly. In just a week or so, she was walking around pretty well and able to go out to dinner. Her chemotherapy was scheduled for the middle of August in 2001. She had one week to enjoy her food before again facing the ravages of the poison they would send into her body. I tried my best to keep her spirits up.

"I guess we will see the return of the 'ghost,'" I joked. Once again she would be losing her hair.

Maggie's first chemotherapy was simply horrible. She was wiped out that same night, suffering severe stomach cramps, nausea, and pain in her joints, and I am not talking about minor pain. It was the kind of pain that caused her to squirm and moan. I could not stand to see her suffer, but there was nothing I could do to help her. Arlana tried every trick in the book to relieve her misery, but the pain medication she had been given was too weak. Then Maggie was scared to death the next morning when she lost almost all of her sight and saw grey blotches instead of objects. Arlana came back to our condo with about three hours sleep. We called the oncologist, Maggie's eye doctor, and everybody we could think of who might be able to help. Thankfully, Maggie's eyesight—such as it was—returned after a few hours. Whatever drug caused it apparently had moved through her system. She was still a mess, and it took almost a full week for the chemo and the pain to totally wear off.

"If this is how it's going to be," Maggie said, "I don't know if I can make it."

I immediately thought of what her mother had told me when she was devastated by chemo twenty-five years before.

Maggie's second chemo session had to be scratched. Her blood count was too low, which meant she simply was too weak. While it was a relief, there was also the psychological burden. Maggie, of course, hated the suffering, but she also hated not getting the chemo. She knew it was her only chance to stay alive. It was a "Catch 22" with a life on the line. She was grateful when the blood test in October was good enough to allow another chemo.

It was during this session that I was again jolted by something I found out completely on my own. While Maggie was being examined, I saw her thick file sitting on a table. I really was trying to find out if there was any good news written down but instead, by accident, I discovered the exact opposite. I looked at what the doctor had written about her ovarian cancer: it said Stage Three! We had been under the impression it was Stage One. I looked at it for several minutes, hoping I was mistaken. Maggie's regular oncologist was on vacation that day, so a substitute doctor was filling in. I cornered him in the hallway and asked point blank if Maggie had Stage One or Stage Three ovarian cancer. He stumbled a little bit and then said: "Oh yeah, it is Stage Three, but don't read too much into that."

The news sent me reeling. Stage Three had only a 20 percent survival. If you are supposed to avoid "reading" anything into that then why put out the damn brochure? I was depressed and angry at the same time, still I held my tongue. I took Maggie home without telling her what I had discovered. Completely out of sorts by the shock, I was glad to be going to work.

When I got to the office at WGN-TV, I just sat at my computer, stunned. I looked up the ovarian cancer website, confirming my fears. Stage Three meant death in almost all cases. I sat there with a glaze in my eyes and my producer, Joel Libertore, leaned over and asked me if I was okay. To avoid breaking down,

I got up and went for a walk outside. It was a repeat of the misery I felt when we got the diagnosis that Maggie had ovarian cancer.

Then a strange thing happened. Back at my desk, I tried calling my mother, as I usually did every night. But I simply could not remember her phone number. It was the same one she's had for thirty years, but the correct sequence of numbers would not register in my brain. No matter how hard I tried, it was a "no-go" for a number I had dialed thousands of times over the years. The human mind in shock simply does not function properly. It took me a half hour to finally remember the number.

I really don't know how I got through that night. I had given her up for dead right after the operation, then talked myself into believing she would be okay. Now I was back to square one, fearing the absolute worse. I realized my whole reason for living was about to be taken from me, and in a very short time. It was as if I was again living the nightmare Arlana and I suffered in July on that park bench after Maggie's surgeon shockingly told us about the malignant tumors.

The next day, I decided to tell Arlana about my finding. She was equally stunned. In her case, she wanted answers. We both agreed we would descend on Maggie's oncologist when she got back from vacation.

"I don't like to put numbers on it because I want my patients to have hope," the doctor said. "Yes, it is Stage Three. That does not mean she does not have a chance. We'll see how it goes when I repair the hernia in February."

By then she was hopeful the chemo would have begun to shrink the tumors. She also wanted to get a firsthand look. As for a cure, there was none.

"We are just trying to give her a few more years of life," she said sadly. At that point "years" sounded pretty good.

Maggie, meantime, never asked her doctor any questions about the outlook, at least not when I was with her. It was as if she did not want to know the odds. Maggie was not one to accept defeat. She had an iron-clad will and had willed to win this latest battle. Her friend, Robert, called her a "pure fighter." I also knew part of her silence was to protect me. We discussed the issue only once on an evening when I was tucking her in bed. It was the week the doctor changed her chemo because a cat scan had showed that the cancer had not been halted.

"It's amazing," she said, "how many chemos there are. I hope they find the right one."

I had no hope that they would, but my reply seemed to cheer her up: "We have a lot of bullets left, don't sweat it. Something will work."

That was it. She never brought up the subject again.

Autumn gave way to winter, and we had our usual low-key Christmas. But we both missed dearly the chance to blow it out on New Year's Eve. We always celebrated big, spending the night at a downtown hotel or taking an exotic trip somewhere. This time, Maggie was too weak even to go out for a light dinner. The one treat we had was a fireworks display at Navy Pier, which we could see clearly from the window of our condo. I held Maggie's frail body tight as we gazed into the night. Maggie acknowledged that she saw the sparkles of the fireworks but could not muster the old goofy enthusiasm she usually enjoyed for such events. She was simply too worn out from the chemo. I had a bad feeling that this was the last time I would be with her on New Year's Eve. It made my stomach twist in fear, and I don't know how I kept my poise. I finally excused myself and went to the washroom where I bent over in stifled agony, choking back tears. I could not linger too long. When I came out, I began joking around. It was madness.

In February, Arlana and I took Maggie back to the hospital for yet another operation, this one to repair her hernia. She also hoped the doctor would have some good news about her cancer.

"I need a rabbit's foot," she laughed. The operation turned out to be a long one where Arlana and I learned the true definition of hell. We knew any good news was a long shot, but we were still hoping for a break. We paced the halls, sat in the waiting room, paced the halls and sat in the waiting room—for six hours! We saw doctors come out and tell relatives good news about various operations that were performed.

"Maybe we'll get some good news, Arlana kept saying. We must have paced fifteen miles and talked ourselves silly in what seemed like an endless afternoon.

When the doctor finally came out, she was fighting back her tears. Not only had the cancer not been halted, but it had spread. It was now in her liver and in her colon. It was just a matter of time. How much time? At first she would not say, but I insisted.

"I know Maggie may not want to know, and I will honor that wish, but are we talking a year, months, weeks?" Finally, after repeated grilling, she admitted it was a matter of months.

"How will it happen?" I asked.

Still fighting back her tears, she told me Maggie most likely would starve to death. The cancer would spread to her colon and her digestive system would begin to shut down. I felt totally devastated, but it was hardly a shock by then. Arlana and I went to Maggie's room to await her arrival from intensive care. We sat there in total silence. The rationalizing was over.

My heart was broken that afternoon. From that moment on, I knew I would never be the same. I had now lost all hope. The only thing left to do was make her final days peaceful. I had to dig deep into my depleted reserve of courage. When Maggie awoke from the operation, Arlana and I were at her bedside like a pair of centurions. We each held one of her hands.

"It's sure good to see you guys," she said with a weak smile as she opened her eyes. It was a good thing she could not see very well because both Arlana and I had tears streaming down our faces. It was impossible to fake it anymore.

I truly expected that Maggie would fade fast. She was weakened by two serious operations and a rugged and draining chemotherapy, not to mention the cancer that was ravaging her insides. But after arriving home, she made an amazing recovery.

"Look at my belly," she said with pride, noting that the hernia was gone. In a week or so, she was up and around and able to go out and even had thoughts of going back to work. It was gut-wrenching to hear her talk to her boss on the phone: "I likely can be back full time by December, after all this chemo is over," she boasted.

Either she was doing the best acting job of her life or she was really in denial. There is no way she could *not* know the extent of her cancer, but the strangest thing is that she never talked about dying, not once, not even when I gave her a chance to get some things off her chest. Only on three occasions did we even come close to broaching the subject. There were never any dramatic "good-byes" or long talks about her life.

The first time she addressed her mortality was quite matter-of-fact. We were sitting on the couch, and I could tell she was in pain. I don't know how she was able to cope with it. Her threshold for misery was sky high, a toughness that defies description. She was trying to get up from the couch but could not. I reached over to help her, and of all things, she laughed.

"I *was* lucky to get fifty-three years out of this God damned body," she said. "It sucked." There was no elaboration.

The second time was similar. We were in our bedroom walking in different directions when she suddenly turned around, groped for my hand and hugged me. She then looked my way ever so sweetly and said in a longing and appreciative voice: "Richie, thanks for a great life!" I hugged her tight, using every single muscle I had in my body to not break down.

"And the great life ahead," I replied. Again, that was the end of the conversation.

The final time was an evening when she was in pain and getting depressed. I simply laid down next to her in bed and started talking about going on a vacation. We then talked for what seemed like an hour, about all the places we had been and all the good times we'd had. Acapulco, St. Thomas, San Juan, Puerto Vallarta, the drive along Highway 1 in California, Cooperstown and upstate New York, during the first year of our marriage. We laughed a lot that night, forgetting, for awhile at least, that she had terminal cancer. It was a brief escape from reality.

"It's been a big bash, hasn't it been, Richie?" she said, and you could see 'good-bye' in her eyes, but she never said it. I made her a cup of tea. Soon her depression subsided, and so did her pain. Once she had dozed off in a peaceful sleep, I retired to the living room where I cried long into the night.

Spring had always been my favorite time of year. Its renewal of life always filled me with joy and anticipation. That ended in 2002. I knew time was now the enemy; thus, the coming of spring only brought Maggie closer to the end. Even though she was weak, Maggie kept planning ahead. She stayed in touch with all her blind friends, even managing to squeeze in a few half days at work. She went in at 8 a.m. and left at noon. When she came home she would be exhausted and head off to bed. Her energy level was slipping badly. Her spirits were not.

Robert told me about the last time he had lunch with Maggie at the office. It was a week or so before she had to quit work, shortly after her operations in February. They always ate in the peace and quiet of Maggie's office because the cafeteria at the Lighthouse was too noisy.

> *"She appeared totally wiped out from all the chemo, but she was not in a bad mood. Maggie never seemed to be down. We talked about life, and Maggie told me something that will stay with me until I die.*
>
> *'You know, Robert,' she said 'I am nearly blind, I am almost deaf, and I am full of cancer.' Then looking upward toward the ceiling she added in a happy and wistful voice, 'But I am married to a wonderful man, and I feel like the most completed person in the whole world.'"*

Robert had tears in his eyes when he told me that story long after Maggie had died, and when he finished, my emotion boiled over. It was as if Maggie was speaking to me in death. The word "completed" is exactly the kind of word she would use. I could hear her saying it. I longed once again to tell her she had also completed my life. I found considerable comfort in the knowledge that I had told her countless times how much I loved and appreciated her. It left me with a wonderful peace. You can never say "I love you" too much in a lifetime.

It was quite obvious to me that Robert loved Maggie, but I was not in the least jealous. I was actually happy that Maggie had touched his life. As brief as it had been, Robert had the good fortune to feel her magic.

Robert also told me she never discussed the possibility of dying. She simply lived on trying to be as normal as possible.

Even a surprising tragedy did not shake her resolve. She had been trying to call her friend, Ted, in Florida for two days, but kept getting his answering machine. She had wondered if he had found another woman and took off somewhere with her. Finally, as I was heading out for work one afternoon, she gave me a yell to come to her room.

"Rich," she said, somewhat startled, "I am calling Ted, and a police officer is on the line. I can't make out what happened."

I grabbed the phone, and the officer asked me who I was. I explained that I was Maggie's husband and that she and Ted were close friends.

"Well," he said, "I am sorry to inform you that he has passed away."

When I pressed for details, the officer told me he could not tell me anything. We needed to contact the family.

After I hung up the phone, I took Maggie in my arms as I conveyed the news that Ted had died. I expected Maggie to start crying, but she did not.

"Oh my God, poor Ted," she said softly. That was it. No tears, not many questions, and no need for consoling. I asked Maggie if she wanted me to stay home from work. She said no, then mentioned that she had the phone number for Ted's brother to seek further information. I have no explanation for Maggie's lack of emotion. Maybe she was totally drained from her own situation. I held her for a few minutes more, but she clearly was not going to lose her composure. As I released my embrace, she said she would be okay. Her reaction remains a total mystery.

Later she found out that Ted had died of a heart attack. He had been left alone for three days before someone found him. The body was flown back to Chicago, where the service was held two weeks later. It was late February 2002 by then. At the service,

Maggie was barely able to sit up. And when Karen McCulloh saw her there, she was obviously shaken by Maggie's weakness. While her body was failing, her mind and her will were not. When we got back from Ted's funeral, Maggie startled me with a request.

"Let's go to Vegas!" she announced to Arlana and me. "I want to get out of the house."

The prospect of taking her on a plane in such a weakened state bordered on insanity. She insisted she could make it, and in typical Maggie-fashion, she argued her point. It took us more than an hour, but we finally convinced her that we could go to Vegas after her chemotherapy. The compromise was that we would drive to Lake Geneva, Wisconsin and spend a few days there at a resort. Maggie finally bought the idea.

Even though her stomach was giving her trouble, Maggie was able to enjoy the trip. George and I went golfing while Maggie and Arlana did their usual shopping marathon in downtown Lake Geneva. Arlana said Maggie was energized while she was shopping. They took breaks, as Maggie needed, allowing her to sit down and to get drinks. Using what little energy she had, she even got on the treadmill in the health spa for a half hour. She was trying to treat it as a normal trip. But when the four of us went for a walk one day, the dreaded reality was clear to see. As Maggie and Arlana walked ahead of George and me, tears streamed down my face.

In the distance, I could see Maggie in her pretty straw hat, covering a now bald head. Her blue summer dress appeared to be hanging on a shadow, from the increasing weight loss. She now walked a bit hunched over, her youthful pep no longer there.

"She's gone, George," was all I could say.

Near the end of the trip, we were sitting in a restaurant when Maggie suddenly chirped out.

"Okay, let's plan our next trip right now."

There was a pregnant pause from the rest of us.

"What's the matter with you guys?" Maggie said, somewhat annoyed.

We quickly jumped in with some ideas—plans we knew would never be realized. Las Vegas was placed on the agenda but no date was set.

When we got home, Maggie plunged into her next project. She was determined to go to a three-day conference for the blind in River Forest, Illinois, a suburb west of Chicago. Arlana and I tried to talk her out of it, but this time we lost.

"I'm going and that's it," she said.

It required her to sleep in a dorm room for two nights. Her so-called stomach cramps were increasing and her bowel movements were becoming erratic. She was also popping more pain pills with each passing day.

As it turned out, Arlana had the week off and was able to drive Maggie to the conference and spend a lot of time with her. Arlana was totally shocked at how well Maggie was able to perform. She was involved in seminars, luncheons, fund-raising strategy sessions as well as some of the fun activities. It was as if she had blocked out the pain until she got back to her dorm, which she shared with another woman. As soon as she could get her hands on them, Maggie popped more pain medication. Still, she met a lot of new people and was just happy she could make it to the conference. Arlana, to this day, says she has no idea where Maggie got the energy to function at the conference.

I was at home when Arlana brought her back and was shocked at what I saw. In just three days, she had gotten horribly worse. Dark circles engulfed her eyes. Her jacket appeared to hang on a wire frame. Within five minutes of walking in the door, she was in bed.

I don't have the courage to write about the final five weeks of Maggie's life. That misery and sadness is just too painful. I am grateful to have had Arlana with me all the way. I can tell you that Maggie had spunk right up until the last hours of her coherent life. I had to fight her tooth and nail to get a visiting nurse to come in and give her an IV to alleviate her dehydration

"I don't need any nurses!" she scoffed.

So I invited in the nurse on my own, and when I told Maggie about it we had a grand battle.

"I told you I didn't want this, how could you?"

It was tearing me apart to argue with her, but in the end I was vindicated. Maggie got the IV. In fact, she got a couple of bags and perked up, immediately.

"I feel a lot better," she laughed. "Once again, Richie, you knew me better than I know myself."

Her doctor also recommended a hospice service, which would visit the apartment. That turned out to be a major problem. I had to explain to Maggie that a hospice offered better access to pain medication.

"Yeah," she said. "They talk all that psychological crap about dying. I don't want it."

I totally understood and vowed to not let any of that creep into the treatment if she agreed to try it. I explained the situation to the nurse at the hospice center.

"Why can't we just get the medical part of your program?" I asked. "Can't you skip the counseling?"

"Oh no," the nurse said. "It's very important that we prepare people for the end."

"I know it's impossible, perhaps, to fully understand this situation, but I will try to make you aware of how Maggie feels," I said. "This is a woman who has fought all the odds all her life.

She suffered hearing loss at birth, had a tough childhood, fought her way out of poverty, battled progressive blindness, graduated from college at age fifty, not to mention skin cancer, breast cancer, and now ovarian cancer. She is a fighter to the core and is not going to give up even if she has a 1 percent chance to live. She is choosing to die as a fighter. I want you to grant her that final request."

"You feel you know all this about your wife?" she asked.

"Not a single doubt in my mind," I answered, without hesitation. "We are one person, one soul."

The nurse granted my request. The hospice did a wonderful job with the medication, which made Maggie more comfortable. The only flaw was a doctor who came over one night in the final days before Maggie slipped into a coma. After I had spent a half hour telling him what I had told the nurse, he still had his own agenda. When he examined Maggie in our living room, he also began to ask her questions about death and accepting it. I quickly cut him off and asked him to step into the bedroom for a private discussion. It is the angriest I have ever been in my life, and the closest I have ever come to knocking someone's head clean off. I called him every name in the book. His face became white with fear as I towered over him in anger. He quickly apologized and then apologized again. He knew exactly what he had done. He was one of those people who thinks they know more than you and don't really listen to what you are saying. It was arrogance, pure and simple, and with Maggie days away from leaving me, I had no tolerance for it. Fortunately, Maggie was so weak that she was not totally aware of what had happened. I was protecting her to the very end. I had made a promise about the hospice and kept it.

In the days that followed, Maggie's health slumped badly. She slept almost all the time, thanks to the increased used of pain medication. Her food intake was next to nothing. She had a brief period one morning where her mind was relatively clear, and she was able to talk. In that period, she again broke my heart in her iron determination to live. From about 9 a.m. until 11 a.m., she called all her friends and talked with them for just a few minutes. The conversation was almost the same during each call.

"Oh yeah, I have stomach cramps, and I am a little weak, but nothing I can't handle," she would say.

Then she would always talk about "getting together" when she got well. The whole process just ripped out my heart. By around 11 a.m., she was exhausted from the calls and fell asleep in our living room in a puffy leather chair we had bought together just a year ago.

Some of her friends and even her family members did not believe me when I later told them how weak Maggie really was and that it was close to the end. Arlana also felt the same sense of disbelief when she talked to our friends about Maggie.

"How could a woman who talked about the future and sounded halfway decent be so critical?" was the prevailing attitude of her friends and family. If I had been in their shoes, I would probably have felt the same way.

But Andi, Jim, Ron, and Gail knew Maggie and knew the truth. Ron called on a daily basis to offer support, and I heard from Andi and Jim regularly. Their son, Jamie, was now eight years old and offered a rather poignant remark about Maggie, "I don't understand why this has to happen to a good person."

Eventually, she could not walk. The hospice brought in a wheel chair, which we used to take her out on the roof to sit by the pool or to go for a stroll in nearby Lake Shore Park. I was now taking more days off from work. One Saturday night in early August, George and Arlana came over for what turned out to be our final walk to the park. Maggie loved the flowers surrounding the jogging track. The Streeterville Neighbors Association did a fantastic job every year making Lake Shore Park gorgeous. Every time Maggie and I walked back from dinner, we made it a point to walk through the grounds. She would always stop to admire the flowers. Many times, we sat on one of the old beat up wooden Chicago Park District benches and enjoyed the scenery. Those benches were the exact kind we had at Dvorak Park in the old neighborhood. They were like old friends. Now Maggie was sitting in a wheel chair. As always, while I pushed her around the track, she leaned over to see the flowers. Very little was said, and I wondered if her eyes had much vision left at all after all the chemo and pain drugs. Though she spoke very slowly, she was able to talk.

"We sure kept the moving companies in business," she joked, as she looked at all the high rises surrounding the park. We had moved three times since we had been downtown.

Most of our time in the park, we spent just sitting and staring. George and Arlana would say something. I would say something, and Maggie would simply nod or say nothing. Even the simple act of sitting was exhausting for her. Soon, we made our way back to the apartment where she was able to lay down on the couch and get a few hours of sleep. She wanted to be awakened for the fireworks display at Navy Pier around 10 p.m., and she wanted to have her nightly "treat," a dish of sherbet, as she watched the fireworks. So we woke her, and she had a couple of spoons of sherbet and watched the fireworks, but it didn't last long. As soon as the fireworks ended, she was back asleep.

Arlana knew it was time to move in with us. I don't know how I could have done it myself. Without Arlana, I might not be here today. Then Maggie's sister, Patty, also moved in, and so

I had two nurses with me to care for Maggie. One of us always spent the night with Maggie in the master bedroom. Usually that was Arlana because she could handle Maggie's physical needs. There is no sense detailing them, but suffice to say we all had our hands full on a 24-hour basis. I slept on the aero-bed on the floor in Maggie's office or on the couch. Patty slept on the couch or with Maggie. We switched off as needed.

This went on for days and became a hellish ordeal. Maggie's moments of coherence diminished by the day. She experienced one final surge of complete clarity. It's another moment that will be etched in my mind forever. It was around 2 a.m. Arlana was getting some well-deserved sleep in our bedroom. Maggie was sleeping on one section of the living room couch, while Patty was slumped on the other end. I was sitting a few feet away from Maggie in our leather chair, half asleep and half awake—a state of misery that defies accurate description. Suddenly, Maggie shot up from her sleep, moaning and crying. I had seen it before when she had her nightmares during the chemotherapy for her breast cancer. I jumped out of my chair and raced over to cradle her in my arms. I held her tight, kissed her, and stroked her head.

"Richie?" she asked as her mind regained consciousness.

"Yeah, its me," I said. "You're okay."

I could feel her trembling body begin to relax in relief. With a clear mind, as if numbness of the pain medication had been washed away, she said in that sweet, soft voice, for the last time in our lives, "Richie, I love you so!"

"I love you too, Bags," I replied. I held her tight for as long as it took for her to once again fall asleep. I then went to the bathroom, closed the door, and collapsed in tears.

The next day, flowers arrived at the condo from Maggie's niece, Nicole. Arlana read the card and was choking back tears.

She tried to read it to Maggie, but she could tell she was not getting through.

"Maybe if you try it, she'll get it," Arlana said, "you have a deep voice."

It was yet another gut-wrenching experience, but I did read the card.

"To Auntie Mood, I hope these flowers brighten your days, as you have always brightened ours."

Maggie's pause lasted about thirty seconds, but she finally responded in a weak and drawn out voice: "I will have to call Nicole tomorrow to thank her." That was the last coherent response of her life.

She went to sleep that night and when she awoke the next morning, she did not know who Nicole was, who Arlana was, who Patty was, and she did not even know my name. She was awake for sure. She was taking liquids and was even able to ask for sherbet, but she had no idea who was taking care of her. We tried everything to jog her memory, old nicknames, old stories, favorite restaurants but nothing worked. She was in what I called a "living coma." Her movements became involuntary, and it was surprising to me that she could still move at all. The hospice nurses came in and predicted she would be dead in three or four days. There were only off by a week and a half! They could not explain why she lasted so long; but I knew, because I knew how Maggie thought. I still do. Somehow deep in the recesses of her drug-laden mind, there was still a will to live. Her fifty-three year-old heart was strong. She was clinging to the hope that she would somehow survive and we would once again walk along Lake Shore Park to enjoy the flowers and life itself. She would never give up.

In the final week, I had booked a hotel room two blocks away. It afforded Arlana, Patty, and me a chance to get away for six or seven hours and get some decent sleep—although we slept only out of exhaustion. On Saturday morning, August 17, 2002, I came back from breakfast to find Arlana and Patty huddled over Maggie in the bed. Her breathing had become very labored during the night.

"This is it," Arlana said.

As I watched Maggie struggle to breathe, I thought about a conversation we once had over dinner.

"Look," she said, in that strong opinionated voice that I longed to hear just one more time, "if I am ever hooked up to any machines, pull the damn plug. I don't want to lay there like a vegetable."

As she lay dying, I wished I had a plug to pull, but there was nothing to do except to suffer the hour.

The digital clock in our bedroom read 11:55 a.m. when Maggie finally, and most unwillingly, gave up the life she had lived to its last precious moment. Arlana, Patty, and I were all holding her. If Maggie had one of those after death experiences that allows you to see the scene below as you drift upward, she would have seen me reach for a picture of her mother that we kept on the bed stand on Maggie's side. Every night when I tucked her in, I glanced at that picture. I had promised Maggie's mother I would take care of her and make her happy. I had tried with every ounce of energy I possessed. Every night when Maggie was warm and secure under my body, I knew I had also made her mother happy. Now it was as if I had to give her back—give back the only real truth I had ever known. I grabbed the picture and gave it to Patty.

"This is yours now," I said, barely able to speak amid the tears.

I took one final look at Maggie and left the room.

Crazy In Love

Maggie would have killed me if I had ended this book with sadness. I knew that going in, and I also knew that when she died she would have wanted no prolonged mourning period. The immediate mission on August 17, 2002, was to have a service that celebrated a phenomenal life. Maggie's idea for her own memorial was typical of her thinking.

"When I kick the bucket, just have a few people over, have some drinks and then get on with your lives and enjoy them," she had told me more than once.

I would always disagree and explained to her that I was going to throw a huge party and pointed out it was an argument I was guaranteed to win.

"You'll be bitching at me from somewhere in the sky with the rest of the spirits," I joked.

So I planned a big service for a variety of reasons. Many of Maggie's friends, blind and otherwise, did not have a chance to talk with her in the final weeks of her life. Maggie had tons of friends. I wanted to give them a chance to mourn her in a public setting. I also had a big service for selfish reasons. I wanted to talk about Maggie's great life and see her in her prime and, hopefully, begin to deal with the horrors of the final weeks.

So the very next day after her death, I took my mother, along with George and Arlana, to a huge church in west suburban Oak Brook. It was a state of the art building complete with TV monitors to play videos. The place was gorgeous and had abundant parking. There was a reception room for a buffet right on the premises. If she had ever agreed to a large service, Maggie would have wanted things first class. As we pulled into the parking lot, I quickly got out of the car and as usual raced to open the passenger side. It was as if I had forgotten Maggie was dead. I opened the door and extended my arm to my mother, who didn't need any guidance. It was a sad and strange feeling not to have Maggie on my arm.

I explained to the pastor of the church that I did not want a lot of prayers at the service. I wanted to handle it myself as the emcee. He tried to talk me into letting him do it, but a handsome donation and my persistence paid off. Arlana and I basically ran the whole thing. We wanted a short service that lasted no more than an hour. I had seen memorials where an endless stream of people get up to talk about their experiences with the deceased. After a while you get tired of hearing it. We asked six people to speak and told each of them we wanted no more than two or three minutes per speech. Each person was from one key part of Maggie's life: her sister and brother, fellow nurses, our good friend Andi Wiley, who represented the Hinsdale Rat Pack, George and Arlana Fako spoke together, and finally, Jim Kesteloot of the Lighthouse for the Blind and Karen McCulloh, who talked about the challenges as a blind and deaf person.

I also made a video, which was heartbreaking, but turned out to be the best way to celebrate her life. A good friend and one of the best broadcast editors in the business, Steve Scheuer, helped me put the piece together at WGN. It was only four and a half minutes long, but it was powerful. From baby pictures to the end of her life, Maggie filled the screen with grace, beauty, and fun. I needed to see her face and her body in happier days.

The music I chose to accompany the video was, in a way, actually selected by Maggie. It was one of her favorites—the theme song from the movie *Somewhere In Time*. It was a touching love story starring Christopher Reeve and Jane Seymour that had become a cult classic over the years. I bought a cassette of the movie and Maggie had seen it several times. The classical music theme created by Jon Barry spoke of eternal love. Ironically, Barry said he wrote the music in the months after he had lost his father and his mother in a short period of time. Now his theme would be played under pictures and video of Maggie, a week after she had passed away.

Maggie's body was cremated on the Tuesday after she had died. She had often told me she hated graves.

"They take up land, valuable land," she insisted.

"When I go, just burn me, and throw my ashes on some flowers."

She got no argument from me on that point. Although when Arlana and I went to scatter the ashes on a sweltering night, in August, it was rough. When we got back to the apartment, we both had a couple of drinks to calm down.

The service turned out to be as beautiful as the life Maggie had lived, with more than 400 people in attendance.

"Maggie would be ecstatic with this turnout," I said to start the event.

The service lasted just over an hour, and the last thing people saw was the video. The first shot was Maggie being held in the arms of her mother. The last shot was Maggie in my arms waving good-bye on that gorgeous beach in Maui. She was in the glory of her youth, smiling and happy, when she waved good-bye to the video camera held by Andi in 1989. Now, she was waving goodbye to everyone at her service thirteen years later.

Two comments stuck in my mind after the service. One came from one of my colleagues at WGN-TV, Robert Jordan. He had not known Maggie, but he said after the service, "I feel like I really know her now. It was inspirational."

My mother also had an interesting comment, "This is the big wedding you and Margie never had," she said.

I felt as if I had accomplished my goals for the service as a final act of love for Maggie.

Instead of flowers, all donations in Maggie's name went to the Lighthouse for the Blind. I also donated all of Maggie's office machines and materials to the Lighthouse. She would have loved to know that someone was enjoying her valuable VTech and even her hearing aids and FM system. All of Maggie's clothes were donated to the American Cancer Society. Arlana and I both joked that if we had sold them, we could have both retired.

When it was all over, Arlana and I were totally exhausted. I had cared and sweated for Maggie all my life and Arlana for the better portion of hers. To watch helplessly as Maggie died sent a trauma through our system that is hard to explain. It's almost as if you are dying yourself. I kept telling Arlana we had to stay busy. I had a chance to take a week off to regroup and someone suggested I rent a cabin somewhere in Michigan to spend some time reflecting. I passed it up.

"If I do that," I said, "you might find me hanging from a tree."

Arlana and I both returned to work within a few days. We felt that we would be depressed anyway, so why not be depressed at work. At the time, we did not know if we had done the right thing by getting back to work so fast, but as I write this two years after Maggie's death, I can honestly say that for me, at least, it was a wise decision.

Soon after her death, I received letters from people about Maggie's life. One was especially touching. It was from a woman named Mary Holden, who had met her briefly at that last blind conference in June of 2002, when Maggie was in the last weeks of her life. Mary attended one of Maggie's seminars and escorted her back to her dorm, called Krueger Hall. She wrote Arlana and Patty a note and told them to forward it to me. It read:

"Maggie had such a profound effect on so many people at the conference. Her presence is still felt because of her leadership and example. Hers is the spirit that can never die; her spirit seems to multiply in conversations we have about her. Perhaps that is one of the best things one can hope for, to be so fondly remembered and with such admiration. I have enclosed a poem about Maggie."

For Maggie:
Guiding to the conference from Krueger
Five short minutes and it was over
knowing you took my arm to guide me forward.
our relationship; one short stroll'
the illness soon would take its toll
but not before I knew with certainty
I had met an angel (or soon to be)

You left me not with broken heart
too short a time to impact that much
Can a heart be touched so fast?
Yes, I whisper, especially by you

and I think back on who was guiding who.

I received similar notes from a wide range of people. The reaction to Maggie's death was extensive. She had touched a lot of lives in her life. A week after I got the letter from Mary Holden, Karen McCulloh wrote me a note, and I could hear Maggie's voice in what Karen wrote:

> *"I have thought of the love you had for Maggie and I remember you telephoning her every night when we traveled together in Washington DC. The greatest gift of love you could have given Maggie, and you did, was to give her the gift of freedom of travel and 'do her thing,' when I know you were concerned about her safety and her health. I admire this gift you gave to Maggie because other spouses may not have let her go. Certainly with her being sight and hearing-impaired, she faced many real obstacles of travel and challenge. Thank you for giving her the gift of freedom. Maggie and I had some wonderful times together, and I know that we loved one another."*

Karen then talked about all the good work Maggie had done and how tragic it was that she was taken from this life so early:

> *"It is our heartache that she did not live to continue. God only knows what Maggie would have done as she was such an intelligent, loving, and caring human being."*

That was the ultimate heartache for Arlana and me. Even though we knew life was unfair, it still leaves a burning anger that someone who had so much to give loses her life so early, while others who offer nothing, or might even contribute to the evil in the world, live on. In the weeks and months after her death, that anger was intense and mixed in with a deep depression. It was a rather toxic formula.

Just before I had the idea to write this book, I began to lose some of that anger, which put Maggie's life into perspective. Call it rationalization. Call it positive thinking. Call it what you want, but I began to accept what had happened, and I began to feel grateful I had Maggie for so long. I even felt bad for the friends she had made in the final years of her life. They had not enjoyed being with Maggie for an extended time. I also felt sorry for some of her family members who didn't take advantage of the time they could have spent with her. I felt sad for all those who did not have what I had experienced. I enjoyed the most of Maggie going back to childhood, and that is the best gift anyone could receive. I had lived with her a life of fulfilled dreams. Not many people are as fortunate.

One cool autumn evening, two years after her death in 2004, I went for a walk by Lake Shore Park where Arlana, George, and I had taken Maggie for the last outing of her life. The sun was sinking behind the giant Loop high rises. I was thinking of Maggie as I always do in that park, but on this night, I felt she was with me. I was listening on my Walkman to a cassette of Julio Iglesias. I had learned a lot of Spanish over the years thanks to his silky soft love songs. But one song on the album is in English, and the words had a huge impact. The song is called *Crazy in Love*. The words that jumped out were these:

> "I could get intoxicated just by looking in your eyes.
> Babe is there anything we can do because I know you're
> missing me like I am always missing you. I do miss the

*days when we were crazy in love. When you were not
sure of me, and I was not sure of you. Bring back the days
when we were crazy in love."*

Maggie and I were crazy in love. It was not just some romantic notion. It was the real thing that transcended the physical world. How else could I describe what had happened? She was an awkward tomboy with hearing aid wires tangled in her dress at the play lot in that now distant innocence of our youth in the 1950s. I was there. She was a blossoming beauty in her teens with that gorgeous long flowing blond hair. I was there. I was there in Wauconda seeing the breathtaking eternal love in her eyes. I was her soul mate for all the happiness that filled our lives as husband and wife. I was with her for all the hard work, the exotic vacations, the zany antics, and the great friends. I was there throughout the bad times—the hearing loss, the blindness, and the cancers. It was enormous adversity that we did not let break us, but instead used to bind us even tighter. I was there for it all. Nobody else had as much of her. Yes, there should have been more—but I can hear her softly telling me now:

"But Richie, there wasn't."

Our magical time was cut short, for sure. What Maggie gave me was so powerful, I could no longer feel cheated.

I kept playing that Julio Iglesias song over and over again, and as I walked along, I could feel Maggie with me in the melody and the words. I did not want to stop the CD. We had really lived the American dream. It was a journey from the concrete of Pilsen to the green summers of the western suburbs then the breathtaking views of the Chicago Gold Coast.

"Can you believe it, Richie?" Maggie would say. "It's a great life, isn't it?"

She was my summer peace, my safe haven in the storm. She was everything. How else could you explain the feeling of total euphoria every time I came home from work and she leaped into my arms? We had thirty-two years of married life where everyday seemed better than the one before. I could try, but I really could not feel sorry for myself around her. She wouldn't let me. The example of her life alone was enough to make me feel ashamed if I failed to enjoy a summer's day, a slice of veggie pizza, or a cup of soy latte. I had her magic everyday, and I still have it.

She would have acknowledged my deep pain over her loss, but she would have quickly added, "Don't waste your life moping around." She also would have chastised me if I had failed to point out her imperfections in this book.

"I'm hell on wheels," she once told me after one of her verbal barrages.

While most of the friends she met later in life did not know it, Maggie struggled greatly with her blindness. She knew she made Arlana and me jump through hoops.

"I wonder," she once joked, "if I had perfect eyes and ears maybe you would have kicked me out a long time ago."

She knew her disabilities had humbled her. In the final years of our lives, Maggie and I often talked about all the scuffles we'd had over the years.

"Why was all that crap so important?" she would laugh. I guess we came to a true sense of understanding; in the final ten years of our life together, we had no major problems or arguments. If there was a disagreement and her temper flared, it lasted just a few seconds, and we both laughed it off.

I could see right through her sometimes fiery exterior, just as I had seen through her mother's so many years before. I saw right into Maggie's heart. Deep down, there was a pure sweetness and a total appreciation of life. When I was going through some of her college papers, I found a fitting epitaph. She was writing about how people perceive her.

> *"In Walden, Henry David Thoreau wrote, 'our outside and often thin and fanciful clothes are our epidermis, or false skin, which partakes not of our life. Likewise, I perceive my hearing aids and white cane as 'false skin.' I consider myself fortunate to have learned this important lesson early in life."*

Maggie and I talked often about life and death. In her endless reading, she often showed me quotes she found to be poignant. A PBS television documentary series on the Civil War provided a quote, which I read after Maggie died. While it applies to war, I also think it applies to the kind of intense life and love that Maggie and I enjoyed. It was written by Supreme Court Justice Oliver Wendell Holmes, a Civil War veteran, and it written in the twilight of his life. I have changed the word "war" to "love" to indicate just what Maggie meant to me.

> *"We have shared the incommunicable experience of love. We have felt, we still feel, the passion of life at its top. In our youth our hearts were touched by fire."*

The fire I saw in Maggie's eyes still burns brightly in my heart. In that same PBS documentary, they shared a letter written by a Union Army Lieutenant to his wife shortly before he was killed in the first battle of Bull Run. He wrote tenderly that if he did not return to "never forget how much I love you, and that when my last breath escapes me on the battlefield, it will whisper your name."

"Isn't that beautiful, Richie," Maggie said. That's the way it will be for us when we die, right?"

Maggie could not talk when she took her final breath, but I am sure that if she could have mustered up the strength, she would have whispered my name. Whatever happens in the years I have left, and however long the rest of my life may be, I know that I will find great peace in my final moment when I whisper, "My Maggie."

Photographs

Maggie at age 2 in 1950 with her mother, Ann Smith.

Maggie at age 4, circa 1952.

Maggie, age 4, and her brother Eddie, age 6
circa, 1952.

From left to right: Friend, Father Dominic, her sister, Patty, and Maggie.

Maggie's St. Procopius High School
picture in 1964.

Maggie at the Statue of
Liberty in October, 1971.

Maggie in Sarasota, FL on
vacation in 1980.

Rich, Maggie, and Arlana at nurse's graduation, circa 1975.

Out for a bike ride with our friends,
Andi and Jim.

The Hinsdale "Rat Pack." From left to right:
Maggie, Andi, Jim, Gail, and Ron.

Maggie and me in Acapulco, circa 1986.

Maggie and me in Puerto Rico in 1994.

From left to right: Annie Smith—Eddie's daughter, Nicole Cook—Patty's daughter, and Aunt Maggie.

From left to right: Patty, Maggie, and Eddie.

Seated: Maggie and Karen McCulloh surrounded by friends at a
Foundation for Fighting Blindness event in 2001.

Maggie at a picnic for the sight-impaired.

Maggie and Cathy Klein (in Harvard T-shirt)
along with friends at a sight-impaired cooking
gathering.

Maggie and a ski guide at a Skiing for
the Blind Ski Club event in 2000.

Maggie and her friend, Trish, taking a stroll in 2001.

Maggie and me getting ready for her
graduation in June 2000.

Arlana with Maggie at her graduation.

Maggie and me at the wedding reception for George
and Arlana Fako.

Maggie and me at our last gala. The Chicago
Lighthouse Annual Gala, 2001.

The CHICAGO LIGHTHOUSE
for People Who Are Blind
or Visually Impaired

1850 West Roosevelt Road
Chicago, Illinois 60608-1298

Telephone: 312-666-331
TTY: 312-666-8874 (for hearing impaired)
Fax: 312-243-8539
http://www.chicagolighthouse.org

Maggie in an advertisement for the Chicago Lighthouse.
Photo courtesy of the Chicago Lighthouse for People Who Are Blind and
Visually-Impaired. All Rights Reserved.